Praise for *Backyard Bounty*

Backyard Bounty is very likely the best book ever written on growing food in the Pacific Northwest, and it sets a whole new standard for garden writing. By acknowledging the impacts of climate change on our gardens, Gilkeson further elevates the literature. This is the first "real time" gardening book. It is fresh and timely, and every page courses with practical advice and revelations. All growers should own this amazing and insightful book, and we should refer back to it often.

—MARK MACDONALD,
West Coast Seeds

Ideal for both new and seasoned gardeners, this new edition adds more listings to the detailed fruit and vegetable profiles, updates variety choices, and supplies practical information on dealing with common pests and diseases, including new ones to our region. Tips on adapting gardening practices to changing weather patterns are eminently helpful, as is a focus on the soil as a life force that fosters health in plants.

—HELEN CHESNUT,
Garden columnist, *Times Colonist*

As usual, Linda Gilkeson is spot on with her trademark down-to-earth advice to Pacific Northwest Gardeners. If, like me, you sometimes find your vegetables bolting before their time and falling short of your expectations, if you're wondering how climate change is affecting what you should plant and when, if you're perplexed about pollination and the impact it is having on your garden's productivity, struggling with organic pest management, or wondering how to achieve year-round bounty in your outdoor space, you'll find these pages brimming with seasoned wisdom and practical common sense.

—CAROL POPE,
Editor, *GardenWise*

Whether you have a small or large lot, little or plenty of time, this book shows you how to grow your own toxic-free fruit and vegetables the whole year round. From preparing the ground to harvesting and storing the ripened produce, all is clearly explained. An invaluable book for novices and experienced gardeners.

—BARRY ROBERTS, Past-President,
Master Gardeners Association of BC

Linda Gilkeson has paid some tuition in the garden. *Backyard Bounty* is remarkably thorough, from roots to pests to pruning to crowns, and it inspires even the experienced grower. Just like homemade soil for a bedding plant, this book is loaded with the richness we need in order to feed ourselves.

—LYLE ESTILL, author,
Small is Possible: Life in a Local Economy
and *Industrial Evolution: Tales from a Low Carbon Future*

BACKYARD BOUNTY

The Complete Guide to Year-Round
Organic Gardening in the Pacific Northwest

SECOND EDITION

Linda Gilkeson, PhD

new society
PUBLISHERS

Cover design by Diane McIntosh.
Cover images: ©iStock: main veg image 695090862; red wood 643825432.
Page 1: woodcut © Christos Georghiou / Adobe Stock.

Printed in Canada. Second printing June 2020.

Inquiries regarding requests to reprint all or part of *Backyard Bounty*
should be addressed to New Society Publishers at the address below.
To order directly from the publishers, please call toll-free (North America)
1-800-567-6772, or order online at www.newsociety.com

Any other inquiries can be directed by mail to:

New Society Publishers
P.O. Box 189, Gabriola Island, BC V0R 1X0, Canada
(250) 247-9737

LIBRARY AND ARCHIVES CANADA CATALOGUING IN PUBLICATION

Gilkeson, Linda A., author
Backyard bounty : the complete guide to year-round
organic gardening in the Pacific Northwest / Linda Gilkeson.
—Second edition.

Includes bibliographical references and index.
Issued in print and electronic formats.
ISBN 978-0-86571-841-8 (softcover).—ISBN 978-1-55092-636-1 (PDF).—
ISBN 978-1-77142-230-7 (EPUB).

1. Organic gardening—Northwest Coast of North America.
2. Backyard gardens—Northwest Coast of North America.
I. Title.

SB453.5.G538 2018   635'.048409795   C2017-907283-8
                                                    C2017-907284-6

Funded by the   Financé par le
Government   gouvernement
of Canada   du Canada

Canada

New Society Publishers' mission is to publish books that contribute in fundamental
ways to building an ecologically sustainable and just society, and to do so with the least
possible impact on the environment, in a manner that models this vision.

new society
PUBLISHERS

Certified
B
Corporation

MIX
Paper from
responsible sources
FSC
www.fsc.org
FSC® C016245

Contents

Tables

Acknowledgments

The information in this book is the sum of far more than just my own experience. It is thanks to many others over the years that have shared their knowledge, observations, and most importantly, their questions, that I have learned so much about growing food in this climate. As the weather becomes less predictable in the changing climate and as new pests and diseases arrive, it is more important than ever that we continue to share tips, best varieties, and new ideas to keep our gardens productive and resilient. Many thanks to all of you enthusiastic gardeners for sharing your experience!

Introduction

I was very happy to be given the opportunity to produce this new and improved edition of *Backyard Bounty*. It allowed me to add crops that were not in the first edition, to expand on certain topics—such as the amazing role of soil micro-organisms in keeping plants healthy—to update the pest and disease information, and add pests that have recently arrived in the region. I have also included a substantial amount of new material on gardening in the increasingly variable weather we are experiencing as the global climate changes.

Gardening the easy way leaves me time to sit in my favorite chair under the apple tree and enjoy the view.

My original reasons for writing this book haven't changed—in fact, after years of teaching gardening classes, I am more convinced than ever of the need for practical information on how to grow food in the unique climate of the coastal Pacific Northwest. With the right varieties and planting schedules, it is possible to harvest vegetables twelve months of the year and to produce a surprising amount from even the smallest plot. These days, busy people also need information on efficient, low-maintenance ways to fit gardening into their full timetables.

Growing an organic food garden is a practical skill anyone can learn: it doesn't have to involve a lot of work and certainly doesn't require a big investment in special products or equipment. Despite increasing challenges from variable weather and new pests, I hope that this book will show you that it still isn't hard to grow food in your own backyard.

Of course, there are many other compelling reasons to grow your own food: from enjoying the delightful flavor and quality of fresh crops to the indisputable health benefits of eating plenty of fruits and vegetables. Not least, there is the sheer pleasure of working among the plants, picking this and that, observing bees, birds, and other creatures—a wonderful antidote to today's high-speed world.

CHAPTER 1

Our Gardening Climate and How Plants Grow

This chapter covers basic information to help take the guesswork out of growing vegetables and fruit in the Pacific Northwest coastal climate. It starts with an overview of the climate and weather along the coast and how it is being affected by the changing climate. The final section reviews how plants grow, flower, and fruit.

Gardening in the Coastal Climate

What's different about gardening on the Pacific Northwest (PNW) coast? The climate here is generally characterized by mild winters and warm summers. Only rarely has it been too hot in the summer to grow vegetables that do well in cool conditions (such as broccoli, lettuce, and peas), yet it is almost always warm enough to allow warm-season crops to be grown reasonably well in most gardens. This is actually a wonderful place to garden because so many vegetables can be harvested fresh out of the garden *all winter*. Because garden beds can produce food all year, you can grow a surprising amount in a small area—and you don't have to spend the time that gardeners from less "fortunate" climates do preserving food for the winter. (When those gardeners move to the Pacific Northwest, it can take them a while to adjust to the idea that our planting season lasts for six months and our harvesting season lasts all year.) That isn't to say there aren't challenges, however. One is adapting to the increasingly variable weather and higher average temperatures resulting from the changing climate; another is learning how to deal with the new pests and diseases that continue to arrive in the region.

Microclimates on the Coast

Within this generally mild climate, the varied geography of the region—from mountains to seashore—holds many local microclimates. The complexities of West Coast geography mean that the USDA climate zone maps are not much use here. While roughly USDA Zone 8 for much of the lower elevation coast, there are large differences in local microclimates.

These microclimates differ in:

- total rainfall and the timing of rainfall
- amount of local fog, marine clouds, and direct sunshine each year
- average low winter temperatures, frequency of frosts and snowfall
- average warm temperatures in the summer
- amount of shading from trees, buildings, even mountain tops

1.1 What's for dinner in January? Carrots, kale, komatsuna, Brussels sprouts, parsley, and radicchio.

Effects of Elevation

Elevation affects microclimates, but not always in obvious ways. The higher the elevation, the lower the minimum temperatures are in the winter. But higher elevations also get more snow. With an insulating blanket of snow providing cold protection, overwintering plants often have a *better* chance of surviving an Arctic outbreak at *higher* elevations than at sea level. With precipitation falling mostly as rain at lower elevations, the ground is often bare during cold snaps, so plants are less protected.

Higher-elevation gardens (up to 1,000 feet), if they are on open slopes, can sometimes have a longer frost-free growing season than valley gardens because cold air flows down the hillsides and pools in the valleys. On very still nights, even in the winter, the air may be even a few degrees warmer at higher elevations than down in the valley due to temperature inversions. This can be an advantage for higher-elevation tree fruit production because there is less chance that a late frost will kill the blossoms of peaches and other early flowering fruit.

The effect of all this is that two gardens only a short distance apart may have the same average annual temperature but quite different gardening climates. A garden close to the ocean or the Strait of Juan de Fuca will have a cooler summer with more fog than a garden a short distance inland, but the winters won't be as cold. Gardeners may need a greenhouse to ripen tomatoes in an oceanside garden, but winter crops such as broccoli and salad greens will grow beautifully without one.

On top of variations from geography, weather patterns in the coastal region vary over cycles of a few years to a few decades, due to two cyclical atmospheric patterns affecting the Pacific Ocean:

- El Niño–La Niña events: Occurring on cycles of 2 to 7 years, with each phase lasting for 8 to 18 months, these result from complex oscillations of warmer and cooler water and high and low atmospheric pressure in the south Pacific Ocean. The effect differs depending where you are on the continent, but for the Pacific Northwest coast, the El Niño phase usually brings warmer and drier than average winters; the ensuing La Niña phase usually brings cooler and wetter weather.
- The Pacific Decadal Oscillation (PDO): This is a variable 10- to 30-year pattern of alternating cool and warm cycles in Pacific Ocean water temperatures. It appears we are now in a warm cycle. The PDO is not well understood, and the pattern may or may not continue as the changing climate affects ocean currents. When an El Niño phase occurs while the ocean is in a warm cycle of the PDO, temperatures are even higher than usual, as occurred in the extreme El Niño of 2015–2016.

A feature of winters on the south coast of British Columbia and north coast of Washington State is the occasional Arctic outbreak. These blasts of frigid air break out of higher latitudes, bringing periods of much colder than average temperatures. There may only be one or two such outbreaks in a winter, and they usually only last for a few days at a time, but the abrupt drop in temperatures can be very damaging to plants.

Rainfall patterns also vary widely around the region. Gardens in the rainforest microclimates receive far more rain than gardens in the rain shadow of the Olympics or other coastal mountains only a few miles away. (A rain shadow is the dry zone on the opposite side of a mountain range from the prevailing direction of wind and rain; as storms pass, they dump rain on one side of the mountain, leaving little to fall on the other side.)

Gardening in a Changing Climate

By now, most people are aware of the increasingly variable weather that is the result of a changing global climate. It isn't your imagination that extreme weather in recent years is making gardening more difficult than it used to be. Information on how to adapt our gardens and methods to meet the challenge of a changing climate is a significant part of the new content I have added to this revised edition of *Backyard Bounty*.

The coastal regions of British Columbia have warmed by around 2°F (1.1°C) over the last century. Climate projections for the 2050s show that average temperatures will likely increase by 3° to 4°F (1.8° to 2°C), compared to 1961–1990 averages. As of 2017, the 15 warmest years ever recorded had occurred in the previous 16 years, with 2016 setting a new global record for the amount temperatures increased in one year. An important factor contributing to higher average temperatures is higher nighttime temperatures, which have been rising steadily.

Average temperatures don't tell the whole story, however, because extreme minimum and maximum temperatures can average out to a normal temperature range. While extremes of heat are becoming more frequent, that doesn't mean that periods of extreme cold are less likely (the prolonged cold of midwinter 2016–2017 was a harsh reminder). A particular concern is that warmer average spring temperatures cause fruit trees to bloom earlier, increasing the risk of damage to the crop from a late frost.

Periods of extreme temperatures are lasting longer because of the weakening polar jet stream, another effect of the warming global climate. With a weaker jet stream, weather systems that should move along across the continent from west to east stall for longer over one region. The result is prolonged periods of extreme heat or Arctic cold or record-breaking rainfall causing severe flooding. As the global atmosphere warms, it holds more energy and more water vapor, which also means an increased potential for stronger windstorms and heavier rainfall. As with temperature, however, the effect is variable. We are seeing shifts in when and where precipitation (mostly rain) occurs, leading to increased flooding in some places and longer droughts in others.

For the PNW coast in the long term, climate modeling shows that we can expect a continuing trend toward warmer average growing seasons, with less rainfall in the summer months. The models show the region can expect about the same amount of precipitation in the winter, but it is likely to fall over a shorter period, in more intense storms. More of it is expected to fall as rain rather than snow at higher elevations. Early drier springs and less snowpack in the mountains means a higher risk of summer water shortages for communities dependent on snowmelt to fill rivers and reservoirs.

While the record-breaking drought and heat of 2015 in the coastal PNW was unprecedented, meteorologists say that it was a preview of what may be an average summer by the middle of the century (and that's only 30 years away). And if that is what an average summer by mid-century might look like, then the variability in weather patterns means some years are likely to be even hotter or drier (or colder or wetter…) than anything we have so far experienced.

Adding to the stress on water resources from a changing climate is the fact that the growing population in the region is also increasing demand for water. Limiting water for gardens is usually one of the first restrictions imposed by water districts when supplies are low. Where once gardeners could irrigate as much as they liked to keep plants growing, water conservation is now an important—even critical—issue for many.

Plants are able to handle variable weather, but the more we know about how plants are affected by weird weather, the better prepared we will be to protect plants from extremes and to design gardens to adapt to these changes.

The Basics of Plant Growth

You might be tempted to skip this bit, but I urge you to read on because so many crop problems that perplex gardeners have to do with growing conditions (weather, nutrients, irrigation) that affect plant growth, flowering, and fruiting. When plants do weird things—such as bursting into flower when they shouldn't—we need to understand why, so we can avoid it in future.

Photosynthesis in plants is a truly amazing process. It allows plants to take energy from sunshine, carbon dioxide from the atmosphere, and water from the soil and make it into sugars. Plants use these sugars as building blocks to make fats, starches, proteins, plant hormones, and other compounds. Through a process called respiration, plant cells burn sugars to get the energy needed for growth and metabolism. If they are making more food than they can use, plants store the surplus sugars and starch in storage organs, such as roots, for later use. Some necessary elements, such as nitrogen, sulfur, calcium, and micronutrients, come from the soil, but surprisingly, most of the weight of the solid material that makes up a plant is actually built out of carbon from the atmosphere, rather than elements from the soil.

Water and nutrients move through a vascular system that reaches to all parts of the plant. Water moving upward from the roots and evaporating from the leaves travels in the xylem vessels. Another set of vessels, called the phloem, carries sap with nutrients and metabolic compounds to other parts. This process, called translocation, moves food internally from a source, such as a photosynthesizing leaf, to a part of the plant that needs it for growth. Surplus food can also be translocated to storage organs, such as roots or fruit. There is one more very interesting place that plants send their sugars and starches: they leak a significant amount of what they make into the soil around their roots. This sounds outlandish, but plants actually benefit a lot by providing food for beneficial soil bacteria and fungi around their roots (more on this interesting relationship in Chapter 3).

Sunlight Is Essential

To make a very complicated story simple: exposure to sunlight is vital. Vegetables and fruits need bright sunlight for as long as possible to produce the building blocks that make leaves, seeds, roots, and fruit. Leafy greens can grow adequately—though slowly—with half a day of direct sun each day, but most plants do much better with eight hours of direct sun in the summer. Gardens in open areas with even longer sun exposure will grow even faster, as they simply have more hours of light to photosynthesize.

The efficiency of photosynthesis depends mostly on light levels, but it also depends on temperature. The best range for photosynthesis is 50° to 85°F (10° to 30°C); photosynthesis stops when it gets too cool (below 40°F or 5°C) and when it gets too hot (above 95°F or 35°C) for most temperate zone plants.

Plants Are Mostly Water

Water is an essential ingredient for plant growth and survival. Evaporation from the leaves pulls moisture up through the plant, moving water from the roots to the leaves and shoots (called transpiration). This flow carries nutrients from the soil up through the stem to the photosynthesis "factories" on the leaves. When the water reaches the leaves and evaporates, it cools the plant. Cooling is essential to prevent leaf temperatures from rising too high and damaging leaf cells. Almost all of the water (97%) taken up by plants passes into the atmosphere in this process.

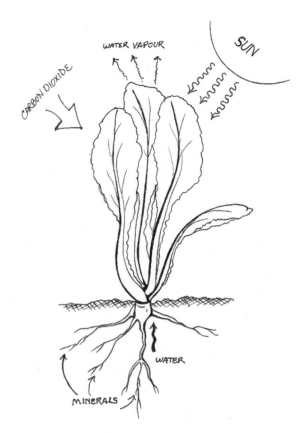

1.2. With energy from the sun, carbon dioxide from the atmosphere, and water and minerals flowing upward from the roots, plant cells produce the building blocks that become leaves, flowers, and seeds.

Plants must have a film of water around their roots so nutrients from the soil can pass into the cells of the roots. If this film dries out, even temporarily, fine root hairs die. The movement of nutrients from the soil and through the plant ceases and growth stops. Because the leaves also lose their cooling system when evaporation stops, it means that, in hot weather, leaf cells can (rapidly!) overheat in the sun and die. Plants may be so severely stressed or injured that, even if they survive, they may never be as productive as they could have been.

Soil Has a Supporting Role

The soil physically holds up plants and anchors them. It is the source of water and essential major and minor elements needed for photosynthesis and respiration.

A healthy soil contains a complex, interdependent community of organisms that range in size from microscopic bacteria to (relatively) huge earthworms. This vitally important community includes decomposers that digest organic matter and release nutrients in forms that plants can use, fungi that penetrate root hairs and ferry nutrients into root cells, and bacteria that colonize the surface of roots and produce compounds that actively protect plants from pathogens. Soil bacteria are also the main diet of protozoa (single-celled microorganisms), and in turn, protozoa are the main diet of earthworms.

The larger soil inhabitants include insects, mites, nematodes, earthworms, slugs, and snails, crustaceans (e.g., pillbugs), millipedes, and centipedes. While a few of these characters attack plants, our gardens couldn't do without the others because they play so many roles essential to the cycling of nutrients, aerating and mixing the soil, and keeping plants healthy. The soil *surface* is also the hunting ground for predators, such as large purplish-black ground beetles, centipedes, and many kinds of spiders.

Plants Need Nutrients

Crop plants need some elements in larger quantities for growth. These major nutrients are: nitrogen, phosphorous, potassium, calcium, magnesium, and sulfur. The first three elements are main ingredients in fertilizers. Local soils usually also need additions of calcium, sometimes magnesium, but rarely sulphur to grow crop plants.

A second group of nutrients is essential too, but in extremely small amounts. These micronutrients or trace elements include iron, manganese, chlorine, zinc, boron, molybdenum, and copper. The tricky thing about this group is that most are toxic to plants in large amounts or if soil conditions (such as acidic soil) make them too easily available to plants.

Chapter 3 covers nutrients from the soil in greater detail and describes how you can make them available to the roots of plants.

How Plants Grow

Plant growth depends on external factors such as weather, sunlight, and nutrients, as well as on the internal workings of the plants.

Annuals, Biennials, Perennials

Vegetables are mostly either annual (go to seed in the first year of growth) or biennial (go to seed the second year). Many crops (lettuce, radishes, mustard greens, beans, and squash) are annuals wherever they are grown, which means they will flower and produce seeds in the same summer if left in the garden long enough. Practically speaking, however, in the Pacific Northwest most garden vegetables are treated as annuals, which means we harvest crops the same year we sow the seeds.

Crops such as carrots, cabbage, kale, leeks, beets, Swiss chard, and parsley are biennials. Left to their own devices in the garden, they would have a two-year life cycle. From a spring planting, they grow all summer without going to seed. After spending the winter in the garden, they send up a flower stalk the following spring. The seeds ripen, and the plant dies in its second summer. The hardy winter broccoli and winter cauliflowers are also biennials; these are sown in June or July, but don't produce heads until early the following spring. For biennials, the cold chill of winter is the signal that tells them they are beginning their second year.

Some plants that we treat as annuals, such as tomatoes and peppers, are actually *perennials*; in a subtropical climate or heated greenhouse, they could continue to produce flowers and fruits year after year. Tender herbs, such as sweet basil and sweet marjoram, are also perennials, but they are often grown as annuals because they are not hardy enough to survive winter outdoors.

There are a few hardy perennial vegetables, such as artichokes, French sorrel, and asparagus. And of course, all fruit trees, grapes, berries, and rhubarb are hardy perennials in the garden.

Effects of Temperature

Plants grow best when it is warm; when it turns colder, growth slows, then stops altogether. The cut-off point at which growth stops differs among plants. Frost-hardy vegetables continue to grow (very slowly) even in the winter, whenever temperatures rise enough for photosynthesis to continue. Heat lovers, such as corn or melons, however, pack it in and die. Eventually, when the days are shortest and temperatures are cold enough, all plants stop growing.

Perennials, such as fruit trees, have a natural dormancy in winter. They drop their old leaves in the fall and withdraw the sap from their stems so they can survive very cold weather without damage. They won't suddenly start to grow if there is a brief period of warm weather in midwinter because they also need the lengthening days of spring to break the dormant state and stimulate growth. Leafy vegetables, on the other hand, are just resting in the cold; they can take advantage of warm spells in a mild winter to resume growing a bit.

How well plants withstand winter temperatures depends on when, how quickly, and for how long it turns cold. As days get shorter and temperatures gradually drop, plants harden off, becoming used to the cold. If there is unusually cold weather in late November, before plants have hardened off completely, they can be injured by temperatures that wouldn't hurt them in midwinter. In spring, if there has been mild weather for a month and plants start to grow again, a late cold snap can cause far more injury than the same temperatures would have done earlier.

At the other end of the thermometer, as temperatures rise, plants grow faster—but only to a point. When it is too warm (above 82° to 95°F or 28° to 35°C, depending on the crop), plant growth slows or may even stop temporarily. In hot weather, the balance between photosynthesis (making sugars) and respiration (using sugars for energy) gets out of whack—and plants become stressed as their stores of sugars are used up in hot weather faster than they can be replaced. Vegetables lose their sweetness, and flavors become bitter (e.g., lettuce) or bland (e.g., tomatoes).

To avoid a disastrous loss of water when it is too hot, plants have to close the pores (called stomata) on their leaves during the hottest part of the day. This shuts down photosynthesis; plants cannot start making food again until it is cool enough for the pores to open. Closing the stomata also shuts off the plant's cooling system because water is no longer evaporating from leaves. So not only does a prolonged hot spell mean a prolonged inability to make food, but it also leaves the cells of fruit and foliage vulnerable to heat injury (sunscald).

Growth and Flowering

While they are young, vegetable plants should be growing quickly. This period of vegetative growth gives the plants more leaf area (more capacity to photosynthesize) and bigger roots (more access to water and nutrients from the soil). If all goes according to plan, by the time conditions are right for them to produce flowers and fruit, plants will have accumulated enough food reserves to support a good crop.

For vegetables such as lettuce, leafy greens, or root crops, the vegetative growth period should be as long as possible because we harvest the leaves or roots, not the flowers and fruit. For these plants, fertile soil, high levels of nitrogen, and regular watering help prolong their vegetative growth period. For fruiting plants, however, such as squash or tomatoes, a prolonged period of leafy growth isn't desirable, because it delays flowers and fruit production. Such plants would eventually produce a large crop, but in the coastal climate, we usually don't have a long enough growing season to reap the full harvest.

Once a plant switches over to flowering mode, its vegetative growth slows, at least until the fruit is picked. If a squash plant or a very young fruit tree, for

1.3. A tale of two squash: The plant on the left was sown April 6; the plant on the right May 6. Vegetative growth of the older plant was stunted by being held too long in a pot. Now it is flowering, but it is too small to carry a crop.

example, is allowed to carry fruit while the plant is too small, the plant has to divert energy into the fruit, resulting in stunted growth. To avoid this, simply pick off early flowers that form when plants are too small.

Several things can cause plants to flower:

- Day length is a signal to some. At these northern latitudes, spinach, for example, resolutely flowers in response to the long days of June, no matter how early or late it is sown in the spring.
- Temperature is a signal for others. Biennials flower after experiencing the cold of winter; other plants flower in response to the heat of summer.
- Stress from a poor nutrient or water supply, from being root-bound in a small container, or from unseasonably cool weather can cause plants to flower prematurely (see Vernalization section below). This is why it is so important to grow seedlings under good conditions, and to do what you can to avoid stressing them.

1.4. Leeks flowering in response to a cool spell that happened shortly after they were transplanted. Only the largest one has gone to flower, but if they had all been that large, they might all have flowered this summer.

Vernalization (or Why Vegetables Unexpectedly Go to Seed)

Vernalization is a plant's response to low temperatures that results in flowering. After the cold of winter, biennials normally bolt, meaning they send up flowers. But if a seedling is big enough, a spring cold spell can fool it into behaving as if winter has passed, so it grows a flower stalk in its first summer instead of waiting (as it normally would) until the following spring. Crops readily vernalized by cool temperatures in the spring include beets, Swiss chard, cauliflower, cabbage, onions, leeks, celery, and celeriac. Temperatures of 40° to 50°F (5° to 10°C) for one to two weeks, for example, can be enough to cause onions to bolt.

Plants can only be induced to flower if they have grown large enough to have sufficient food reserves to devote to flowering. If the cold period happens while seedlings are still tiny, they won't flower because they are too small. Plants don't have to be very large, however, to respond to cool temperatures. Onion sets larger than a nickel and cabbage or leek transplants with stems the thickness of a pencil are big enough to be induced to flower prematurely by a cool spell. The larger the seedlings are when the cool weather occurs, the more likely it is that they will switch to flowering mode.

Vernalization is a particular problem for coastal gardeners eager to get a jump on the season. In our mild climate, it is often possible to sow seeds of hardy vegetables as early as February. If there is a nice long period of mild weather, these early seedlings grow big enough that a late cold spell (and we always seem to get a late cold spell!) can cause them to flower. You don't see the flower stalks immediately, but the plants get set on a growth path that will result in premature flowers later on.

Vernalization is also a problem if you try to get a head start by starting seeds indoors too early. If you do a good job of growing large healthy transplants and set them out early, it can take as little as a week of cool weather to induce some of them to flower. Our spring weather is so variable that it is more reliable to start seedlings later and plant out small plants that can tolerate a late cold spell without bolting.

Pollination and Fruit Set

For many vegetables, flowers are only important if you want to save seeds. For fruiting plants, however, such as tomatoes, squash, apples, or blueberries, there can only be a crop if the plants flower and the flowers are successfully fertilized.

Pollination occurs when the dust-like pollen from the male parts (stamens) reaches the female parts (pistils) of the flower. The flower is successfully fertilized when the pollen grain sends a pollen tube into the egg cells in the ovary of the female flower. Most vegetables and fruit have flowers with both male and female parts in the same flower. Most are also self-fertile, meaning that pollen from the same flower only has to drop onto the pistil within the flower for fertilization to proceed. Bean and pea flowers, for example, are already pollinated by the time the flowers open.

1.5. Bumble bee working an apple blossom. Bees are called "nature's sparkplugs" because, without them, many plants can't start to produce a crop.

Were Your Squash Flowers Pollinated?

Many disappointed gardeners want to know why their squash plants produce flowers but no fruit. It happens because the flowers were not pollinated. The flowers need bees to pollinate them, but wild bees are scarcer now, and few people keep domestic honeybees in populated areas anymore. Bees are also less active in cool weather, so flowers go unpollinated when it is cool and rainy. The bottom line is that nowadays gardeners need to know how to hand pollinate flowers (for instructions, see the entry for squash in Chapter 10, A to Z Vegetables).

Many species of bees, flies, and other insects have a vital role in pollinating flowers. As they collect nectar and pollen, they move the pollen from one blossom to another. Bumblebees, because of their large size, also vibrate flowers as they work, which causes the pollen to fall onto the pistil inside the flower. People can be another pollinating agent: gardeners can hand pollinate flowers to improve fruit set or to make sure seeds they save are true to the variety.

Some crops, such as squash, cucumbers, and melons, have separate male and female flowers on the same plant. They depend on insects (or people) to carry the pollen from male to female flowers. This is also the case for kiwi fruit, which has male flowers on one plant and female flowers on a separate plant. Corn has separate male and female flowers on the same plant, but it depends on wind to shake the pollen from the male flowers at the top of the plant onto the silks of the ears (female part) lower on the stalks. Other plants pollinated by wind include tomatoes and grapes. The flowers are self-fertile, but they need the wind to shake the pollen onto the pistils within the flowers.

Despite having flowers with both male and female parts, many varieties of fruit can only be successfully fertilized if the pollen comes from flowers of a different variety. This is called cross-pollination, and it complicates your choice of what to

1.6. No pollen equals no squash. The shriveling small zucchinis at the bottom of the picture were not fertilized.

grow in a small garden. Without a suitable variety for cross-pollination, flowers of apples, pears, and many other fruits can't be successfully fertilized. Some crops, such as blueberries, do have self-fertile flowers, but cross-pollination from other varieties helps to increase the amount of fruit set.

When I was a child, no one hand pollinated squash, fruit trees, or other crops. The many species of native bees and other pollinators were out there, so we didn't even think about it. Since then, the loss of native pollinating insects and domestic honeybees has meant that pollination is no longer guaranteed. For how to pollinate fruit flowers, see Chapter 6, Basic Methods for Growing Fruit).

Fruit without Fertilization

Parthenocarpic varieties of plants set fruit whether or not the flowers were successfully fertilized. For example, the early tomato varieties Oregon Spring and Siletz can set fruit when it is too cold for tomato pollen to successfully fertilize the flowers. The unfertilized flowers develop seedless fruit; later, in warm weather, they produce normal fruit.

Long English cucumbers also set fruit without pollination. In fact, greenhouse growers take care to avoid letting the fruit be fertilized. They remove all male flowers and screen bees out of greenhouses because fertilized cucumbers have a bulbous end instead of the long slender shape desired.

What's Next?

I imagine you are wondering whether you really need to know all this and when we are going to get to the hands-on gardening information. I have spent so much time on vernalization and pollination biology because in my experience those are the two main sources of grief for gardeners in this climate. When plants bolt prematurely or flowers go unfertilized, it results in a partial or even complete crop failure—and there is nothing more discouraging after all the work you put into to the garden.

Now, on to planning that garden!

CHAPTER 2

Planning a Productive Garden

Vegetables and fruit are all sun lovers: the less direct sunlight there is, the slower they grow. Sadly, the amount of sunshine is the factor that you may have the least power to change (especially if it is your neighbor's house that is blocking the sun!). Happily, you can improve many other things—soil depth and quality, drainage, and irrigation—so before you pick your site, start with finding out where the sun shines the longest in your yard. If that is a concrete patio, not to worry: you can build vegetable beds on top of concrete if you have to.

The ideal site for a garden is where it will receive full sun for six to eight hours of the day from March through September, when plants are most actively growing. But also keep in mind that, for plants harvested from November to February, the best location is where they also have the most protection from cold and wind.

Lettuce and salad greens can grow fairly well in gardens that offer about half a day (four hours) of good sunshine during the summer, but tomatoes and other heat-loving crops must have more than that. The warm midday sun is the most important. Most gardens do get enough direct sun in the middle of the day from early May through late August because the sun is highest in the sky then. Some fortunate people have gardens in open sites that receive sun all day, but most of us have to work around obstacles that block the light in the morning or afternoon when the sun is lower in the sky.

As the angle of the sun and the length of day changes over the year, the amount of sun reaching a garden depends on neighboring buildings, trees, and other objects. With the sun low in the sky in December, even a short fence

Will Anything Grow in a Shady Yard?

If you have a spot that gets half a day of direct sun over the summer months, by all means experiment with growing some vegetables. Start with lettuce, spinach, arugula, or Chinese cabbage and other leafy greens—and be patient: the less sunlight the plants receive, the slower they grow.

casts a long shadow (if the sun ever comes out, of course). It is too cold for plant growth anyway, so exposure to direct sun isn't that important in midwinter. For example, my garden receives only about one and a half hours of direct sun in December, due to a neighboring mountaintop, but my winter harvests are plentiful because the plants have already done their growing in the growing season.

Get to Know Your Garden

Even in a small yard, there are microclimates that can make a difference in which crops will grow best there.

Light and shade: Some parts of the garden are likely to be more shaded than others, and this changes over the season as the angle of the sun changes. Once they reach their full

2.1. Vegetables and fruits need as much sun as they can get during their growing seasons.

height, tall crops eventually shade other plants, so there may only be certain places where they can be grown (usually along the north side of a garden). Reserve the places that receive the most sun for heat-loving crops.

I find it useful to periodically note where the sun and shade falls on my garden beds as the season goes by. For one thing, knowing the hours of sunlight on a particular date in the spring will also tell you what it will be like in the fall. Dates that are an equal number of days before and after the summer solstice (June 21) have the same day length. So the sun exposure on April 12, ten weeks before the solstice, will be the same as ten weeks after the solstice on August 30. Over the years, occasionally checking where and when the sunlight falls on your garden is useful, because it is hard to see slow changes, such as the growth of trees that gradually block the light. What might have been a very sunny bed can become too shady to grow vegetables in later years.

Gardeners are usually looking for more space to grow crops, and you might find there are some useful places you haven't thought of as garden space. When the sun is lower in the fall, it can reach under decks, porches, and building overhangs that would have been too shady to grow vegetables in June. Such protected spots make good places for hardy greens to spend the winter. (You can sow them in August or transplant them from the main garden later.) And don't overlook the possibilities of expanding into your flower beds: many vegetables are beautiful and look lovely mixed with flowers or even by themselves in ornamental beds.

2.2. Late-August peas happily growing at the shadier end of the garden in the summer.

Soil drainage: While you *can* grow summer vegetables on low-lying wet ground by planting late, after the soil has dried out, such sites won't be good for growing winter vegetables. For overwintering crops, either choose a site that is already well-drained or improve a poorly drained site—by installing a raised bed, for instance.

Air circulation: The flow of cool air depends on the terrain. You may find frost pockets in slightly lower spots where cold air settles on clear cold nights in spring or fall. When there has been a light frost overnight, note where the frosty patches are in your garden. These won't be good spots for the most frost-sensitive crops, such as cucumbers or squash. These are also likely to be the coldest areas of the garden in the winter, so avoid planting overwintering crops in these areas, or reserve them for the hardiest plants, such as kale, corn salad, or parsley.

Tree roots: Encroaching roots from yard or boulevard trees, even nearby hedges, are always a problem when they get into garden beds. They spread much farther than you might think and well beyond the dripline of the branches. Vegetables simply cannot compete with tree roots, which suck up huge amounts of water and nutrients, yet in some yards, the best sunshine may be found on the south side of a tall hedge. Removing the trees is rarely an option, so what can you do? One approach is to set large planters on top of the soil, and another is to build beds with solid bottoms (such as boards, marine-grade plywood, or concrete patio squares) that don't let in tree roots. Some people build their boxes raised an inch or two on short legs to make sure roots can't invade. The soil should be at least 18 inches deep for best results growing vegetables. Another approach is to dig a deep trench along the edge of the garden where tree roots are coming in and bury barriers. Commercial root barriers are widely available from hardware stores and online in US and Canada. Some barriers are rolls of heavy black plastic, others are rigid sections that lock together; they come in different widths to block roots at different depths. You can also bury recycled galvanized sheet metal or 18- to 24-inch-wide metal flashing. Do not use landscape fabric or plastic sheeting for this purpose, as tree roots will bust right through such materials.

Keeping roots of vegetables and fruit well away from roots of black walnut trees is particularly necessary, because they exude a compound called juglone that is toxic to nightshade family plants, apple trees, and berries. The toxic zone from a mature black walnut tree can extend 60 feet or more from the trunk. If you can't plant far enough away from the tree to avoid its roots, then grow vegetables in planters or build beds with a solid bottom.

Garden Bed Design

Gardens are as personal and varied as the people who make them. Authors of garden books are an opinionated bunch, and we all swear by our own ways of designing gardens. But, really, plants don't give a hoot about that; they seem to grow fine regardless of human opinion. Personally, I'm glad I didn't read a lot of gardening books when I started gardening because the amount of work some people go to would have stopped me in my tracks. Since this book is about my own intensively planted, organic, low-maintenance, year-round coastal garden, that's what I am going to describe. But ultimately, the best design for your garden is the one that works for you.

Permanent Beds

Growing crops in permanent beds is popular in this region for good reason. Compared to a garden plot that is tilled from edge to edge every year, there are several advantages to permanent beds:

- Once beds are laid out, pathways and growing areas don't change over the years.
- Only planted areas need be fertilized, watered, and weeded, which saves work and resources.

2.3. Permanent beds are very productive and save a lot of work.

2.4. A common ground beetle—one of the good guys you want to encourage to live in your garden.

Credit: E. Cronin

A Stable Home for a Gardener's BFFs

Ground beetles eat slug eggs, root maggots, and other garden pests. Because they are territorial and long-lived (for an insect), they appear earlier in the season and in higher numbers in gardens with undisturbed areas. They use these areas as refuges while garden beds are being dug and planted.

- Soil in beds doesn't become compacted, because you don't walk on it.
- It can be easier to control weeds between beds when the pathways are permanent.
- Permanent pathways can provide a refuge for beneficial insects that eat plant pests.

Beds can be any length or shape, but should be narrow enough that you can reach the center easily without stepping off the pathway. Four feet is a width most people find workable. If they are too wide, you will end up walking on them, which compacts the soil.

Beds should also be designed with the irrigation method you plan to use in mind (see Chapter 4). Despite our wet winters on the coast, there are several dry months in the summer when crop plants need irrigation. The drier the summer climate is where you are, the more important this consideration will be.

Do you need raised beds?

Permanent beds do not have to be raised beds. Whether you decide to build up the height of the soil in raised beds depends on your site and on personal preference. Vegetable beds must have soil at least 12 inches (30 cm) deep. A depth of 18 inches (45 cm) is better—and deeper than that is better yet. If the soil in your garden is very shallow, you can increase the depth and also improve drainage by building raised beds. If you have deep, well-drained soil, however, you might be better off not building raised beds. Permanent, but not raised, beds usually need less water during the summer, and the root zone stays cooler in a heat wave.

Raised beds may or may not have sides to hold the soil in place. Soil on garden beds can be mounded up a foot or so deep without being supported by sides. Building a bed without sides is cheaper and easier to make, initially, and beds can be quickly changed as plans change.

2.5. Raised beds don't need to have sides.

If deeper soil is desirable, sides for beds can be made of any material, including untreated wood (scrap lumber, utility-grade cedar boards), recycled plastic landscape "wood," or stone, brick, or concrete blocks. Treated wood is not acceptable for certified organic growers, and no one should use wood treated with creosote, pentachlorophenol, or chromated copper arsenate (CCA). These are toxic chemicals that can leach into the soil and should never be used around food crops. Some people now use borate pressure-treated wood, which is considered a more benign treatment. I would still advise lining it with heavy plastic as a barrier to prevent leaching into the soil. Though I have used wood to build garden beds in the past, I don't like it because wood attracts such large numbers of pillbugs (see Chapter 9) when it starts to rot in a few years.

2.6. Well-built stone sides on permanent beds.

To summarize, raised beds have several advantages:
- They provide improved drainage for the root zone in low-lying wet soils.
- They can be used to terrace steep slopes so the soil is held level in a bed.
- Soil warms more quickly in the spring, which is particularly desirable in cool, foggy regions and for gardens with heavy clay soils.
- Beds several feet high can make gardening more comfortable for people who have trouble bending down to ground level.
- Gardens can be built on rocky surfaces (or concrete or asphalt).

Raised beds also have disadvantages:
- Plants generally need more irrigation in the summer dry season.

2.7. Deep soil in planters built on top of concrete.

- Soils may be too warm and too dry in midsummer, especially sandy soils that are already well-drained.
- They take work to build and maintain, and they require some investment in materials.

For many gardeners, the choice comes down to personal preference. You may find that raised beds suit some parts of your garden, but not necessarily the whole garden.

Pathways

Paths can become weedy messes if not maintained. As you might expect, I try to keep maintenance to a minimum. Here are a couple of ways to handle the pathways between garden beds:

Mulches: The best option for most gardens is to use a thick, fairly permanent mulch of some kind on pathways to control weeds. You can use wood chips, shredded bark, leaves, straw, newspapers, or any combination of these and other materials. Laying a solid mat of newspapers or cardboard along a path and covering it with a layer of wood chips or leaves gives a neat, weed-free appearance for the whole season. Tough leaves, such as oak and arbutus/ madrone, make especially long-lasting mulches for pathways. For the small intensively planted space I have now, narrow well-mulched paths have been easy to maintain; they look good and don't require periodic mowing or clipping.

Permanent sod: You can also sow pathways with lawn grass or white clover to make a permanent sod. If you make the pathways wide enough to accommodate a lawn mower, you can maintain them by periodic mowing. This works better for permanent beds without solid sides because the mower wheel can ride along the soil edge of the bed, giving a clean cut. Once a year, you'll probably need to recut the edge along the sod with a spade or edging tool to prevent the sod from taking over the bed. This method isn't quite as low-maintenance for raised beds with sides because the mower leaves an untrimmed strip along the sides where the wheels travel. Where wireworms are a problem (which, unfortunately, is pretty much everywhere on the coast), permanent sod invites adults to lay eggs and can harbor large numbers of larvae that continually move sideways into the garden beds to infest roots of crops.

Pathways are much easier to manage when you use a drip or seep irrigation system as opposed to sprinklers. Without overhead watering, there is considerably less weed growth in pathways.

Breaking New Ground

In the first year or two of a new garden, it usually takes extra work to establish the beds. You might have to put up a fence, build beds, or bring in more soil. There's no way around it: this takes work. But, the long planting season on the coast means that not all of your beds have to be done at once. Get one done and plant it before building another. If you plan on building five beds, you can make one every month from March through July and plant as you go.

To make the job of converting lawn or weedy sod into a new garden easier, cover the area with a thick mat of newspaper or sheets of cardboard, old tarps, or other light-excluding materials to smother the sod. A huge thick pile of leaves left on the spot over the winter will have the same effect. Ideally, you should do this in the fall, to be ready to garden in the spring, but it can be done anytime, as long as it is at least three months before you want to plant. When you smother the sod in place, it is much better for your soil, because it preserves every bit of top soil and the dead roots add substantial organic matter. You won't believe how much easier this is than digging up sod!

If you *do* have to remove sod, shake as much soil from the roots as you can, then compost the rest. That layer of soil still clinging to the roots is the best topsoil you have, so you will want to return it to the garden eventually.

Choosing What to Grow

Now that you know *where* to garden, it is time to figure out what to grow. If you have limited space, you might want to concentrate on a few favorite vegetables or special crops that are expensive or hard to find in the market. Some gardeners, for example, don't bother with potatoes or carrots because they are relatively cheap and always available. I do grow them, however, because the flavor of a carrot right out of the ground is irresistible, and tiny new potatoes are a gourmet treat.

Start with the Easiest Plants

Some vegetables are easier to grow than others in the coastal climate. If you are a beginning gardener, the vegetables on this list are usually good ones to start with:

- lettuce and other salad greens
- onions from sets
- garlic
- some plants in the cabbage family (broccoli, cabbage, kale)
- summer squash (zucchini, crooknecks, patty pan)
- beans
- peas
- beets, radishes, turnips, rutabaga
- potatoes
- Swiss chard
- parsley and annual herbs (dill, cilantro)

In addition, perennial herbs such as chives, thyme, sage, and mint are easy to grow, as are hardy perennials like French sorrel and rhubarb.

Some vegetables grow well in the coastal climate, but are a bit more of a challenge:

- Carrots germinate slowly, making it difficult to get a good stand of seedlings; once established, carrots are not hard to grow.
- Cauliflower is very sensitive to cold, heat, lack of nutrients, and irregular watering.
- Brussels sprouts are frost hardy, but quite sensitive to hot weather.
- Leeks, onions from seed, celery, and celeriac have to be started indoors very early in the season (if you are a first time gardener, try to buy seedlings).
- Globe artichokes need special care to survive the wet winters (see entry for artichokes in Chapter 10, A to Z Vegetables).
- Asparagus takes up a lot of space and needs high fertility.

Vegetables that need a long warm season have traditionally been the most difficult for coastal growers to manage, especially along the ocean and straits where it is much cooler than inland areas. Tomatoes, in particular, are generally quite vigorous and put up with more cool (but not cold) weather than other heat-loving plants. The following are heat lovers that can be challenging to grow in cool years and in the cooler parts of the region:

- sweet and hot peppers
- winter squash
- cucumbers, melons
- eggplant
- sweet corn

All but sweet corn either have to be started early indoors so they have time to mature, or you should buy started seedlings in the spring. Also, some of these—winter squash and sweet corn, in particular—take up a lot of space.

Among the fruit, I think June-bearing strawberries are the easiest and most reliable. They are well-adapted to the climate, and the early ripening berries miss the peak season for an invasive fruit fly (spotted wing Drosophila) that has become a serious fruit pest in the region. With controls in place for the fruit fly (see Chapter 9), however, everbearing strawberries, blueberries, currants, and gooseberries are also easy to grow. Raspberries and other bramble fruit are well-adapted to the climate, but do require more pruning and training to keep the canes within bounds, and are prime hosts for pest fruit flies.

Among the tree fruits, apples and plums are probably the most reliable, but tree fruit (and vine fruit, like grapes and kiwi) generally can be more challenging to grow than berry crops. Most have pests that require some knowledge to deal with, some have cross-pollination requirements, they take up more space, and they require at least some pruning (or a lot) every year. That said, well-chosen and maintained fruit trees and vines can provide harvests for many years.

Choosing Varieties

There are hundreds to thousands of varieties of every kind of vegetable and fruit, each with different characteristics. To a botanist, a variety is a naturally occurring subgroup within a plant species; a particular variety has characteristics that differ in some ways from the main species (such as growth habit, variegated leaves, fruit qualities). A cultivar is a cultivated variety, usually selected for certain desirable characteristics (the equivalent of breeds in animals). I will stick to the term "variety" to cover both for the purposes of this book.

By some counts, there are over 7,500 tomato varieties worldwide, ranging from pea-sized yellow to gigantic green-and-red-striped. Lettuce varieties include leaf, buttercrunch, romaine, and iceberg—in various leaf shapes, textures, and colors. Some are adapted to spring planting, some tolerate summer heat, and others are frost-hardy.

So, how to choose? Read the seed descriptions in catalogs, particularly those from local and regional seed suppliers; they will have prescreened varieties to find the best for the region. Ask local gardeners (join a local garden club or veggie group). Some of my favorite varieties are the ones I've grown from seed given to me by neighbors.

Keep trying different varieties. After a while, you will discover which ones you like the most for taste, how well they grow in your garden, and other characteristics. In fact, given the variable weather patterns coming our way as the climate changes, it is a good idea to always grow several varieties of each crop, even when you only want a few plants. There are notable differences in how

A Cautionary Note

If you are tempted to grow interesting varieties from international seed houses or heirloom seed banks, do some research first on what they require. Some vegetables are sensitive to day length, such as onions, spinach, and Chinese cabbage; varieties adapted to the southern United States (e.g., southern California or Texas) might not behave as desired at our latitude, which has much longer days in June. Short-day onions, for example, may only form small bulbs in a region with long days such as ours. Many heritage varieties of tomatoes, sweet corn, and winter squash need the long hot summers of the Midwest and southern United States to mature. Varieties from British and Dutch seed suppliers, however, usually do well in the Pacific Northwest because of the similar climate and latitude.

well varieties handle heat waves, late frost and cold snaps, drought, waterlogging, diseases, and other stresses. In the drought summer of 2015, three of the six onion varieties I planted failed—but three varieties, growing in the same bed, did much better. If I had only grown one of the failed varieties, I would have had no onions that year (and also wouldn't have known that some varieties could handle the stress). Which reminds me to remind you: *always* records the names of varieties you plant so you can grow more of the successes and avoid the failures.

When you are perusing the descriptions in seed catalogs, look for the following:

Climate and season adaptation: The coastal zone is relatively cool in the summer, with few really warm days. Therefore, look for "short season" or "early" varieties of tomatoes, corn, peppers, cucumbers, and melons. In the cooler, foggier region along the ocean, even the earliest varieties may not ripen unless they are grown in a greenhouse or plastic tunnel or under row covers to trap heat. If your garden is in a warm, protected location on the inner coast, though, you might find you can usually grow warm-season varieties that take longer to mature.

For winter vegetables, look for descriptions of cold hardiness and suitability for winter conditions, such as "frost hardy" or "stands all winter." There are big differences in cold hardiness among varieties of leeks, lettuce, other leafy greens, endive, broccoli, cauliflower, and other crops. Choosing the right varieties can make all the difference in the success of your winter harvest.

Days to harvest/days to maturity: Where seed catalogs give a number after the variety name, it refers to the number of days from planting to harvest. For example, "Sturon, 110 days" means that this onion would take 110 days to mature under ideal conditions. For most crops, the days are counted from the time the crop is seeded. For commonly transplanted crops, however, such as cabbage or tomatoes, the days are usually counted from the date of transplanting.

Since growth rate depends on temperature, soil fertility, and water supply, how long it will take a particular variety to actually mature in your garden can vary from the number given—often by quite a bit. The "days to harvest" figure is most useful as a guide for comparing varieties: a 110-day variety will obviously take longer to mature than a 90-day variety.

Open pollinated vs. hybrid plants: Open pollinated, or OP, varieties are like purebred animals, which have both parents of the same "breed." Seeds of each successive generation should produce plants that look and taste just like the parents. A great advantage of growing OP varieties is that you can save seed and know that the next generations will have the characteristics you expect.

2.8. For hardy varieties of leeks and leafy greens, winter temperatures are no problem.

There are many excellent OP varieties, well adapted to the coastal climate, but the selection has dwindled over the years as the large seed companies focused primarily on developing hybrid varieties that could be patented. Most OP varieties left have been those kept going by the smaller local seed companies and are those maintained in seed banks such as Seeds of Diversity (Canada) and Organic Seed Alliance (US). These are often called "heritage" or "heirloom" varieties, but there is no standard definition of these terms. Basically, they are tried and true varieties that have been grown for many years. Opinions differ on how old a variety has to be to be called heritage. I was surprised to see Sugar Snap peas billed as a heritage variety because I remember when they came out as a new variety in the 1970s. That certainly made me feel old!

In the last decade, there has been a revival of interest in actively breeding new OP varieties with characteristics valued by organic growers. Led by the Organic Seed Alliance in the US, breeding programs involve growers and university researchers. The first release, in 2015, was the sweet corn Who Gets Kissed, disease-resistant and adapted to cool conditions and short seasons. It was released as an "open source" variety, meaning no seed company owns a patent and growers can save their own seed. Breeding programs for zucchini, purple sprouting broccoli, spinach, and other crops are in progress.

Many vegetable and fruit varieties are hybrids. Hybrids are common in nature (for example, nearly all apple varieties are really hybrids, because apple flowers have to receive pollen from a different variety to be fertilized). The names of horticultural hybrids usually show the term "F1" as part of their name (sometimes seed suppliers omit this). It means that the parent plants come from two different "lines" of that crop. When the male from one line is used to pollinate the female from a different line, the next generation of plants (the F1 generation) has a predictable and unique blend of characteristics from the parents.

There are many excellent hybrids that give good results in home gardens under a variety of weather conditions. Hybrids, like cross-bred animals, tend to be robust due to the phenomenon known as "hybrid vigor." Hybrid seed is usually more expensive, but the main problem with hybrids is that they don't come "true" from seed. If you save seeds, the next generation will show a mix of characteristics that won't be the same as the parent plants.

I like to save as much of my own seed as possible, but do grow a few hybrids because they have characteristics I haven't, so far, found in OP plants. For example, the hybrid zucchini Partenon F1 is parthenocarpic, meaning it can set fruit without being pollinated. In my garden, it produces fruit into early November, far longer than OP varieties, because it doesn't depend on bees being able to fly in good weather for pollination. It is difficult to save squash seed, and I only use a few seeds each year anyway, so I don't mind buying a package of hybrid zucchini seeds every five or six years.

Disease resistance: The moist, cool climate of the coastal region favors many plant diseases. Fortunately, among the many varieties of fruit and vegetables, some are notable for their disease resistance. Growing disease-resistant varieties is the easiest and most effective way to avoid many plant diseases (see Table 2.1 for examples).

Careful reading of variety descriptions will turn up information on disease-resistance characteristics. It is a good idea to cross-check with various seed suppliers (online catalogs are great for this), as some don't list disease resistance. For example, Marketmore cucumber is widely available, but the fact that it is more disease resistant than other open pollinated varieties is not always listed.

Disease Resistance Terminology

Some varieties are listed as "immune" to a particular disease, meaning they won't be infected even if conditions favor the disease. Others are described as "resistant," meaning they won't be infected unless condition are very favorable for the disease, in which case, infections will likely be minor. Varieties listed as "tolerant" can be infected but should continue to produce reasonably well unless conditions are highly favorable for the disease.

2.9. Leaves of powdery mildew-resistant zucchini (*center*) are undamaged even though they are surrounded by infected crookneck squash leaves.

Table 2.1. Varieties of fruit and vegetables resistant to plant diseases of concern on the West Coast.

Fruit	Disease	Examples of Resistant or Tolerant* Varieties Available at Time of Writing
Apples	Apple scab	**Resistant:** Akane, Bramley's Seedling, Elstar, Enterprise, Fiesta, Goldstar, Jonafree, King, Liberty, Macoun, Mutsu, Priscilla, Redfree, Spartan, Sunrise, Wagener, Wolf River, Yellow Transparent **Immune:** Pristine, Williams' Pride, Prima, Dayton, Releika, Rajka, Liberty, Belmac, Goldstar
Grapes (table)	Powdery mildew	**American hybrids:** Himrod, Interlaken, Reliance, Coronation, Vanessa
Peaches	Peach leaf curl	Frost, Pacific Gold, Renton, Avalon Pride, Oregon Curl Free
Pears	Pear scab	Orcas, Harrow Delight, Bosc, Rescue, most varieties of Asian pears
Raspberries	Phytophthora root rot	Cascade Bounty, Cascade Delight, Latham, Newburgh, Prelude, Autumn Bliss
Vegetables		
Beets	Cercospora leaf spot	Red Ace F1, Pacemaker F1, Merlin F1
Beets	Powdery mildew	Detroit Supreme
Cucumbers	Powdery mildew	Marketmore, Slice More F1, General Lee F1, Fountain F1, Olympian F1, Excelsior F1
Peas	Powdery mildew	**Pod:** Maestro, Sabre, Perfect Arrow/Grundy, Serge **Snap:** Cascadia, Sugar Lace II, Sugar Ann, Sugar Bon, Sugar Sprint **Snow:** Avalanche, Oregon Giant, Sweet Horizon
Peas	Pea enation virus	**Pod:** Aladdin, Maestro **Snap:** Cascadia, Sugar Lace II, Sugar Sprint **Snow:** Oregon Giant, Oregon Sugar Pod II
Potatoes	Potato scab (tolerance only)	Chieftain, Norland, Viking, Russet Burbank, Satina, Seiglinde, Goldrush, Orchestra, Colomba, Warba
Spinach	Downy mildew	Seaside F1, Escalade F1, Samish F1, Corvair F1, Yukon F1, Giant Winter/Viroflex, Speedy F1
Squash	Powdery mildew	**Winter Squash:** Golden Nugget F1, Orange Summer Kuri F1, Tiana Butternut F1, Autumn Delight F1, Bush Delicata, Honey Bear F1, Fairy F1, Butterscotch F1 **Summer Squash:** Yellowfin F1, Grey Griller F1, Astia F1, Anton F1, Emerald Delight F1, Delta F1 (crookneck)

*Note: Tolerance to disease is more common than true resistance; tolerant varieties can be infected when conditions are good for the pathogen, but usually suffer smaller losses.

How Much to Plant

Quantity is something that is very hard to judge when you are new to gardening. Over time, of course, as you keep records, you will learn how much your household generally uses of each crop.

There is a big difference in space requirements between a summer and winter crop of the same vegetable. For example, 2 to 3 square feet of lettuce and salad greens for a small family is plenty for each successive planting in April, May, and June. For winter salads, however, one big planting in early August has to last all winter, so you might need an area about five times larger (i.e., 10 to 15 square feet). The same for carrots: sowing 4 to 5 square feet in May might be plenty for summer eating, but if you want fresh carrots all winter, you would need to sow a large enough bed in early July to last you for 6 to 8 months.

If you aren't sure how much to plant, I suggest you start with the following space allotments for summer crops:

- 1 to 2 square feet for each tomato, pepper, and cucumber plant; Three to six plants of each usually provide enough for a small family's fresh eating. Grow more plants if you plan to make tomato sauce, pickles, etc., to store.
- 2 to 4 square feet each for these fast-growing vegetables: lettuce, other salad greens, scallions, spinach, Chinese cabbage.
- 8 to 12 square feet for vegetables that occupy the beds all season: beans (one pole bean tepee trellis takes about 8 to 10 square feet of soil area), leeks, broccoli, kale, cabbage, Swiss chard.
- 20 to 40 square feet for each of the "big" vegetables: that's a patch of twenty to forty sweet corn plants, three summer squash, or three winter squash.

When to Plant

Gardeners unfamiliar with the mild coastal climate don't realize that we have a six-month planting season, which provides us with a twelve-month harvest. In the course of a growing season, some garden beds will be used to grow several crops, one after the other. When planning the garden, prepare to have space available to sow crops in June, July, and August. You can grow early crops in these beds, but just make sure they are empty when you need them for summer sowing.

Table 8.1 (p. 186) shows a list of crops with typical planting dates that work for the coastal region. The timing of spring planting depends on the weather and soil temperature: it may be a month earlier in warm springs or a month later in cooler years. Planting dates from June onward, however, do not vary with the weather because the soil is usually warm enough by then to seed anything. In fact, for crops sown June through August for winter harvests, it is the planting *date* that is critical. Plants have to be sown in time to reach full size by the end of the growing season. As the summer draws to a close, day lengths get shorter faster, and with the sun lower in the sky then, many gardens also have more shade. By September, the hours of full sun on the garden each day is much shorter than in midsummer. If crops are planted too late, there just aren't enough hours of sun and warmth left in the growing season to produce a good crop.

Think of the winter garden as a "living refrigerator": plants are alive, but it is too cold, and days are too short for anything to grow. Crops have to do their growing in the growing season; therefore, planting dates have to be early enough to fill that living refrigerator by late October.

Crop Rotation

Rotating crops is a method of managing pests and diseases by depriving them of their host plants for years at a time. The general practice is to leave three to five years between crops in the same family. For example, after potatoes have been harvested, the same soil would not be planted again to potatoes or related plants for several years. Crop rotation is very effective for controlling root diseases and can help with managing a couple of root insects. Crop rotation is not effective for insects that feed on many different plants, such as wireworms or cutworms, or for leaf diseases, such as rusts or powdery mildews.

Some books have made planning garden crop rotations sound complicated, but it can be kept fairly simple. For a home garden, attempting to rotate *all* crops is not only unrealistic but also unnecessary. Only a few families of plants are critical to rotate because of the risk of diseases that live in the soil. Many other common vegetables, such as lettuce, spinach, and Swiss chard, are rarely troubled by soilborne diseases and can be planted anywhere, anytime, without worrying about rotation.

The most important plant families to rotate in a home garden are the carrot, mustard (cabbage), nightshade, and onion families. They are most at risk from soilborne disease or root insects (see Table 2.2). Among the nightshades, potatoes bring the highest risk of disease to the garden, whereas tomatoes or peppers grown from seed present hardly any risk. Rotating potatoes is essential, and they should never be followed by other nightshade family plants—but growing tomatoes or peppers in the same place year after year rarely causes a problem in a home garden (so don't worry if you only have one or two really good spots for your tomatoes).

To simplify crop rotation, try to grow plants from those four key families together in blocks (e.g., keep all onion family crops together in the same area). And, remember that related weeds and self-sown plants, such as kales (mustard family) or dill and cilantro (carrot family), all count in the crop rotation. They must also be kept out of the beds during the rotation period. The only time I covered carrots with insect netting and had it fail to produce a clean crop was the year I didn't pay attention to the fact that self-sown cilantro had come up in the bed earlier. I weeded, sowed the carrots, and covered the seedbed, trapping the carrot rust flies that had been in the cilantro roots under the netting for the rest of the season—they really had a party!

When Crop Rotation is Important (and When It Isn't)

For diseases: Crop rotation may be the only method we have for controlling most root diseases, but it can be very effective. It works because plant pathogens are generally host specific, meaning they live and grow only on closely related plants. Allium pathogens, for example, grow only on onion family plants. If onions and garlic are grown in the same bed for several consecutive years, high numbers of infective spores build up in the soil. If there is a gap of four or five years between onion family plantings, however, most of those dormant spores expire for lack of host plants.

For pest insects: Crop rotation can help to prevent damage from root insects that limit their attack to only one family of host plants: for example, the carrot rust fly only attacks carrot family plants. If you cover carrots with insect netting to prevent rust flies from laying eggs, rotate crops to make sure rust fly maggots are not still in the soil from a previous crop. Root insects become adults and fly away within a few weeks, so crop rotations for the purpose of managing insect pests can be quite short. After a couple of summer months without carrot family plants, you could plant carrots in the same bed again, if necessary (though it would still be better to wait longer between carrot crops as a precaution against root disease). Other pests that live in the soil, such as wireworms, pillbugs, and climbing cutworms, attack such a wide range of plants that crop rotation doesn't help control them (for more on pests and diseases, see Chapter 9).

For fertility: Growing the same crop year after year depletes the soil of the nutrients it uses, which is why you see recommendations to alternate "heavy feeders," such as potatoes or corn, with vegetables that enrich the soil with nitrogen, such as beans or peas. While this is very important in agricultural crop rotations, it doesn't make much difference for a garden because, on such as small scale, you can easily add more compost or fertilizers to compensate for nutrients used by a previous crop.

The following plant families have the lowest risk of soil-borne pests or diseases in the coastal Pacific Northwest (not necessarily the case elsewhere). These can usually be grown without concern for a crop rotation schedule:

- Amaranth family (Amaranthaceae): Beets, spinach, Swiss chard
- Grass family (Poaceae): Corn
- Gourd family (Cucurbitaceae): Cucumbers, squashes, melons, gourds, pumpkin
- Pea family (Fabaceae): Beans, peas, lentils, chickpeas
- Sunflower family (Asteraceae): Lettuce, endive, radicchio, salsify
- Honeysuckle family (Caprifoliaceae): Corn salad

Table 2.2. Vegetable families for planning crop rotation.

Plant families	Family member plants	Root Insects and Soil-borne Diseases in the Coastal Region*
Carrot family Apiaceae	Carrots, celery, celeriac, dill, parsnips, parsley, cilantro	Carrot rust fly, Erwinia root rot
Cabbage (Mustard) family Brassicaceae	Broccoli, cabbages, Brussels sprouts, kales, cauliflower, Chinese cabbage, mustards, arugula, kohlrabi, radishes, rutabagas, turnips	Cabbage root maggot; clubroot of cabbage; black rot
Nightshade family Solanaceae	Tomatoes, peppers, eggplant, potatoes, ground cherries, tomatillo	Scab (potatoes), soilborne wilt viruses; late blight
Onion family Alliaceae	Onions, leeks, garlic, shallots	Onion maggot; many onion and garlic root rots

*Note: This column only shows diseases and pests unique to each plant family, for which crop rotation is helpful.

Making the Most of Your Space

Land is expensive, and few people can afford the large lots or rural properties that make it possible to have a large garden. However, the point of this book is that you don't need to have much space to grow a surprising amount of food, especially if you adopt some of the intensive methods described below. There are several ways to increase productivity so that your garden is full of food most months of the year.

Grow more plants in the same space:

- In fertile soil, you can grow vegetables closer than the spacing recommended on the seed package, sometimes much closer. A bonus is that densely planted crops help control weeds by shading them out.

- Space vegetables out evenly over the garden bed rather than planting in rows with wide spaces between them: you waste much less space on unproductive rows and have a smaller area to weed.

- Within a bed, set individual plants in a staggered pattern, which allows closer spacing while giving each plant the maximum room for its roots. To see how closely you can plant small plants (lettuce, radishes, salad greens, scallions), lay a piece of 2-inch stucco wire or 2-inch chicken wire down on the soil and put one seed or plant in the center of each cell.

2.10 Spacing seeds using 2-inch chicken wire as a template for high-density planting.

Table 2.3. Examples of close spacing.		
Crop	**Inches/feet**	**Centimeters/meters**
Onions, garlic	4–6 inches apart	10–15 cm apart
Celery, celeriac, leeks	6–8 inches apart	15–20 cm apart
Squash: 3 plants per hill	3 feet between hills	1 m between hills
Broccoli, cabbage	12–16 inches apart	30–40 cm apart
Peas, beans	1.5–3 inches apart	4–8 cm apart in wide rows

2.11 Weeds don't have a chance in densely planted beds. I was too busy to weed this bed all summer (the few trying to hang on are along the edge).

- In the first years of a new garden, the soil might not be fertile enough to plant too densely, so keep an eye on how your plants look. You might need to apply liquid fertilizer, such as compost extract, a few times over a summer to keep them growing well. Thin the plants if it looks like they are struggling. Over time, as you continue to add compost and other amendments, your soil will improve and you can grow plants closer together.

Take advantage of vertical space. Crops with sprawling vines take up more space on the ground than their roots do in the soil below. Trellising them off the ground opens up more space for planting:

- Stake up tomatoes, cucumbers, melons, and rambling winter squash or train the vines on a trellis. (You can make slings of cloth or netting to support squash and melons so they don't pull the vines off the trellis.)
- Grow pole beans instead of bush beans; they produce more over a longer season in the same amount of space.
- Use the space along fences and walls to grow plants you can train vertically, such as pole beans, peas, and grapevines.

As well as using vertical space, sometimes you can use non-garden space to accommodate plants temporarily. For example, you can plant winter squash (most are notorious ramblers) where you can direct the vines between corn plants, over a patio or other non-garden space.

Avoid wasting space on unproductive plants. Gardeners soon learn that a small patch of lettuce can provide a lot of salad, and that radishes shoot past their prime in days. To avoid wasting space on crops you won't use, sow smaller amounts of the quick-maturing vegetables at two- to four-week intervals. That way you don't have too much of any one vegetable to deal with at one time, and you can enjoy a longer harvest of vegetables in prime condition. The coastal growing season is quite long for crops that thrive in cool conditions, making second, third, or even fourth plantings of peas, lettuce, and cauliflower possible (see Table 2.4 for other examples).

Keep trying out different planting dates for your favorite vegetables: you might discover how to enjoy them longer. It was only after years of sowing peas in early spring (having given up on them as a fall crop) that I realized how well they do when sown in mid-June in the shady end of my garden. I now enjoy peas through October! And a few years ago, I learned that seeding a second crop of zucchini plants in the third week of June results in robust young plants producing fruit late into the fall.

2.12. An astonishing quantity of pole beans grow in a few square feet of space.

Get Rid of Surplus Plants!

It seems like a waste to discard unused plants—but it isn't nearly as much of a waste as an unproductive garden bed. Give the vegetables away or pull them out (and make a note not to plant so many next time). But if you do overplant, you can console yourself knowing they will make great compost or mulch.

Table 2.4. Examples of succession planting.

Crops	Schedules
Radishes, lettuce, mixed salad greens	Every 2 to 3 weeks until mid-August
Peas	Monthly, March to end of June
Sweet corn, early variety (65–70 days)	Two-week intervals, early May (started indoors) to mid/late June
Bush beans	Three weeks apart, mid-May to late June
Cauliflower, spring/summer varieties	Monthly, March (started indoors) to late July
Potatoes, for harvest as new potatoes	Two or three plantings between March and June
Zucchini	Second sowing 3rd week of June for young plants resistant to powdery mildew in late summer

Minimize the time garden space stands empty: A Dutch grower once told me "never leave a space empty more than a day." In our climate, this is quite possible. Many vegetables for winter harvests can be sown immediately after spring crops are finished. For example, the earliest sowings of peas, radishes, lettuce, and other salad greens are usually exhausted by July. Garlic (planted the fall before) and onions (from onion sets) are also harvested by mid-July or even earlier in some years. July is a perfect time to sow hardy greens, such as kales, komatsuna, and leaf beet, which will occupy the garden bed until the end of the following May.

Table 2.5. Approximate dates when early crops are finished.

Planting Date and Crops	Harvest Usually Completed
• March–April-sown peas, lettuce, mixed salad greens, radishes • Early garlic (planted the previous fall)	Last week of June to 1st week of July
• March–April planted onions (from sets), Chinese cabbage, cauliflower, carrots • May–June sown lettuce and greens, radishes • Main crop garlic (planted the previous fall)	2nd to 3rd week of July
• May-sown bush beans, cauliflower, carrots • Sweet onions (from March sown seeds) • Early potatoes	Late August to early September

Be ready to fill gaps as they arise by keeping a small area in one of your beds as a seedling nursery. Crop such as cauliflower or corn, for example, leave spaces as they are harvested one by one. You can fill them immediately with seedlings of lettuce, kale, Chinese cabbage, leaf beet, and other plants you have already started in a nursery bed.

You can also use the seedling nursery to make a winter crop planting schedule work when plants that should be finished are lingering later than expected. A cool summer can jam up the schedule for hardy vegetables that should be sown in July. But you can start your winter crops in a seedling bed (or in flats) and move them to growing beds when space opens up. It depends on the crop, but most transplants can be set out three to four weeks later than they would be seeded directly. This buys you an extra month to allow a crop still occupying a bed to

Credit: E. Cronin

2.13. A small seedling bed provides transplants to fill gaps or get winter crops started while you are waiting for their space to open up.

mature. Or, because some local nurseries carry winter crop seedlings in the summer, you can skip sowing seeds altogether and just buy transplants to fill gaps as needed.

Interplanting: Some combinations of vegetables can share the same garden space. Plants that occupy different root zones or mature at different times make good partners. For example, lettuce, which has short roots and grows quickly, can be tucked in around a variety of larger deep-rooted vegetables. The lettuce is harvested and gone before the other crop needs the space. I never plant lettuce separately anymore because there are so many places to fit it in among other crops.

One of my favorite combinations is planting lettuce between Brussels sprouts, which, because they grow quite large, need to be widely spaced. The same goes for winter cauliflower and winter broccoli, which occupy garden space in beds from mid-June to the following spring. When they are still small, interplant them with lettuce (or other salad greens). Or plant cauliflower and broccoli between cucumbers or melons. The low vines shade the soil, which is good for the cauliflower and broccoli roots in the summer.

Some of my other favorite combinations include:

- Leafy greens (Swiss chard, Chinese cabbage) can be planted in alternating rows between root crops (carrots, beets).
- Green sprouting broccoli (a very large, productive summer broccoli) can be interplanted with early cauliflowers, which are harvested by the time the broccoli expands to fill the space.
- Radishes sown sparsely in carrot beds break the soil for the carrots and are half-grown by the time the carrots germinate.
- Lettuce grows well between first-year plantings of strawberries, asparagus, and other plants.
- Onion sets planted along the edges of garden beds mature in mid to late July and leave the space to the other crop.
- Set out small plants of winter cabbage and broccoli in July between established cucumber plants: the cabbage enjoys the cooler soil under the vines.

Whatever the combinations you try, be alert to how the plants are growing. Thin or remove the interplanted crop if the main crop is struggling or supplement with liquid fertilizer as needed.

2.14. Interplanting green sprouting broccoli (*circles*) with summer cauliflower and lettuce. By the end of the summer, the lettuce and cauliflower have been harvested and the (now huge) broccoli plants have all the space they need.

Underplanting: Also called relay cropping, underplanting is starting the next crop in a bed before the previous crop is

2.15. Squash vines underplanted with corn salad broadcast over the soil in late August.

finished. It works particularly well for fast-growing greens (corn salad, lettuce, spinach, leaf mustard, leaf radish), which can be sown underneath warm-season plants that will be finished in the fall. For example, in late August, I lift up winter squash vines, pull the mulch back if necessary, and broadcast corn salad and lettuce seeds over the soil. The seedlings grow well in the shade of the vines and are a good size by the time cold weather puts an end to the squash.

You can underplant squash, cucumbers, melons, tomatoes, and peppers. To avoid disturbing the new crop, cut the spent plants at the soil line rather than pulling them out.

Developing a Planting Plan

I hope your head isn't spinning with how complicated this all sounds. Garden plans can be as simple or as complex as you want, but the more planning you do, the better use you will make of your garden space. I find a plan really helps me be sure I save enough space for winter crops that won't be sown until mid-summer.

Here are my suggested steps in developing a garden plan:

1. Make a list of what you want to grow. Check your seed collection to make sure you have enough of each variety for the year's plantings.
2. Sketch a plan of your garden beds, marking areas that might be limited to certain crops. For example, I look for:

An Example of Intensive Planting

Here is an example of how interplanting and underplanting worked over the course of a year in one of my garden beds:

1. **April:** Set out mixed lettuce seedlings.
2. **Early June:** Set out Brussels sprouts plants between the remaining lettuce. About half of the lettuce has already been harvested.
3. **Late June:** The lettuce is all done. Set out cucumber plants between the Brussels sprouts.
4. **August:** Gently lift the cucumber vines and broadcast corn salad seed under the living vines.

5. **October:** Cucumbers are all done and vines removed. For the rest of the winter, the bed is occupied by the mature Brussels sprouts plants with corn salad covering the soil between them.

Although this bed produced lettuce, cucumbers, Brussels sprouts, and corn salad over the season, for the purpose of figuring out the crop rotation, the only plant family of concern is the mustard/cabbage family. Because of the risk of overwintering root maggots in the soil, I would not plant any mustard family vegetables in the bed until late summer of the following year.

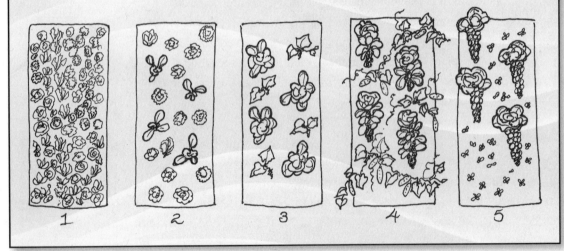

1   2   3   4   5

- sunny, warm spots: best for tomatoes, squash, cucumbers, corn;
- areas with a little less sun: could grow lettuce, peas, Chinese cabbage;
- places for tall crops: on the north side of the garden for corn or pole beans;
- areas with well-drained soil: good for overwintering crops;
- beds under roof overhangs or decks: suitable for winter crops sown in August, such as spinach and winter lettuce.

3. Next, identify the space needed for winter vegetables because planting these at the right time is critical. That means beds have to be empty and available when it is time to plant. Decide where to locate the big blocks of winter crops, and note when they should be planted (for a suggested planting schedule, see Table 8.1, p. 186). For example:

   - Carrots, beets, and other root vegetables for an eight-month supply (seed July 1).
   - Cabbage family: winter broccoli and cauliflower, cabbages (transplant to growing beds in July).
   - Hardy lettuce and other leafy greens (winter lettuce, kales, leafy mustard, Swiss chard, and leaf beet, arugula, radicchio, Chinese cabbage, komatsuna, etc.) (seed late July to early August).

4. With the winter crop beds reserved, decide which early- and short-season crops (e.g., onion sets, early lettuce, radishes, peas) you can fit into those spaces before you need the beds for winter crops. You don't have to plant these beds, of course, but it makes the most use of garden space if you do.

5. Now assign the remaining crops to the available garden space. Try to keep together plants in the four most critical

2.16. The same bed shown in **2.15** after the squash were removed, ready to produce salad greens all winter.

The Simplest Plan of All

If you have a level sunny area for your garden, large enough to lay out five or six parallel beds of equal size and sun exposure, you can develop a plan for each bed that you can shift over by one bed each year. For example, you might have one bed for nightshade family crops that has vine tomatoes staked up at the north end, bush tomatoes and peppers in the middle, and potatoes at the south end (because they are low growing and won't shade the other crops). The next bed over might have pole beans and peas at the north end, bush beans at the south end, with the peas followed by winter greens. The next bed could have sweet corn at the north end and squash and cucumbers on the south end. One bed could have all kinds of mustard family crops and blocks of Swiss chard and other greens, while the last bed could be devoted to leeks, garlic, onions, and other roots. Next year, you could use the same plan, but shift it over by one bed. In this example, the beans and peas would move to the bed where the nightshade crops were growing, the corn and squash would go to where the beans and peas were, and so on. This would give you a crop rotation cycle of five or six years. Once you figure out how much of each crop you need and the succession plantings to make the most of the space, you will have a perennial garden plan.

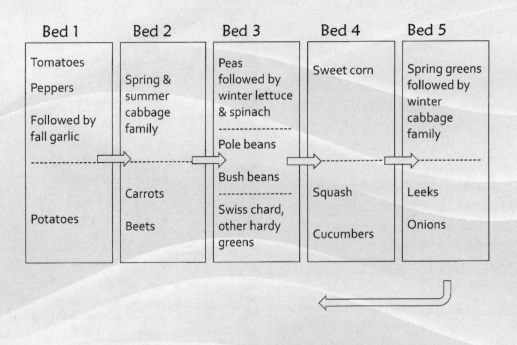

2.17. Plan to have space open for sowing winter crops. These beets were sown July 1; the lettuce and endive, August 8.

plant families (carrot, mustard/cabbage, nightshade, and onion families) to make it easier to rotate crops (see Table 2.2). Pencil in where each crop or family of crops could go on your plan.

6. When you are happy with the plan, you might want to make a chronological list of what you will plant. See Chapter 8 for a step-by-step year-round planting schedule.

7. Keep records so you can perfect your planting plan next year. I know we all think we will remember what was planted and how it went—but next season rolls around, and we are left scratching our heads. So, really, write it down! Things to keep track of include varieties, planting dates, garden maps and plans, harvest dates and pest problems.

CHAPTER 3

Preparing the Soil

Soil chemistry is a complex subject. Fortunately, if you follow a few basic rules for managing soil, you can grow a perfectly good organic garden without getting too technical. Think of the soil as a living, breathing, densely populated community of organisms (roots, fungi, bacteria, insects, mites, worms, and a lot else besides) living in a moist, dark world. Keeping this community happy, rich, and busy is the essence of organic gardening. If you can do that, you will reap the rewards of a thriving garden.

The Ideal Garden Soil

The best soil for a vegetable and fruit garden is deep, fertile, and well-drained. Prime agricultural land has these characteristics, but your garden soil might start out far from this ideal. Not to worry—even the worst soils can be amended to grow a garden. The better your soil conditions are to start with, however, the less work and time it will take to make it into a productive garden.

Deep soil: A garden should have soil deep enough to provide a root zone that anchors plants and allows roots to reach sufficient nutrients. A small annual plant like lettuce can grow in a foot of soil, if necessary, but obviously, a fruit tree has much a larger root zone.

On natural undisturbed land, the top layer of soil (the topsoil) is several inches to over a foot deep. This is usually darker than the layers of soil below (the subsoil) because it contains more organic matter. Ideally, there is a thick layer of topsoil sitting on subsoil that is several feet to several yards deep. If your soil profile is like this, you are fortunate indeed!

It is more likely that, when you start digging up the yard for a garden, you will discover there isn't an obvious topsoil layer—or there is, but it is only an inch or two deep. Unless care was taken to preserve topsoil when the building was originally built, the topsoil was probably mixed with excavated subsoil (or even stripped off and sold). The builder may have then trucked in a

Special Case: No Soil?

If you don't have a patch of soil to cultivate, try for a plot in a community garden. Or, if you have a sunny deck or balcony, many vegetables can be grown in containers (see Chapter 7). If you have a large sunny area, but it is paved or covered with gravel or rock, you could still have a productive garden if you invest in building large planters. They should be at least 18 inches (45 cm) deep (deeper is even better); they can be any length and width, as long as you can easily reach to the middle. Buy the best soil available, and mix in a generous amount of compost, leaf mold (well-rotted leaves), and other organic matter as you go (1 to 2 parts compost to 9 parts soil as a rough guide).

soil-like substance to spread on the yard after construction. It could be a thin layer, barely enough to grow grass, which can grow in practically anything. This situation is all too common, but it can be remedied: If there is hardly any soil before you hit gravel, rock, or very stony subsoil, you could build raised beds and bring in good soil to fill them. If there seems to be a foot or two of workable soil, but it is of poor quality (it is light-colored, for example), work with the soil you have and enrich it on the spot with compost, fertilizers, and other amendments.

Fertile soil: Good garden soil has an adequate supply of the major and minor nutrients as well as a good supply of organic matter. Soils almost never have enough of all of these, which is why they are added by the gardener.

Crop plants use large quantities of some elements, major nutrients, for photosynthesis and growth processes. Three of these (nitrogen, phosphorus, potassium) are the primary elements in fertilizers, but they are not the only ones used in large amounts. The elements below are listed in order of the relative quantities used by plants:

- **Nitrogen:** This main element for plant growth is used in greater amounts than any other major element. It promotes rapid leafy growth and is a key building block of proteins. Microorganisms breaking down organic matter in the soil or capturing it from the atmosphere release nitrogen in a form usable by plants. Until there are good levels of organic matter in the soil, however, nitrogen is the element most likely to be in short supply in the first few years of an organic garden.

- **Potassium (potash):** This regulates the production of proteins and starches and makes for sturdy plants. Second only to nitrogen in the amount plants use, it plays an important role in disease resistance and heat and cold tolerance. Root crops tend to need more potassium than other vegetables. It leaches out of the soil with heavy rain, but the more organic matter there is in the soil, the less likely this is to happen.

- **Calcium:** A key element for the functioning of plant cells, calcium is involved in regulating many processes, including how plants respond to the environment. Deficiencies show up in the death of cells in actively growing parts, such as tips of shoots, roots, and fruit (see Disorders). Horticultural lime applied to make coastal soils less acidic also supplies plenty of calcium.

- **Magnesium:** This has a critical role in processes essential to respiration and photosynthesis. Sandy acid coastal soils in high-rainfall areas can be low in magnesium, but it is unlikely that you have to worry about a deficiency in garden soil amended with compost. Using dolomitic lime to make soils less acid provides a good balance of both calcium and magnesium.
- **Phosphorus:** This promotes flowering, fruiting, and strong stems and roots. It doesn't move much through the soil, but it does travel on eroding soil particles and can pollute water bodies. Soils usually have plenty of phosphorus, but only a fraction of it is available to plants at any one time. It is most available in slightly acid soil with a good supply of organic matter and a healthy community of fungi and bacteria.
- **Sulfur:** This is an important component of proteins, vitamins, and other metabolic compounds that plants need to regulate growth. Sulfur deficiency isn't usually a problem in garden soils amended with organic matter and complete organic fertilizers.
- **Silicon:** The second most abundant element in the soil, silicon is important in building strong cells, which resist disease and pest attack and help withstand heat and drought. There is no need to add it because the action of soil microbes in a healthy soil makes enough silicon available to plants.

Another group of nutrients is essential for growth too, but in amounts hundreds to thousands of times smaller than major nutrients. These micronutrients, or trace elements, listed in order of the amount used by plants are: chlorine, iron, boron, manganese, sodium, zinc, copper, nickel, and molybdenum. For every atom of manganese, a plant uses one thousand atoms of nitrogen—but without that tiny amount of manganese, photosynthesis can't proceed, so you can see that trace elements are vital. However, in higher amounts, most of these become toxic or may prevent other nutrients from being available to plants. So don't add these as amendments because it is highly unlikely you would have micro-nutrient deficiencies in a garden fed with compost and complete organic fertilizers.

Well-drained soil: Soil organisms and plant roots suffocate in waterlogged soil. Poorly drained soils can successfully grow summer crops that are sown after the soil has dried out, but such soils won't be good for winter or early spring crops. Plants suffer if they are planted where water stands for more than twenty-four hours. When it rains day after day in midwinter, however, water may pool anywhere temporarily. As long as the water drains within a day or two after the rain finally stops, plants and their microbes should be fine.

Poor drainage can be improved by digging trenches to channel water away from beds to a nearby drainage ditch or by installing subsurface drain pipes. The latter is costly, and neither approach may be feasible on small properties because there is nowhere to direct the water. The most practical solution often is to mound up the soil or build raised beds high enough to elevate the root zone above the water line.

Soil texture: This depends on the proportion of clay particles (the finest), silt particles (medium-sized), and sand particles (the largest). Ideally, soils have balanced proportions of these particles; such "loam" soils are the gold standard for horticulture. I don't know why I bother bringing this up, though, because so few gardeners are lucky enough to have loamy soil. It is a good idea, however, to have some idea of the texture of your soil so that you know how to improve it and the best way to irrigate it.

- **Sandy soil:** Sandy soil feels gritty when rubbed between your fingers and may have small stones mixed in. Such soils are strong (don't compact easily), well-aerated, and usually well-drained (or even too well-drained). In the spring, they warm up quicker and can often be worked earlier than other soils. The downside is that they don't hold water and nutrients as well as soils with higher proportions of silt or clay particles. Sandy soil can be greatly improved by adding organic matter and fertilizers.

- **Clay soil:** Soil with a high proportion of clay leaves a sticky coating when you rub the wet soil between your fingers. These soils are "heavy," meaning dense and easily compacted because the particles are so fine. They are sticky when wet and make hard clods if cultivated while too wet. They are often found in low-lying or poorly drained sites, but not always. The upside of clay soil is that these very fine particles are great at holding water and nutrients and making them available to plants. They make excellent garden soils when amended with lots of organic matter.

Sand Amendments for Clay Soil?

Adding sand to clay soil in an effort to improve the texture is a logical, but flawed, idea that researchers now know makes problems with compaction and drainage worse. Although I recommended this in the first edition, I changed my tune after learning more about it (for more on this and other questionable horticulture practices, read research papers by Washington State University researcher Linda Chalker-Scott; see Resources). The fine clay particles fill in between the sandy particles and actually make the soil denser. It would require additions of unrealistically large proportions of sand (something like over 50% by volume) throughout the whole root zone to change the texture of a clay soil. For that matter, adding clay to sandy soil apparently causes the same problems. Compaction and lack of aeration, however, improve markedly in any kind of soil if the soil is managed in a way to improve its structure (see below). So don't try to change soil texture by adding sand or clay. If you have done this in the past, then from now on focus on improving *soil structure*.

Soil structure: In an ideal soil (regardless of texture), the tiny particles are clumped together in larger "crumbs" with stable air spaces between them. Well-aggregated soil, with pores of various sizes, looks a lot like a cross-section through a piece of chocolate cake. The soil structure dictates how quickly water drains through the soil, how rapidly oxygen gets in and carbon dioxide gets out so roots and soil organisms can breathe. Humus, the dark brownish residue of decomposed organic matter, coats soil particles and sticks them together. Soil particles are also stuck together by the activity of earthworms, by gums and glues made by bacteria, fungi, and plant roots. The structure of all soils, especially clay soils, improves as organic matter and the activity of soil organisms increases.

You can destroy soil structure by walking (or driving!) on the soil, which crushes the air spaces, and by careless cultivation. Rototilling, for example, dashes apart the crumb structure and can be especially destructive. As the air spaces collapse, the soil becomes compacted, which slows drainage and the movement of air. Cultivating of any kind while soil is too wet also destroys the structure, particularly in soils with a high proportion of clay. When such soils dry out, there are often rock-hard clods to contend with, or you may be left with a hard crust on the surface. Pounding winter rain is another force that destroys soil structure. Luckily, the best ways to improve soil structure are also the least work: don't walk on the garden beds, minimize cultivation, and protect the soil with mulch.

Soil Organisms

A healthy soil has a rich community of organisms ranging from microscopic bacteria to the much larger insects and earthworms. These essential partners make nutrients available to plants and perform many other functions that maintain plant health. Without these, plants could not get enough nutrients or defend themselves against pathogens. Just as we have an enormous community of microbes in and on our bodies, called our microbiome, the same thing applies to plants. They rely so much on microbes that you could consider a plant plus its microbiome as one big functioning organism.

You won't be able to see the smallest microbes, but they are there and thriving if conditions are right. For most, this means good drainage, organic matter for food, and soil that is not too acid or too alkaline (these are all discussed below). Most organisms live in the top 4 inches (10 cm) of soil, and nearly all live within the top 10 inches (25 cm), where most feeder roots of plants, including trees, are also found.

I think one of the most interesting discoveries in recent years has been how much energy plants use to feed bacteria, fungi, and other microbes in the soil. It is estimated that over 20% (and possibly much more) of the carbohydrates plants make through photosynthesis leak from their roots into the soil. Bacteria feed on this rich food supply, and their numbers are hundreds to thousands of times higher in the root zone than in soil without roots—and that's a good thing! They make nutrients available and actively protect roots from disease, both by forming a barrier to block invaders and by producing antibiotics that kill pathogens. Bacteria and other microbes help plants regulate root development, adapt to poor growing conditions, and even (amazingly!) help plants resist feeding by leaf-eating insects.

Fungi are also essential plant partners involved in every aspect of decomposition and nutrient cycles in the soil. Within their filaments (called hyphae) they move water and nutrients throughout the soil. Some, the mycorrhizal fungi, actually penetrate into roots or form a net of fungal strands around root tips and are especially important in making phosphorus available to trees, shrubs, and other plants. Their hyphae radiate out from each fine root in a wide network, in effect giving each root its own fungal "root" system. This allows a plant to receive nutrients and water from a much larger volume of soil than it could reach with its roots. The fungi receive carbohydrates from the plant in exchange for shuttling nitrogen, phosphorus, and other elements into its roots. Oddly, plants in the mustard/cabbage and amaranth/spinach families don't seem to have mycorrhizal associations.

There are myriad soil organisms (e.g., actinomycetes, protozoa, nematodes, mites, insects) linked together in a network of eating, being eaten, and interacting with plant roots. For example, single-celled organisms called protozoa are the main predators of bacteria (protozoa also eat fungi). Because bacteria have more nitrogen in them than any other living thing, when protozoa consume them, they excrete excess nitrogen. This is in a form plants can use, making protozoa "poop" a key source of nitrogen. Protozoa are also the main diet of earthworms; therefore, a soil rich in bacteria feeds lots of protozoa, which in turn feeds lots of earthworms, who in turn aerate and enrich the soil as they burrow. Along with soil insects, earthworms start the process of decomposition by shredding fresh plant material and pulling it into the soil. As the plant material is shredded into finer pieces, a succession of fungi move in, digesting the tougher components and making it more digestible for bacteria. Bacteria continue chopping the molecules into ever-smaller bits, and protozoa thrive on eating the bacteria. The fertility of the soil increases year after year as these processes make more nutrients available to plants.

3.1. The white crust on the roots of this healthy beet are beneficial soil microbes, likely actinomycetes, among others.

Organic Matter

Adding organic matter to the soil provides food for soil microbes, and they in turn, slowly release nutrients to plants. And slow release does mean *slow*; studies show that the rate of nitrogen released from mature compost can keep increasing for at least eight months after it is applied to the soil. It continues to release small amounts for much longer, which is why garden soils fed with compost every year become more and more fertile as the years go by.

No matter what type of soil you have, the one thing that improves most soils is the addition of organic matter: coarser compost improves aeration in clay soils; mature compost improves the moisture and nutrient-holding capacity of sandy soils. For all soils, the activity of microbes and the formation of humus from organic matter improve structure, hold carbon in the soil, and provide nutrients. Because organic matter is continually being digested into humus, you need to add more every year.

Sources of organic matter for urban gardeners:

- **Homemade compost:** Use it when it has become dark, crumbly, and well-digested. The nutrient content will vary, depending on the ingredients.
- **Commercial compost:** Several brands of composted fish and wood waste are made on Vancouver Island and in Washington State (see Resources). Some are certified for organic growers by OMRI (Organic Materials Review Institute). They are available bagged or in bulk quantities. There are also bagged mushroom, steer, and poultry manure composts (these are cheaper, but inferior in quality to the fish/wood waste composts, and most are not certified for organic growing).
- **Municipal compost:** Some municipalities collect yard waste, compost it, and sell the finished product back to residents by the bucket, bag, or in larger quantities. Because the sources of material are unknown, this is not allowed for certified organic growers. Years ago, there were problems with persistent herbicide residues in municipal compost in Washington State; however, those herbicides were not available to home gardeners in British Columbia. With the use of most pesticides by home gardeners now restricted across the province, there should be a very low risk of persistent residues in municipal compost. In US states where people could be using lawn herbicides, you might want to stick to your homemade compost or buy certified organic commercial compost products.
- **Leaf mold:** Pile any kind of well-moistened leaves in a bin for the winter, and you will have leaf mold by spring (it takes longer in climates with cold winters). A deep mulch of leaves applied to garden beds in the fall also

Walnut Worries

Trees in the walnut family contain a chemical called juglone that stunts or kills some other plants. Levels of juglone in most of these trees are low and not a problem, but levels in leaves, roots, and bark of black walnut and butternut are high enough to be toxic to tomatoes and other nightshades, some berries, and other plants. Juglone can also be high in leaves of English walnut that has been grafted onto black walnut rootstock. Juglone breaks down during composting, and a few walnut leaves mixed in with lots of other leaves or materials in a compost bin is not a concern. If you have a lot of black walnut leaves to compost, though, mix them with other materials and hot compost for at least a month or cool compost it for a year before using.

3.2. Roots of corn plant at harvest (*left*), a few weeks later (*center*), and after decomposing for a few months (*right*). By spring the roots have added substantial organic matter to the soil.

decomposes right on the spot. With the exception of black walnut (see text box above), all kinds of leaves are fine, including oak and big-leaf maple.

- **Plant roots:** Don't overlook the important contribution of crop plant roots to organic matter levels in the soil. Rather than pulling up the roots after harvesting, cut stems at the soil line and leave the roots to decompose undisturbed. In fact, the next crop only benefits from nitrogen formed in the roots of legumes if the roots *are* left in the soil. Although a little nitrogen leaks into the soil as legumes grow, most isn't available to other plants until the legumes die.

Since beneficial soil microbes are mostly around the roots of plants, I think it is better for them, and for soil structure, too, if they are not dragged off to a compost pile. Even roots of sweet corn, which has a large, dense root system, are best left in the soil over the winter to decompose. By spring, only a small core of woody stalk remains. As long as plants don't show any sign of a soilborne disease (see Chapter 9), I leave as much of the root system as possible in the soil, only removing woody stumps if they are in the way of the next crop.

Two other sources of organic matter are animal manure and green manure (discussed below), but for most gardens, I recommend sticking with the above sources.

Animal manure

Older garden books always talk about digging in "aged manure." These days, it is pretty rare for an urban or suburban dweller to get ahold of livestock manure. If you *do* get cow, chicken, or pig manure from a commercial farm, you must compost it carefully in a well-turned, hot compost pile before using it. Disease organisms that cause serious illnesses in people, such as *E. coli*, *Salmonella*, and *Campylobacter*, are now common in the livestock industry. It is no longer considered safe enough to pile manure and wait for it to age.

If you can get rabbit, goat, sheep, or llama manure, you can use it without necessarily composting it first. These manures are lower in nitrogen, so they don't burn plant roots, and they generally don't carry the risk of human disease that other manures do. They should be composted before use, however, if there is a lot of straw, sawdust, or shavings mixed in with the manure (more than 10% of the volume); composting also reduces the survival of weed seeds in the manure. Many gardeners find it makes the most sense to buy commercially composted manures at garden centers. These don't carry the disease risk that handling raw manure does.

For many people in suburban areas, the most readily available manure is horse manure. Even though it isn't a human disease risk, there are reasons to compost horse manure for at least three months before using it:

- Many seeds pass right through a horse's digestive system, so the manure can be a source of agricultural weeds you may not have in your garden. Composting reduces the survival of seeds in manure.
- It usually has bedding mixed in with it. How much and what kind will dictate how long it should be composted. Straw bedding composts quickly, but

if there is a lot of sawdust or wood shavings, it may need to be composted for a year or more, until it is dark and crumbly.

- Most horses are given deworming medication regularly for intestinal worms (unrelated to earthworms). Although much of it stays in the horse, there may be residues in the manure right after worming. Avermectin-based products (e.g., Ivermectin) are commonly used; they are extracted from cultures of a soil microorganism. These products are allowed on certified organic farms and break down quickly during the composting process. Other products may also be used.

Green manure

These are living crops, such as fall rye or clover, grown for a short time and then turned under in the soil. While this is an essential way to add organic matter, build nutrients, improve soil structure, and suppress weeds on a field scale, green manures make less sense for backyard gardeners for several reasons:

3.3. Turning under a fall rye crop in the spring must be done at the right time.

- Most people with small intensively planted gardens don't have the space. If you are growing food year-round, and the garden can be filled with crops most of the year, why take space out of production? You can add all of the necessary organic matter and nutrients in the form of compost, mulches, and organic fertilizers.
- Much of the benefit from green manure crops comes from the mass of roots they produce. You achieve a similar benefit by leaving the roots of your crop plants in the soil to decompose.
- A cover crop is tricky to manage because it must be turned under when it is a few inches to a foot high, while it is still lush, green, and easy to handle. A delay of a week or two in the spring can result in vegetation that is too tall and woody to be a green manure, or that has become nearly impossible to turn under without a rototiller. What could be more discouraging?
- Where wireworms are a problem, green manure plants present in the garden in the spring when the adults are laying eggs make the problem worse. Wireworm adults (called click beetles) are especially attracted to lay eggs on grasses, such as fall rye, but will lay their eggs on clover and other plants (see entry for wireworms in Chapter 9).

Composting

One of my goals in writing this book is to banish "composter's guilt." I believe this widespread (in gardeners) anxiety comes from comparing those ideal instructions found in garden books with what really happens in a home garden. When I ask people in my gardening classes, "Who turns their compost regularly?" it is rare to see even one hand go up—and that one usually belongs to an energetic new gardener going by a book (written by someone who works too hard!).

After years of making "proper" compost when I had a market garden, followed by decades of *intending* to make good compost, but not quite getting around to it for my home garden, I finally realized my crops were not suffering. In fact, yields appeared to be increasing, not decreasing.

I often just leave crop waste on the ground to decompose where it grew. The rest goes into a bin to decompose at a leisurely rate or is thrown into the chicken yard, where my two spoiled hens go over it, shredding and manuring the mix. After a few months, I fork that well-shredded material into a bin with other garden waste and leaves to finish composting. Easy as pie!

The following notes on the various methods of making compost start with the simplest. Although it has been many years since I bothered with hot composting, I have included a procedure to follow in case you have farm manure to compost.

Sheet composting: This is how nutrients are recycled in nature: organic material lying on the surface of the soil decomposes in place. The material disappears as it is first shredded by worms, insects, and slugs, then further digested by a myriad of other organisms. Green soft materials disappear quickly, while drier woodier materials break down more slowly. When leaves and other materials are used as mulch, they continuously break down and feed the soil. Layering organic matter on the soil surface actually builds soil organic matter and improves soil structure more rapidly than cultivating it into the soil.

I routinely leave green crop waste, such as cut pea vines and bean plants, on the ground where they grew, and transplant seedlings for the next crop through the mulch. In fact, you can leave any material on the soil to decompose, including pulled weeds; old leaves of cabbage, squash, and other plants; stalks from harvested corn, etc.

An extreme variation on this is "lasagna" gardening, which involves spreading layers of crop waste, leaves, manure, spoiled hay, or other readily available organic matter on the soil surface until it is a foot thick. The layer takes the place of topsoil; you plant directly into the mix. This method works, but you have to be able to get ahold of *a lot* of organic material—and have a means of hauling it to the garden. While this is a "no till" method, it is not a "no work" method.

3.4. This cabbage seedling has been planted through cut-off pea vines now mulching the soil (the white barrier visible under the mulch protects the roots from cabbage root maggot attack).

3.5. The wire compost bin holds layers of crop waste, horse manure, and leaves. Kitchen scraps are composting in the closed composter.

Cold composting: Most home compost is made using this method: simply pile materials in a compost bin as they become available and leave them there. After about a year, pull apart the pile, and use the well-digested crumbly brown material in the center and bottom of the pile. Undigested stalks and other coarse materials that haven't decomposed go into another bin to become the bottom layer of the next pile.

Bins or Piles?

Either works fine, however, bins usually look better in a landscape setting than an open pile. A good size for a pile or a bin is at least 3 x 3 x 3 feet (about a meter square by a meter high). Bins can be as simple as cylinders of fence wire or more sturdily built of wood, plastic "wood," or other material. Beloved of composting enthusiasts, a system of three side-by-side bins allows you to turn compost from one to the next and have an extra to accumulate material until there is enough to make a new pile. Sides of bins should be slatted to allow air circulation.

You can build a more organized cold compost pile if you can stockpile enough materials to build a pile all at once (see below).

Cold composting won't kill weed seeds. It also won't heat up enough to kill all plant disease organisms, but it does kill those that can only survive on intact or living plant material. Once the infected leaves decompose, spores of rusts, powdery mildews, apple scab, and other pathogens die, even if the compost doesn't heat up.

Hot composting: This labor-intensive way to make compost results in a pile that heats up and is ready in months. If piles are carefully made, turned, and managed (see below), the temperatures reached during the heating phase of the decomposing may be high enough—and last long enough—to kill plant pathogens and weed seeds. This is the only way that cow, poultry, or pig manure from commercial farms should be composted.

The Well-Organized Compost Pile

A good time to make any compost pile is in the fall, when there is usually lots of garden waste, leaves, and other materials available at the same time. Whether you are going to leave the pile to compost slowly (cold composting) or keep turning it to make hot compost, the decomposer organisms need the following:

- **Good ventilation:** The organisms that digest organic material need to take in oxygen and get rid of waste carbon dioxide, so you need to build piles with good ventilation. An easy way to do this is to stand a length of wide plastic pipe (a 4-inch drain pipe works well) in the center. Pull the pipe out when the pile is built, leaving a donut hole in the center. Some people make a cylinder of wire mesh and leave it as the core of the pile.
- **Moisture, but not too much:** In the summer, make sure the materials throughout the pile don't dry out. In the winter, cover the top of piles with a plastic tarp, sheet of plywood, or other material to shed rain and prevent the pile from becoming waterlogged.
- **Balanced ingredients:** Use whatever materials you can get most easily. Ideally, ingredients used to build the pile should roughly balance material with a high carbon content with material that has a high nitrogen content: "Brown" dry materials are higher in carbon and include bulky materials such as straw, mature crop residues, corn stalks, and shredded paper. "Green" materials are higher in nitrogen and include fresh garden waste,

Coffee Grounds

Don't overlook the value of coffee grounds, a significant compost ingredient in some households. Since grounds aren't attractive to rats, they don't have to go into a rat-proof composter as for other kitchen waste. They are a good source of nitrogen and decompose readily (earthworms seem to like them). If you have large quantities, layer the grounds with other ingredients in a compost pile. In small amounts, they can be mixed directly into the soil or sprinkled lightly on the surface. Just don't use a lot in the same place; thick layers may temporarily inhibit the growth of some plants until the grounds have decomposed.

most fresh manures, leafy weeds, and kitchen waste. Try to layer twice as much brown as green material. Some materials already have a pretty good nitrogen-to-carbon ratio: leaves, ground-up yard and tree trimmings (not sawdust or wood chips), and horse manure (as long as there is a minimum of sawdust or shavings mixed in) can be used in any quantity in compost piles.

Composting don'ts: Things *not* to put in a compost pile include pet poop, dairy products, meat, bones, fat, and oil. Starchy or sweet kitchen scraps attract rats to open bins, but can be composted in rat-proof composters. Don't put wood ashes or lime into the compost pile either. It makes the compost alkaline, which allows microbes to grow that release the nitrogen to the atmosphere in the form of ammonia.

Note: The "green cone" type of composter is meant as a disposal system for pet waste, meat, and other materials. The digested contents from such composters should never go into a garden compost pile or be used on a food garden.

Seedy weeds in the compost? Even the hottest home compost piles are rarely hot enough to kill weed seeds. Here are two ways to approach this:

- Just go ahead and throw the weeds on the compost pile, anyway. In the future, try to pull weeds before they flower. If you keep your soil mulched to smother weeds and inhibit germination of seeds, there won't be weeds to worry about.

- Keep a "seedy weed" compost separate from the main garden compost. Use this compost where the seeds won't get a chance to germinate in future, such as to enrich a planting hole for a tree or shrub.

How to Make Hot Compost

1. Keeping in mind the general requirements given above regarding ventilation, moisture, and ingredient mix, here's how to make hot compost: Start with a layer of coarse stalks or small branches at the bottom of the pile to assist aeration.
2. Alternate layers of dry brown (high carbon) and wet green materials (high nitrogen), or mix them together. Use about twice as much brown material by volume as green material. To speed up the process, shred or cut up materials. The smaller the pieces, the faster the organisms will work and the higher the temperature will be in the pile.
3. Water as you go to moisten materials until they feel uniformly damp, but not soggy.
4. Use a garden fork or pitchfork to turn the piles two or three times, a couple of weeks to a month apart, completely mixing material from the outside of the pile into the center. As a pile heats up, the heat drives water out of the center, so you usually need to add more water when you turn it.
5. In warm weather, the heating phase takes about a month. But hot compost is not ready to use at the end of this phase; it must be given another one to two months to "cure" so that organisms that grow in cooler temperatures can spread throughout the compost and finish the composting process. This step is necessary to make nitrogen available to plants and to break down compounds made during hot composting that inhibit seed germination and root growth.

Do You Need Compost Starter?

Nope. There are plenty of native bacteria already on the materials you compost. Researchers say that not only are commercial "activators" unnecessary, but the native bacteria from your own soil are likely to be better adapted to your garden conditions than bacteria grown in a laboratory. If you want to inoculate a new compost pile, sprinkle a little finished compost or a shovel of garden soil into the materials as you build the pile.

Using Compost

Regardless of how it was made, compost is finished when the material is dark and crumbly and has an earthy smell. The

Compost Troubleshooting

• *Pile doesn't heat up.* Conditions for heat-loving microbes are not ideal. Usually you need more materials richer in nitrogen, such as manure or green crop waste. Check that the materials are damp enough, but not waterlogged, both of which conditions will inhibit the growth of microbes.

• *Ammonia or a rotten smell occurs.* The materials are not getting enough oxygen. Turn the compost more often and mix in more carbon-rich brown materials.

• *Rats appear.* Check on what is being composted, and make sure there is no attractive kitchen or crop waste (fruit, starchy or sweet garbage, meat scraps, etc.).

greater the variety of starting materials, the more variety of nutrients there will be in the finished product. Composted straw and manure typically have more nitrogen than composted leaves do. Generally, homemade compost is considered to have about 0.5% to 1% available nitrogen, but it depends on ingredients and whether the pile was protected from rain to prevent nutrients from leaching away.

Organic matter is continually being digested; therefore, compost should be applied every year to a vegetable garden. How to use compost:

- For a new garden in poor to average soil that has not had compost or manure added previously, turn in up to a 4-inch (10 cm) layer of compost to start.
- For an established garden, aim to turn in a 1-inch layer of compost annually, if you have it (who ever has enough?); you can use less if you also build soil organic matter by using mulches and cultivating as little as possible.
- Use screened finished compost as an ingredient in potting soil for containers or seedlings.
- Apply coarse or half-digested compost to the soil as a summer mulch.

You can turn in more compost between crops from spring through late summer, if needed (it usually isn't). But don't spread compost or manure on the soil in the fall on the theory that it will enrich the soil for next season. Plants can't use the nutrients in the winter, and rain will just leach nutrients away. Instead, keep compost or manure piles covered to shed rain and preserve nutrients until spring.

Organic Fertilizers

Fertilizers add major and minor nutrients to the soil in more concentrated amounts than compost alone usually provides. Fertilizer supplements are necessary because vegetables and fruit need much more of these nutrients to produce good crops than they can get from ordinary soil. If you are used to maintaining perennial landscape plants, which need little, if any, fertilizer, you might be surprised at how much more nutrients crop plants need.

Read Fertilizer Labels

When choosing complete fertilizers, read the labels carefully. If you require fertilizers accepted for certified organic growing, look for Organic Materials Research Institute (OMRI) certification on the label. Some products with a blend of natural ingredients and synthetic fertilizers have "organic based" or "organic and natural" on the label, but this doesn't mean they are for certified organic growers.

Check labels to see the differences between similar sounding products. For example, Pro-Mix® Organic Granular Multi-Purpose Fertilizer (7-3-3) is an OMRI-certified product with an excellent ratio of nitrogen to other nutrients. Pro-Mix® Organic Based Multi-Purpose (20-8-8) is not OMRI-certified, and the label says it is "soluble," meaning it includes synthetic fertilizers (the only way the available nitrogen could be that high).

Beware of paying high prices for specialty fertilizers as well. Mother Earth News researchers compared cost and nitrogen content of a range of organic fertilizers to arrive at a cost of one pound of available nitrogen for each product. At 2015 prices, costs ranged from $0 (for lawn clippings) to $365 per pound of nitrogen in worm castings to $14,000 per pound (!) of nitrogen in a liquid tomato food product with a vanishingly low nutrient content.

The series of three numbers you see written prominently on bags of fertilizer is called the analysis. The numbers stand for how much the fertilizer contains of the big three: nitrogen (N), phosphorus (P), and potassium (K). They are always in the same order, N-P-K, so a bag of organic fertilizer with 2-4-3 on the label contains 2% available N, 4% available P, and 3% available K. If the numbers are higher than that (e.g., 20-10-10), it is a synthetic fertilizer. Since this book is about organic gardening, I won't dwell on how to use the inorganic fertilizers. Although application guidelines are given on the fertilizer packaging, don't be too concerned about the rates—as long as you don't use *more* than the suggested amount per area. Not only does this waste money, but overfertilizing with phosphorus or potassium, for example, can make other nutrients unavailable to plants. Consider fertilizers as a supplement to the main food supply for crops, which comes from mature compost and other organic matter. After the first few years of a new garden, you might find that levels of P and K are high enough that you only need to add nitrogen.

Nitrogen sources: Alfalfa meal, fish/wood waste compost, and composted manures supply useful amounts of nitrogen. Blood meal is far and away the highest nitrogen fertilizer for organic gardeners, so you don't need very much of it. The application rate listed on boxes of blood meal is usually about 4 to 8 pounds per 100 square feet (2 to 4 kg per 10 m²). The lower numbers would apply to root and fruit crops or for soils that have good organic matter levels; the higher rate would suit leafy greens or soils low in organic matter. Now that my garden has a good supply of organic matter, I only use small amounts of blood meal at planting time as a nitrogen boost for plants that need a lot (such as sweet corn and squash).

Liquid fish fertilizer is a good source of nitrogen if plants look deficient during the growing season. Signs of nitrogen deficiency are

3.6. Planting corn seedlings: I dig a tablespoon of blood meal into the soil where I plant each seedling.

The Nitrogen Cycle

Nitrogen exists in different forms in the environment—in fact, air is 79% nitrogen. Microorganisms in the soil are a vital part of the natural processes that move nitrogen in a cycle through the environment. Some kinds of soil bacteria combine nitrogen from the atmosphere with hydrogen and oxygen, "fixing" it into a form that plants can use. Other microbes, mostly soil bacteria and fungi and their predators, make nitrogen from organic matter available to plants.

Soluble nitrogen is readily leached out of the soil by heavy rain. It pollutes water bodies when it washes out of the soil or from uncovered compost or manure piles. In waterlogged conditions (called anaerobic conditions because of the lack of oxygen), some microorganisms convert nitrogen from the form plants can use into a gaseous form that is lost to the atmosphere. You could look at a sodden, compacted compost pile as a tragic waste of plant food. Nitrogen in the form of ammonia is also released to the air by soil bacteria in very alkaline conditions (which is why you shouldn't put lime or wood ashes in the compost pile).

stunted growth with leaves turning pale yellow, usually starting with the oldest leaves. Too much nitrogen makes soft, lush growth with large leaves—at the expense of fruiting or root growth.

Phosphorus sources: Although soils generally contain lots of phosphorus, most isn't in a form plants can use; therefore, we usually need to add some fertilizer containing phosphorus to make sure enough is available to crops. It is important not to overfertilize with phosphorus amendments, however, because excess phosphorus interferes with the uptake of other nutrients, such as iron, zinc, and manganese.

Bone meal is one readily available source of phosphorus for organic gardens. Application rates for bone meal are usually given as 10 pounds per 100 square feet (4 to 5 kg per 10 m²). That's quite a lot, so I use half that on *new* garden beds. Rock phosphate (a rock dust), another source used by organic growers, releases very little phosphorus in the first year, as it is a long-term, slow-release source.

Adding fertilizers containing high proportions of phosphorus year after year is not necessary and can impair plant growth if phosphorus levels get too high. Instead, focus on maintaining soil pH between 6.0 and 7.0 and on increasing the organic matter to feed the soil microbes that make phosphorus available to plants. If a soil test shows excessive phosphorus levels, stop adding amendments containing phosphorus, but continue with nitrogen-rich amendments and eventually the phosphorus levels will drop.

Phosphorus-deficient plants are stunted, have less fruit than they should, and often have purplish streaks or patches on the undersides of leaves, but such symptoms can also be due to deficiencies *caused* by excess phosphorus. Both deficiency and excess can be avoided by relying on compost to enrich garden soil and the judicious use of balance organic fertilizers. To avoid overuse of phosphorus, some sources recommend against using complete fertilizers that provide a higher proportion of available phosphorus than nitrogen. Alfalfa meal, which has an N-P-K analysis of 2.5-1-1, is an example of an amendment with a good ratio, as are commercial organic products with a 4-4-4 ratio (e.g., Gaia Green All Purpose Fertilizer).

Potassium sources: Langbeinite (potassium magnesium sulfate) is a mined mineral included in some organic fertilizers to supply potassium, magnesium, and sulfur. Greensand (a type of rock mineral) is also used as an ingredient in complete organic fertilizers to supply potassium.

If you have them, wood ashes can be used a potassium fertilizer. They are high in potassium (also called potash) in a form readily available to plants and also provide calcium and micronutrients. Wood ashes are very alkaline, therefore make soils less acid, which is good for coastal soils that are naturally acidic, but not for soils with a pH over 6.5. You *can* add too much wood ashes, so limit yourself to using no more than 2 pounds per square yard (about 1 kg per m²) in a year. People usually don't have enough ashes to use that amount anyway, so distribute what you do have on the vegetable beds. Ashes should never be put on acid-loving plants, such as blueberries, or used in compost piles (where alkaline conditions drive the loss of nitrogen). As with most elements, applying excessive amounts of potassium can cause nutrient imbalances in plants.

Deficient plants don't have a clear set of symptoms, but generally they are woodier and smaller than they should be (but there are also other reasons for this). Leaves can show browning or yellowing, starting at the tips; brown spots appear along the leaf edges; and leaves often curl more than is characteristic for the plant.

Calcium sources: In most coastal soils, which are naturally acidic because of high rainfall, calcium is easily supplied from finely ground limestone added to the soil to raise the pH (see below). Use the horticultural lime sold at garden centers and farm suppliers. Wood ashes are about 25% calcium, which also makes them a good calcium source for acid soils. Oyster shells and egg shells both contain calcium, but they have to be ground to a powder to make the calcium available. For neutral or alkaline soil (pH 7.0 or more), use gypsum (calcium sulfate) to supply calcium without affecting the soil pH, but *only* do this if a soil test shows the combination of low calcium levels and high pH.

What About Epsom Salts?

Epsom salts (magnesium sulfate) can provide a quick source of magnesium for deficient plants—but it also risks causing excessive magnesium levels, which can tie up other nutrients in the soil or cause toxicity. For example, trying to use Epsom salts on tomatoes to prevent blossom end rot, caused by calcium deficiency in the fruit, only makes matters worse as the magnesium interferes with calcium uptake in plants. It is impossible to tell by looking at leaves whether plants are suffering from a magnesium deficiency, but it is unlikely in garden soils amended with compost and organic matter. Because Epsom salts are so soluble, much of what is applied leaches away anyway, which can cause environmental pollution.

Magnesium sources: Sandy, acidic coastal soils can sometimes be low in magnesium, though it is usually not an issue in soils enriched with compost. If you need to amend with lime to make the soil less acidic, using dolomitic limestone every few years is an excellent way to ensure adequate magnesium. It naturally contains both calcium and magnesium in a safe ratio that does not risk causing a nutrient imbalance. Although you may see Epsom salts (magnesium sulfate) recommended, there is rarely any reason to use this highly soluble magnesium source in an organic garden (see text box on left). Rely on compost, complete organic fertilizers, and the action of soil microbes to provide plenty of magnesium for your crops. The langbeinite included in some organic fertilizers also supplies magnesium.

Micronutrient sources: Compost and organic fertilizers supply micronutrients, so there is usually no need to specially supplement soil. If you are concerned about micronutrient levels, you can amend the soil with kelp or seaweed meal, which are a source of many micronutrients without the risk of causing plant toxicity, but don't take seaweed from beaches. It is an important nutrient source for marine ecosystems—think of it as "compost of the sea." It is also illegal to remove it from beaches in some places.

Easy Fertilizing

Complete organic fertilizer mixes are sold at garden centers and farm supply stores. I highly recommend them for home gardens because they take the guesswork out of fertilizing (follow quantities per square

The Dose Makes the Poison

Don't try to supplement micronutrients without knowing for certain (from a soil test) whether it is necessary because most are toxic to plants in larger quantities. For example, a deficiency of boron causes brown, corky spots in apples and deformed leaves in other plants, but too much boron stunts or kills plants. In fact, boron is used in some kinds of herbicides! Overusing some micronutrients can cause others to become deficient: plant and soil chemistry is really complicated. Stick to using compost and complete organic fertilizers to feed your soil and micronutrients won't be a problem.

Fancy Amendments? Save Your Money!

Is the cost of products such as humic acids, compost starters, cocktails of microbes and special nutrients, mycorrhizal fungal inoculants, etc. justified for a home garden? After all, we don't want vegetables to cost more than at the grocery store! There are remarkably few independent scientific studies showing that such products improve yields or plant health under real garden conditions. One reason is that fertile garden soil with good levels of soil organic matter already has plenty of microbes, humus, and available nutrients. Adding laboratory-grown microbes is just a drop in the bucket compared to the enormous numbers naturally present in soil. Some of these products make sense to inoculate soilless growing mixes or where soils have been badly depleted by heavy cropping and are low in organic matter. But you don't need them for your backyard organic garden.

Table 3.1. Examples of commonly available organic fertilizers and soil amendments; if certified organic products are required, look for OMRI certification on package labels.

Product	% Available N-P-K	Application notes
Gaia Green All-Purpose Organic	4-4-4	Rates on container; as a supplement to compost, half the rate is sufficient
Pro-Mix® Organic Granular Multi-Purpose	7-3-3	Rates on container; as a supplement to compost, half the rate is sufficient
OMRI certified fish compost products: SeaSoil™; Earth-bank™; Oly Mountain®	Approximately [1.5–2]-1.5-0.5	Dig in 1- to 4-inch (2 to 10 cm) layer, depending on soil fertility
Compost, homemade or commercial	Approximately 1-1-1 Highly variable	Dig in 1- to 4-inch (2 to 10 cm) layer, depending on soil fertility Homemade compost may have 0.5% available N; composted manure up to 2–3% N
Alfalfa meal	[2.5–3]–[0.5–2]–[1–2.5] Variable, but good N source	OMRI certified available; livestock pellets are cheapest form
Kelp/Seaweed meal	1-0-2	Micronutrients
Liquid fish fertilizers	Products vary: 5-1-1 Alaska 2-4-1 Neptune's Harvest 2-3-0 BioFish	Dilute in water according to label instructions
Bone meal	2-[11–14]-[0–2] 24% calcium	Label rates: 10 lb/100 ft² (4–5 kg/10 m²); use in first 4–6 years of new garden and when planting fruit trees and grapes; after that only apply if soil test shows low available P
Blood meal Feather meal	12-0-0	Label rates: 4–8 lb/100 ft² (2–4 kg/10 m²); use annually or for N boost at planting time
PNW crab meal	4-3-0 14% calcium	Label rates: 5 lb/100 ft² (2.5 kg/10m²); relatively expensive N source
Wood ashes	0-1-5 25% calcium	1 lb/100 ft² (0.5 kg/10 m²); maximum application rate 2 lb/100 ft² (1kg/10 m²)
Grass clippings	[2–5]-0.4-2	Dig in ½ inch (1 cm) at a time or use 1–2 inches (2–4 cm) as mulch; breaks down quickly

foot on the bag). However, you can also blend your own. For example, if you have wood ashes from a wood stove to supply potassium and micronutrients, you could use blood meal for nitrogen and bone meal for phosphorus and have a balanced fertilizer mix.

Products for vegans (containing no animal products or manures) are available from some suppliers, but at a premium price. Vegan gardeners may prefer to build soil nitrogen by using alfalfa meal or by turning under green manure crops or lawn clippings; other nutrients can be supplied from non-animal sources, such as rock phosphate for phosphorus and wood ashes or glacial rock dust for potassium.

Our Soils Need Lime

Many soils on the West Coast are naturally acidic, though not all. Acidity is measured in terms of pH (which stands for potential of hydrogen, but don't ask, it is very complicated). A pH of 7 is neutral; lower numbers indicate acidic soil, and higher numbers show the soil is alkaline. Most crop plants grow best at a pH of 6.5 to 6.8, which is slightly acidic. The pH of the soil is a factor determining the community of beneficial bacteria present. Although fungi do thrive over a wide range of pH, most bacteria, including those that capture nitrogen in legume roots, thrive in soils with a pH closer to neutral.

In the high-rainfall regions of the coast, most soils have a natural pH of 5.0 to 5.5. Soils in parts of the region that are in the driest rain shadows of the Olympics and Vancouver Island mountains are less acidic and may not need much, if any, lime to raise the pH. If you don't know anything about the soil you plan to use for a garden, it is a good idea to have the soil pH tested (see below).

For acid soils, agricultural lime is the cheapest, most effective amendment you can buy; it

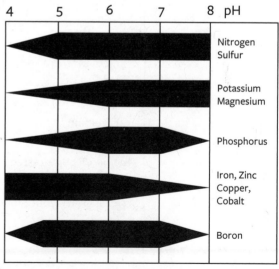

3.7. The relative availability of nutrients at different soil pH is shown by the thickness of the bars. Note that, at a range of pH 6.5 to 6.8, the most nutrients and least heavy metals are available.

raises soil pH and also adds calcium, which crops need. To compress a lot of complex soil chemistry into one short list, here is why you want to aim for a soil pH just on the slightly acid side of neutral:

- Essential nutrients in the soil become more available to plants; therefore, your investment in fertilizer is more effective.
- Naturally occurring aluminum and heavy metals in the soil become less available to plants (this is a good thing to avoid toxicity to plants).
- Slightly acidic to slightly alkaline soil benefits soil bacteria that fix nitrogen, break down organic matter, make nutrients available, protect roots from disease, and improve soil structure.

To make soil less acidic (i.e., raise the pH), dig in agricultural lime, which is ground-up limestone. Any garden center or agricultural supplier sells it. Don't get hydrated or builder's lime from the building supply center; that is for making plaster, whitewash, etc., and can burn plants. Dolomitic lime (from

Should You Have Your Soil Tested?

A soil test done by a laboratory is worth the investment when you don't know anything about the soil you are starting with. The key thing to find out is the acidity (pH). A pH test costs $15 to $20 from most labs in Canada; US gardeners get a much better deal, paying $3 to $10. (See Resources for soil testing labs. And be sure to check their websites for instructions on how to collect the soil for the sample.)

Don't bother with pH test kits or probes sold at garden centers. *Consumer Reports* tested a range of these products, from the cheapest kits to expensive probes, and found they all gave inaccurate and inconsistent results. Save your money!

If plants are not growing well and pH seems to be in the right range, it might be worth having a soil test done for all nutrients. A complete test shows levels of organic matter, nitrogen, phosphorus, potassium, calcium, and other important nutrients. Such tests are quite expensive in British Columbia ($40 to $200), but much cheaper in Washington.

dolomite limestone) is a good choice for coastal gardens because it also contains magnesium. Prilled lime, which is limestone that has been made into pellets so it can be evenly spread on lawns with a fertilizer spreader, is fine for a garden, but it costs more. Only some prilled products are acceptable for certified organic growers, so check for OMRI certification before you buy if that is a consideration.

Add lime once a year until a soil test shows the soil pH is above 6.5. High rainfall leaches calcium and magnesium down through the soil, and a lot of calcium is also taken up by plants. It is important not to overdo lime, but it takes time to increase the pH significantly because lime

3.8. Scab on potatoes only affects the skin and can be peeled away.

works slowly. It takes less lime to raise the pH in sandy soils than clay soils. As a general rule, it takes about 1 pound per square yard (½ kg per m²) to raise the pH from 6.0 to 7.0, but it is best to go by a soil test recommendation.

A pound of lime is not very much—after all, it is as heavy as rock. To make a lime scoop, I take a pint cottage cheese container and weigh out about a pound (½ kg) of lime, which half-fills the container. I draw a thick black line around the inside of the container to mark the level and then use the container as a scoop to measure out enough lime to cover a square yard (or square meter).

Test the soil pH again after four or five years to see if you are on track. Once the pH is above 6.5, stop liming for a few seasons and retest after a couple of years.

You can skip liming the potato bed for a year if you want to. Potatoes produce a bit better in soil that has been limed, but they also tolerate acid soil, which suppresses the growth of the bacteria that causes potato scab. This isn't usually much of a problem in home gardens (unless grocery store potatoes have been used as seed potatoes), so if your potatoes haven't been troubled by scab, lime away (the next crop will appreciate it).

Managing Soil Fertility Year-Round

Managing the soil for all-season harvests in my garden means being generous once a year when adding compost. After that, successive plantings and inter-plantings usually don't require more amendments.

With a year-round planting schedule, the main addition of amendments happens whenever the bed is completely empty between early spring and late summer. At that time, I turn in as much compost as I have (aiming for an inch-thick layer), plus complete organic fertilizer and the annual allotment of lime, if needed.

I don't usually add anything more for the next crop unless the previous plants didn't grow as well as expected. However, for hardy leafy greens for winter, which are sown in July and August, I usually do sprinkle in some blood meal at seeding time to give them a ready supply of nitrogen. There is no point in fertilizing the soil in the fall, because the soil bacteria that make nutrients available are largely dormant in cold weather, and plants can't use the nutrients then anyway. You could lime the soil in the fall if a bed is going to go through winter empty or before you plant garlic in October.

3.9. Spring soil preparation includes turning in compost, fertilizer, and lime, if needed. I don't add any more amendments before planting successive crops during the same season unless the crops look like they need a boost.

If overwintered plants need some extra nitrogen in the spring (leaves are pale yellow rather than darker green), you can give them liquid fertilizer or sprinkle blood meal beside the plants and lightly scratch it in or mulch with compost. It usually isn't necessary because there is a natural surge in available nitrogen in the spring as soil bacteria get back to work digesting organic matter.

Fertilizing during the growing season: It might be necessary to add supplementary fertilizer in midsummer, especially for the first couple of years of a new garden that started on less-than-ideal soil. If plants seem to stop growing or are growing very slowly, it could be a lack of nutrients. If you don't know how quickly plants should be growing, ask an experienced gardener what to expect.

Nitrogen is the nutrient most likely to be in short supply, especially in the first few years of an organic garden. When leaves that should be dark green become a pale green or yellow, especially starting with the lower leaves first,

Making Compost or Manure Extract

Put a shovelful of compost or horse, rabbit, sheep, or goat manure into a 5-gallon bucket and fill with water (avoid pig, chicken, and cow manure due to the risk of human diseases). Let it steep for one to two days, until the water turns dark brown, but don't leave it longer or it will ferment. It now contains whatever soluble nutrients were in the compost, but is too concentrated to use as is. Dilute it with water until it is a pale brown, like weak tea. Water plants with the liquid every week or two or as needed. You can usually brew a couple of buckets of tea from a shovelful of manure or compost.

Note that this is simply a way to extract readily soluble nutrients, such as nitrogen, and not an "aerated compost tea." While aerated teas are purported to improve disease resistance, there is actually little evidence of this in the field (as opposed to laboratory studies). More troubling is the fact that the human pathogens *E. coli* and *Salmonella* have been found growing in such aerated teas, especially when molasses and other ingredients have been added.

3.10. Making compost or manure extract is easy and cheap!

plants are likely deficient in nitrogen (and possibly other nutrients). If plants have adequate sunlight and water, and temperatures are warm enough for growth, slow growth is often due to a lack of nitrogen.

You can deliver a useful supply of soluble nutrients in water for a quick boost during the growing season. If plants are low on nitrogen, they will usually respond in a week or two, with darker green leaves and better growth. If plants needed this boost to keep growing, it is a sign that you should increase the fertility of the soil with compost and nitrogen-rich amendments before planting the next crop.

You can buy liquid fertilizer concentrates (such as fish fertilizer) to dilute in water or you can make your own "tea." (For instructions, see the text box, pg. 81.) There are also various proprietary plant tonics for sale. These may give good results, but can be quite expensive. Why pay, I say, when your own compost extract will do the trick?

Cultivating the Soil

It will take some initial labor to establish a new garden bed: you may need to shovel soil into raised beds or deal with sod, remove large rocks, or hack into poor, compacted soil to turn in amendments. Once this is done, some work is required every year (but much less) to fertilize and prepare seedbeds. Depending on how you choose to cultivate your garden, though, these annual chores can entail a lot of hard work or a bit of light work. Methods based on a "hands-off" approach are healthiest for the soil: "no till," minimum tillage, deep mulching, and permaculture are examples.

We now know that the more you cultivate soil, the more harm it can do to its community of organisms and structure. The greatest variety and number of soil microbes and larger organisms, such as worms and insects, live in the top few inches where there is the most organic matter, warmer conditions, and air circulation. Cultivating methods that bury microbes deeper, such as using a shovel to dig deep and turn over the soil, are detrimental to this community.

Some gardeners advocate annual deep digging (or worse, double digging), but that's hard on the soil community. It is also a ridiculous amount of hard work! Instead, just stir the surface layers enough to mix in compost, organic fertilizers, or other amendments.

Vegetables and fruit can grow under different systems, but some techniques are better suited to the coastal climate or are more appropriate for small gardens than others. Having farmed and gardened over the years on a variety of soils in different climates, I have arrived at the same conclusion as many people before me: minimizing cultivation protects the soil, is a lot less work, and gives excellent results.

The point of cultivating is to mix in compost and other amendments, control weeds, and prepare a bed for planting. Cultivation also loosens and aerates soil in the root zone, but how important this is depends on your soil type and its level of organic matter. The objective in preparing a seedbed is a reasonably level soil surface free of large clods or stones. For transplants, the soil surface can be left quite rough. In fact, there is often no need to cultivate at all if you are transplanting a second crop into a bed that has already received enough amendments for the year. Just open a hole for the transplants and put them in (see Figure 3.4).

Cultivation Methods

After going through a (very short-lived!) deep-digging phase and then a rototilling phase when I had a large market garden decades ago, I arrived at a comfortable system of minimal cultivation that works fine in this climate, is easy, and fits into a busy life.

Minimum cultivation: Once a year, spread compost and other amendments over the surface of the soil. Using a garden fork, lightly fork over the top layer enough to mix

Does Soil Have to Be Cultivated?

It is certainly possible to garden without cultivating at all, as many gardeners attest. "No till" methods usually involve maintaining a thick mulch on the soil for most or all of the year. Here on the coast, heavy mulches should be pulled back in the spring to allow soil to warm up and dry out and discourage slugs and pillbugs from having a heyday at the expense of your seedlings. However, in the summer, planting well-grown transplants directly into a deeply mulched bed works quite well (see Figure 3.4, p. 64). In this climate, where we plant crops through both cool wet springs and warm dry summers, you might apply different methods to suit the season. The important thing is not to bury the topsoil community if you do cultivate.

amendments into the top 4 to 6 inches (10 to 15 cm). The fork easily combs through loose open soil. If the soil stays together when you lift a forkful, turn the fork so that the soil slides off sideways and then lightly fork it into the surface layer. Avoid turning forkfuls of soil completely upside down because this buries the topsoil organisms away from the warmth and air circulation they need. If you want to loosen the root zone below, drive in the fork and rock it back and forth to loosen the soil, without lifting the soil and turning it upside down. If you have a very large garden, you might want to invest in a wide two-handled tool called a broadfork or U-bar digger (see Resources), to make cultivating quicker and easier.

Advantages of this method:

- It maintains a healthy topsoil community of bacteria, fungi, worms, insects, and other organisms.

- It drags fewer dormant weed seeds to the surface to sprout than deep-digging methods (for more on the "seed bank," see Chapter 4).
- It preserves soil structure.
- There is less interruption of the natural upward movement of moisture from the subsoil (called capillary flow).
- It preserves more carbon in the soil, preventing it from reaching the atmosphere and contributing to climate change.
- Last, but certainly not least, it is less work. It takes me about twenty minutes to spread compost and other amendments and lightly fork over a 40-foot-square bed (if it isn't weedy).

3.11. My trusty garden fork is now all I use to cultivate— but I do it lightly and no more than once a year in any one garden bed.

A disadvantage is that surface cultivation doesn't incorporate lime deeply, which is important in the first year or two of a new garden in acid soil. Minimum cultivation works very well, however, for established gardens once lime and amendments have been mixed in more deeply in the first year or two.

Double digging and deep digging: The best that can be said for these methods is they incorporate lime and other amendments deeply. But they have serious disadvantages, not the least of which is that they are a daunting amount of work. The fact that crops grow just fine without all this effort shows how unnecessary they are.

Any kind of deep cultivation buries the community of topsoil microorganisms down where it is cool (even cold, at times) and dark, and there is less air circulation. Because we rely on these organisms to release nutrients, protect roots from disease, and perform many other functions, it doesn't make sense to set them back this way. Deep digging also brings weed seeds from greater depths to the surface, where they will readily germinate in the light and warmth. It can also disrupt the natural upward flow of moisture from the subsoil (the capillary flow) at a point well below the root zone of annual vegetable plants, at least while they are small. Because water conservation is a widespread concern in this region, it is preferable not to interrupt this natural upward movement of water to crops where it exists.

Rototilling: Tillers come in a variety of sizes, including very small models. The tines of rototillers spin around, thoroughly mixing the soil to the depth of the tines. I am not a fan of rototillers because they pound apart the soil structure and chop up fungi and earthworms (plus, they make noise, use gas, and cost money); however, they are useful for breaking new ground if you want to plant a garden immediately. They break up sod easily and quickly compared to hand digging, and the action of the tines can rapidly incorporate large amounts of organic matter into the soil. In fact, soil shouldn't be rototilled unless you *can* turn in lots of organic matter at the same time to help counteract the damage done to the soil structure and soil organisms.

The disadvantages of tillers:

- The action of the tines destroys soil structure. Some soils should not be rototilled at all, because they are too fragile, while other soils hold up pretty well to occasional rototilling, as long as a generous supply of organic matter is incorporated every time.

- Even the smallest models are hard to use in very small areas, and they all require a fairly strong person to control the machine.
- They are expensive to rent or to buy and maintain.

The bottom line: Crops can be grown under a wide variety of cultivation systems, so how you choose to cultivate your garden depends on the time and energy you have available, the tools you want to use, and the size of your garden. Bearing in mind how beneficial it is to minimize cultivation and the fact that my personal objective is to harvest the largest amount of food for the least amount of work, I use a garden fork to disturb the soil as little as possible and mulch to control weeds, feed the soil, and conserve water.

CHAPTER 4

Basic Methods for Growing Vegetables

There was a time was when most people grew up around *someone* who had a food garden, so they were more or less familiar with how to go about it. No longer. These days, many people who are interested in growing their own food are unfamiliar with even the most basic methods. So, this Chapter is geared toward beginning gardeners. You more experienced gardeners can just skip on ahead (perhaps to the section on dealing with extreme weather!).

How to Sow Seeds

In case you are looking at your new seed packages and wondering what's next, here is how to get going on sowing those seeds.

Preparing a seedbed: After you dig in the soil amendments (see Chapter 3), level the seedbed using a rake or the back of a garden fork. Remove stones, clods, and debris from the surface, but don't go overboard working up a fine surface. In fact, depending on the soil type, overcultivating can result in a crusty surface that is hard for seedlings to poke through. Most seedlings can pop up through surprisingly uneven soil as long as they don't have to push up stones or clods.

Remove large rocks as you come upon them. Don't be overly concerned about removing pebbles, however, unless the bed is for carrots. Carrots produce forked roots when they hit stones, so the fewer pebbles the better.

Sowing depth: The general rule is that seeds should be planted three times deeper in the soil than the width of the seed. A lettuce seed is so tiny that in practice this means covering the seeds with the thinnest possible layer of soil. Beans or corn seeds, which are much larger, should be planted about 1 inch (2 cm) deep. This is not an exact requirement, and it should be adjusted for the conditions. For example, in early spring, while the soil is still cool and moist, many tiny seeds germinate well if they are just scattered on the surface of the soil (lettuce, arugula, dill, cilantro).

In midsummer, when the soil temperatures are higher and the surface dries out quickly after watering, seeds germinate better if they are sown a bit deeper than the general rule: Tiny seeds would need about ¼ inch (5 mm) of soil, and bean and corn seeds would be planted about 1½ inches (3 cm) deep.

Seeding patterns: There are several ways to sow seeds. They all work fine, but some suit certain vegetables better than others. Seed spacing information is included under each entry in the A to Z Vegetables section in Chapter 10.

- **Broadcast:** Broadcast sowing is particularly suited to lettuce, other salad greens and mesclun mixes, and annual herbs, such as dill. Scatter seeds lightly over the surface of the whole bed area. "Lightly" means one or two seeds per square inch. Cover them to the right depth by sprinkling more soil over the whole bed. (Before sowing, I usually scrape back a thin layer of soil from the surface of the bed, store it to one side or in a bucket, then use it to cover the seeds.) Crumble the soil between your fingers as you spread it to break up small clods, so that you deposit a fine layer over the seeds. Press seeds into good contact with moist soil by firmly patting the surface of the soil. Some seeds don't have to be covered: corn salad broadcast in late summer germinates even if you don't cover the seed.
- **Furrows:** Sowing in shallow trenches or furrows is particularly suited to bigger seeds, such as beans, peas, beets, and Swiss chard, but it works fine for all seeds. It particularly suits beds irrigated with parallel rows of drip or soaker hoses because you can run a furrow on either side of each hose. Make the furrows with your fingers, a trowel, or a hoe to a depth that fits the size of the seed. Sprinkle seeds along the bottom of the furrow or place large seeds one by one along the row. Push in the soil from the sides to cover seeds to the correct depth. Firm the soil down to ensure good contact

between seeds and soil. You can fill a wide bed with closely spaced, parallel furrows.

- **Hills:** A hill is a mound of soil built up a bit above ground level to make a warmer, drier planting site. Planting in hills works well for large plants that need a lot of space, such as squash and cucumbers. These are not usually sown directly in the garden in this region because the soil warms so late there isn't much time for a crop, but you can set out seedlings in the hills. Dig in an extra supply of compost and fertilizer at the site of each hill. For squash, hills are usually spaced a yard apart.

4.1. Sow bean seeds in a furrow a couple of inches deep, so the seeds can be covered with more than an inch of soil.

- **Individual sites:** Large seeds, such as corn, can also be sown directly in small groups at each planting site. I like to just take a trowel, dig in a bit of blood meal, and plant two or three corn seeds in each place about a foot apart each way. When the seeds come up, the plants are thinned to the strongest seedling.

Watering: Once the seeds are planted, keep the soil damp, but not soaking wet. Seeds take up moisture from the soil and from the humid air between soil

The Marvel of Germination

Each seed has its own food supply inside its protective coat. When seeds are exposed to moisture and warmth (and in some cases, light), they germinate, meaning that they start to grow. The tiny developing plant uses the food stored in the seed as its energy supply. Only when it has pushed down a root and the shoot has opened its first leaves to the sun can the plant start making a new food supply through photosynthesis.

particles so as long as the soil surface isn't allowed to dry completely, they will be fine. In the spring, when it rains frequently, it may not be necessary to water a seedbed at all or after the initial soaking. In the summer, however, be vigilant, because a seedbed can dry out in just half a day.

The gentle sprinkle from a watering can is ideal for watering newly seeded beds. For larger areas, use the gentlest shower setting on a hose nozzle. Take care not to disturb the soil by blasting a stream of water that would dislodge seeds or tear the roots of germinating seeds. Even a heavy rain can wash away small seeds, which is why I prefer a rougher seedbed—it keeps the seeds from being moved around.

When to Sow Seeds in the Spring

This is a vexing question! Some concepts useful in other climates, such as average frost-free dates (see text box below), don't mean much for the coast. And coastal spring weather varies so much from year to year (and is likely to vary more as the climate changes) that last year's timing doesn't necessarily apply this year.

Forget the Average Frost-Free Date

While the average date of the last frost is used in other regions as a marker for spring planting, this concept isn't much use on the coast. Frost-free dates are calculated from many years' worth of weather data at a recording site (usually a regional airport). Because the coast is so geographically complex, even weather records from a site very near your garden may bear little relationship to the frost patterns in your garden. On the coast, there can be striking differences in frost patterns over very small areas.

Another reason the concept doesn't apply here is that spring on the coast is such a long, drawn-out affair; the "last frost" might happen anytime from February through May. The warmest areas might get only one or two frosts all winter. In my garden, the last frost dates over many years has ranged from March 5 to April 30, yet a mile away, in a friend's garden, I have seen ground frosts in mid-May.

Garden books often recommend planting peas and other cold-hardy crops "when the soil can be worked." In this region, there is often such prolonged wet weather in the spring that some soils are too wet to work until quite late. When you plant for year-round harvests, however, this isn't as much of a concern because your overwintered vegetables will be producing good crops in the spring long before you are able to work the soil to sow new plants.

The key is soil temperature. For coastal gardeners, soil temperature is the best indicator of when to plant. This is the only temperature that matters to germinating seeds anyway, and it varies widely from year to year. For example, in a year with a very cold spring, the soil a few inches down in my garden was just above freezing on April 1. The next year, my soil temperature was 48°F (9°C) by March 15. It is handy to have a soil thermometer, but with a little experience, you can also go by how cold the soil feels to your fingers.

Because winters are so mild here and hardy plants grow pretty well all winter, is it easy to

Treated Seeds?
Treated seeds are coated with a fungicide to protect the germinating seed from fungus attack. If you plant seeds when the soil is warm enough (see Table 4.1), there is no need for chemical protection. The faster a seed can germinate and get growing in warm soil, the less time it spends vulnerable to attack by fungi or other organisms. Organic growers don't use treated seed.

Table 4.1. Soil temperatures for germination of vegetable seeds.

Crops	Minimum °F (°C)	Better	Best
Lettuce, onion, spinach, parsnip, endive	32 (0)	60 (15)	70 (21)
Beets, broccoli, cabbage, carrots, cauliflower, celery, parsley, peas, radishes, Swiss chard	40 (5)	60 (15)	77 (25)
Tomato, turnip	50 (10)	70 (21)	77 (25)
Sweet corn (OP and normal hybrids), beans, cucumber, pepper	60 (15)	70 (21)	86 (30)
Eggplant, melons, pumpkins, squash, sweet corn (supersweet and sugar-enhanced hybrids)	64 (18)	77 (25)	95 (35)

Note: Wait until the soil reaches the temperatures in the "Better" column before sowing seeds. Higher temperatures in the "Best" column may only be achieved using bottom heat for seedlings.

4.2. Nitrogen-fixing nodules on the roots of peas. If your legumes have these pinkish lumps on the roots, they are happy and healthy.

Are Legume Seed Inoculants Worth Buying?

Commercial suppliers sell cultures of nitrogen-fixing bacteria for inoculating pea and bean seeds. They usually aren't necessary, however, because most soils already have these bacteria. There is a good chance that the products in the store aren't even viable, because the bacteria don't keep for long. It *may* be worth it to buy seed inoculant the first time you plant in soil that has never had legumes grown in it, such as container mixes with a high proportion of non-soil ingredients (peat/coir, vermiculite, etc.). Follow package instructions for mixing with seeds.

be fooled into putting out very tender crops too early. But waiting until the soil is warm enough for seeds of heat-loving crops, such as corn and beans, could mean waiting until June. Here are some ways around this:

- **Warm the soil before sowing.** For at least a week before planting, lay a sheet of clear plastic flat on the soil surface and anchor it with stones or boards (black plastic is not as effective as clear). If the weather continues cloudy, it won't have much effect, but as soon as the sun comes out, the top layer of soil warms up markedly.
- **After sowing, cover the beds with plastic over hoops to make a tunnel.** Don't lay the plastic down on the soil after seeding, however, as the heat can literally cook the seeds. Alternatively, bump up the temperatures by covering the beds with floating row covers or perforated plastic film (e.g., Gro-Therm).
- **Start seeds indoors.** This is more likely to ensure a higher percentage of successful plants and usually eliminates the need to reseed poor stands of plants. Pre-sprout beans in a tray of vermiculite until they have their first true leaves. Start the first plantings of sweet corn indoors, preferably on bottom heat.

How to Sow Seeds in the Summer

The challenge for sowing seeds in the summer is keeping the soil evenly moist until germination occurs. The surface soil also needs to be below a certain temperature for some seeds. The maximum temperature for seed germination for most crops is about 86°F (30°C); for lettuce and spinach, it is about 75°F (24°C). The solution to both challenges is to shade the soil.

Water the soil well after sowing, then cover the beds with newspaper (anchored with a couple of stones), burlap, woven feed bags, or other cloth (old beach towels work great). If you have a piece of stucco wire or chicken wire the size of the bed, lay that down first, then spread the fabric on top of the wire to give a little air circulation over the surface.

4.3. Plastic trays protect seedlings from hot sun. Burlap in the background is shading a seedbed before the seedlings emerge.

The soil usually doesn't need to be watered again for several days. Lift a corner of the cover to check daily for germination and remove it the minute the tip of the first seedling shows. Seeds sprout very quickly in the summer: leafy greens may germinate in two or three days. If you need to water, remove the cover, soak the soil, and replace the cover.

If the weather is hot and sunny when they first come up, tiny seedlings will fare much better with some shade. I like to use horticultural shade cloth (see p. 114) or plastic latticework trays that hold seed flats, turned upside down and spread out over the bed. You can use anything—branches, latticework, strips of cloth supported on a frame—as long as the seedlings get *some* sun but don't cook. As soon as possible, gently work in fine mulch, such as grass

4.4. Shade cloth makes cool, yet bright, conditions for seedlings on a hot day.

clippings or crushed up leaves, between the seedlings to keep their roots cool and moist; you can beef up the layer of mulch as plants grow larger.

Thinning Seedlings

Whether you intentionally planted too many seeds in the row (a good strategy to make sure enough survive pests) or not, most stands of seedlings will have to be thinned once they come up. Carrots are notoriously hard to sow thinly, and no matter how carefully you place seeds of beets or Swiss chard, you still have to thin them. This is because they have several seeds inside each shriveled up "seed" (botanists call it a seedball).

Remove crowded seedlings while the plants are tiny to avoid damaging the roots of the keepers. You can pull them or clip them off. With care, you can also transplant seedlings from crowded spots to fill in gaps. For beets, lettuce, and other greens that are edible at any size, thin them in several stages and use the thinnings: first time through, thin the plants to an inch apart; next time, thin to a couple of inches, and on a third pass, thin to the final spacing.

4.5. Thin leafy seedlings, and eat the tender baby leaves in a salad.

Buying Transplants

Whether you buy all of your transplants or just a few to supplement what you start from seed, here are some guidelines:

- Choose small young plants rather than larger plants, which may have been in pots too long.
- Avoid plants that appear old, root-bound, or spindly, especially those that have been held on shelves without enough light. Roots sticking out of the pot's drainage holes indicate the plant is becoming root-bound.
- Avoid plants with yellowing leaves or purplish or brown streaks on the leaves. No seedlings should have discolored lower leaves, indicating they are suffering from nutrient deficiency or other stress.
- Check for insect pests and disease; don't take home anything that looks suspicious.

A good tip for getting the best quality is to find out when your local nursery expects new plants to arrive (it is usually weekly); buy your plants the day they are put out for sale, and plant immediately if the weather is suitable. If you buy transplants well before they can go outdoors, it is a good idea to move them into larger pots. This is especially important if you end up with large seedlings of leeks, onions, cabbage, Swiss chard, or other plants that are easily vernalized (see Chapter 1) by a late period of cool weather.

Setting Out Transplants

Before planting out seedlings you started indoors or in a greenhouse, make sure young plants are hardened off (acclimated to being in wind and direct sun. See Chapter 5).

1. In a previously prepared bed, use a trowel or your fingers to scoop a hole a bit bigger than the root ball of the seedling. If the seedlings were growing in individual containers, you can slide the root ball out with little disturbance. For seedlings growing in flats, gently work the roots of each plant loose from the others with your fingers or a small tool, keeping as much soil as possible around the roots.

2. Taking care to disturb the roots as little as possible, set the small plant in the hole and fill in soil around the root ball so that the seedling sits upright. As you fill in the soil, gently poke it around the roots to fill air spaces. The

final level of soil around the stem should end up the same as it was in the original flat or just a bit higher.

3. Gently firm the soil around the roots, but don't press down hard enough to tear the roots. Water well.

This sounds like a slow process, but it can go quite quickly as you scoop out the soil, plunk in the seedling, push in the soil, and move on.

For squash and cucumber plants, set out in hills of three or four plants. I dig a larger hole where the group of plants will go and mix in a generous supply of compost and ¼ cup of complete organic fertilizer at the bottom of the hole, or you could just use 2 tablespoons of blood meal. I replace enough soil to bring the bottom of the planting hole to the right depth for the transplants and carry on from there, planting and watering.

Nursing transplant shock: The ideal weather for transplanting is cloudy and moist. The hotter and drier it is, the more care seedlings will need to help them recover from the shock of transplanting. Because their roots inevitably suffer more damage during transplanting, seedlings that were growing in a flat with others will take longer to recover than seedlings grown in individual pots.

Protect plants from sun and wind for two to four days to give them time to replace fine root hairs. You can use anything to shade them temporarily: a sheet of newspaper over the seedlings, slabs of cardboard or wood shingles pushed into the soil on the south side of the plants, or even a large plant pot turned upside down over the seedlings. The object is to shade them from the midday sun until their roots recover.

If a late cool spell threatens, shelter young plants with floating row covers, cloches, or other covers to keep them warmer. If a heat wave arrives, of course, continue to shade them until temperatures drop.

Irrigation

Vegetables need a lot of water, and they must be watered in dry weather. Coastal gardens on low-lying land may not need water until midsummer if there is enough moisture in the soil. In contrast, gardens with well-drained soils might need irrigation in late May if the usual dry summer weather sets in early.

How much to water: You will read elsewhere that intensively planted annual vegetable gardens need the equivalent of 1 inch (up to 2 cm) of rainfall per week in hot weather. When it doesn't rain, you are supposed to supply the difference. Now, that is a lot of water! I do not come close to providing this much to my own garden, in part because where I live it is necessary to conserve well water. How much you really need to water varies tremendously, depending on the following factors:

- **Soil characteristics:** structure, drainage, and organic matter content all affect the water-holding capacity of a soil.
- **Temperature and wind:** both influence how much water the plants pull from the soil and transpire through their leaves. On a hot, windy day, plants will suck up much more water.
- **Plant spacing:** dense plantings need more water per square yard than plants spaced farther apart (but of course, produce more per square yard too).
- **Mulches:** these prevent surface evaporation from the soil (which accounts for about 10% to 15% of water loss) and prevent weeds from growing and competing for water.
- **Efficiency of the irrigation system:** delivering water through drip irrigation and soaker hoses uses much less water than overhead sprinkling to achieve the same harvest.
- **How much water you have:** what is available for gardening also depends on the water source and whether restrictions to conserve water are in effect in the summer.

If your plants show wilting in midday, they may be water stressed. In a heat wave, though, plants wilt somewhat to protect themselves from disastrous water loss even when the soil is moist. If they don't recover by evening, that is a sign they are suffering, and fine roots have probably been injured. They will need the best of care to recover and may never produce as well as they would have if they hadn't been drought stressed.

How often to water: As a general rule, in deep soil it is better to water longer and less often because it encourages roots to grow deeply as they follow the moisture. The plants reach more nutrients and are less likely to suffer a check in growth in a period of hot weather. Gardens with deep soil probably need to be watered once a week in typical midsummer conditions. Established fruit trees and bushes that are well-mulched usually need deep watering less often (every two to four weeks, depending on how warm it has been).

However, gardens with shallow soils in raised beds over rock or gravel won't hold much water. Gardens on sandy well-drained soils also don't hold moisture well. In these situations, long watering *wastes* water because it drains out of the root zone. These gardens make better use of irrigation water if watered for short periods two or three times a week.

The best indication of when to water is the soil condition. Watering when the soil needs it generally uses less water than watering on a fixed schedule. Poke a finger into the soil to check or take a trowel and open a hole: if you see darker moist soil 2 to 3 inches (5 to 7 cm) down, the moisture in the root zone is fine. Do this in a few places, and you will get a good idea whether some areas of the garden need more or less watering than others.

Irrigation Systems

There are many designs on the market. What you use and the price you pay will depend on the quality of the components, how much assembly you can do yourself, and whether the system has automatic controls. For detailed information on options, talk to local irrigation suppliers and ask other gardeners about their systems. Lee Valley Tools has a very helpful *Irrigation Design Guide* to do-it-yourself design and installation, a free download from their website. Most regional districts, counties, and municipalities also provide information guides and sometimes public workshops on water-conserving irrigation systems.

The following is a brief overview of the different ways to irrigate:

Hand watering: For small urban gardens and gardens on rental property, using a hose or watering can may be the most practical option. It takes time to hand water, but it requires little investment in equipment (and what there is can be taken with you when you move). Sturdy plastic watering cans cost less than $10, and a garden hose costs $20 to $50 (much less at garage sales). If you use a hose to hand water, invest in a nozzle with a shutoff and a setting that delivers water in a gentle rain. In some locations, under the most extreme restrictions on outdoor water use, hand watering may be the only irrigation allowed. For how to measure water applied by hand, see below.

Overhead watering: There are many types and designs of sprinklers. They use more water than the drip or linear systems described below, so are mainly useful when and where water shortages are not a concern or there are no municipal watering restrictions. Sprinklers can be inexpensive, and they are easy to move around to water different areas. You can install a timer (several designs are available) between the hose and the tap to shut the water off automatically.

Note that watering the whole garden area encourages weeds to grow in pathways, so it will take more work to control them. Also, overhead watering can create or worsen slug and disease problems, particularly of tomatoes, potatoes, sweet basil, beans, and related plants. You can lessen the risks by sprinkling early in the morning, so that leaves and the soil surface dry off quickly in the morning sun.

Drip/micro-irrigation systems: These systems use much less water than overhead sprinklers because water is delivered through small emitters right to the plant roots. No water is wasted on non-growing areas, which also helps control weeds in pathways. This is an excellent way to water individual perennial plants, fruit trees, and bushes; it is easy to change or add drippers to the systems as the plants grow. Drip irrigation is less suitable for annual vegetable beds because the plant spacing differs with every crop; the drippers won't be in the right place for every plant. To get around this, unfortunately, some suppliers install micro-spray heads on irrigation systems for vegetable gardens, which spray water onto the plants just above the soil level. Do *not* use these for vegetables because the frequent wetting of the leaves provides perfect conditions for such devastating diseases as late blight on tomatoes and leaf disease on beans.

Linear systems and soaker hoses: Linear irrigation lines (punched with holes at close spacing) and soaker hoses (water weeps from openings all along the hose) work very well for vegetables because they provide continuous strips of water along the length of beds. They also save water since it is only going to the crop and not onto pathways. Some designs emit water more quickly, and some are much slower and for low-pressure systems. Whichever you use, make sure that all of the lines or hoses are of the same type for even distribution of water; if applicable, check that they comply with local water conservation bylaws. If using soaker hoses, get a good-quality product: professional grade hoses (e.g., from Lee Valley Tools) have double walls and can operate at very low water pressure, consistent with water conservation bylaws.

For my vegetable beds, I use a set of four parallel, professional grade soaker hoses. They are attached to a header made up of a 4-foot length of plastic plumbing pipe with four threaded fittings for the soaker hoses and one in the middle to connect to the garden hose from the water supply. Each soaker hose is screwed onto a fitting and rolled out to run the length of the vegetable bed. The soakers stay in place permanently; I cultivate around and under them and plant along both sides of each hose so plants are right beside the water source. When the seedlings are large enough, I top off the beds with a thick mulch over everything to reduce evaporation from the soil.

4.6. Soaker hoses conserve water and can fit any shape of garden bed.

Measuring Irrigation

You can easily find out how much water has been delivered by an overhead sprinkler system by setting out a rain gauge or straight-sided tin can in the middle of the sprinkler zone. Run the sprinkler and check how long it takes to rain down half an inch of water on the garden. Wait for an hour or two to let the water soak in, and then dig down to see how far that water penetrated. Then wait for a week and keep checking to see how quickly soil at 2 to 3 inches (5 to 7 cm) deep dries out. Adjust your watering schedule accordingly.

Use a variation of this to check how much water you are delivering when hand watering. First set out five or six straight-sided cans spaced over a bed to use as gauges. Move the watering can or hose end nozzle smoothly back and forth over the bed until all of the soil in the bed has been hit with water once. Turn off the water and check how much has accumulated in the cans. Make more passes over the bed as needed, until there is half an inch of water. Wait for an hour or two and check depth of water in the root zone, as above.

With drip or linear irrigation systems, the water spreads downward, roughly in a cone shape, with the tip of the cone at the delivery point of the water. That means that the surface soil around the individual emitter or on

4.7. The surface still looks dry, but digging down shows the root zone has plenty of moisture.

Special Case: No Spare Water for Irrigation?

In some places, such as the Gulf Islands and San Juan Islands, households depend on cisterns to hold winter rain for their summer water supply and have no surplus for a summer garden. By thinking of food gardening as a fall-through-spring activity, rather than a summer activity, it is still possible to enjoy garden vegetables for much of the year.

For summer, grow a couple of tomato plants or cucumbers or other favorites in containers or keep a small bed close to the house where it will be easy to water with "light gray" kitchen water—the clean wastewater you can catch in a dishpan from rinsing dishes or washing vegetables. Or keep a bucket in the shower to catch the water while it is warming up enough for you to step in, and use it for your container crops.

For overwintering crops:

• If you have a little gray water to spare, start winter lettuce and leafy greens (kales, Chinese cabbage, leaf beet, spinach, leaf mustard) in early August in a small nursery bed that you can irrigate with a minimal amount of water. Or, buy most of these as transplants from garden centers in mid-August, and put them in a small bed. Transplant your seedlings to the main garden in September. Even if it doesn't rain until October, they won't need much water because of the cooler, shorter days. Once the fall rains start, these plants will do fine.

• If you have no water to spare, sow seeds in September directly in the garden. They will sprout and grow a little in the fall, but they won't yield a crop for fall or winter harvest. They will, however, start growing again in February and produce a good crop, probably until the end of June.

• In late March, you should be able to grow an early crop of peas, potatoes, scallions from onions sets, lettuce, and possibly baby carrots before the soil becomes too dry. Without irrigation, plants will stop growing sometime in June or July. In most areas, you can grow a good crop of garlic without irrigation. Plant the cloves in October and harvest the mature crop in early July. Early garlic varieties can be out of the garden before the end of June.

Vegetable Watering Requirements

Vegetables need more water than other kinds of plants, but even among the vegetables, there are some differences in water needs and no vegetables appreciate irregular watering (alternating too dry and too wet), which causes growth disorders (see p. 97).

Vegetables that can handle less water:

• **Snap and pole beans** (not broad beans) fare better on less water than other vegetables, but if kept too dry, flowers drop and pods become distorted or won't fill evenly.

• **Tomatoes** can grow relatively deep roots; therefore, plants in deep soil can be watered less in the latter part of the season. Don't try this for young plants or plants in containers or in shallow or sandy soils.

• **Winter squash**, once plants have become well-established and set fruit, can make do with less water, though the fruit may be small.

Vegetables to keep well-watered, with a thick mulch:

• **Cabbage family (broccoli, cabbage, cauliflower, Brussels sprouts)** don't tolerate dry conditions any time, but adequate water is most critical when heads are developing.

• **Carrots and other roots** need evenly moist soil throughout their early development, but once parsnips and long-rooted carrots reach a good size, they can reach deeper moist soil. Drought-stressed roots crack, split, or become knobby.

• **Corn** has shallow roots and needs a lot of water, most critically during pollination and ear development. Drought stress causes the pollen to be shed before the silks on the ears are ready to accept it, resulting in poor kernel development.

• **Lettuce and leafy greens** need a constant supply of moisture. They tolerate some shade, so grow them under latticework or in dappled shade to cut down on watering.

• **Onion family, celery, celeriac, and endive** all have short roots and need a ready water supply. Fall-planted garlic is an exception because its roots become established over winter when there is plenty of moisture; depending on the site, garlic may need little or no irrigation before harvest in July.

• **Peas'** demand for water is most critical when the seeds are developing and filling pods.

• **Potato** yields are low and tubers are knobby or develop a hollow heart if they get too dry during tuber development.

either side of the soaker hose stays dry no matter how long you water, which makes you think you haven't watered enough. To check, run the system for a set time (e.g., ten or twenty minutes). Turn off the water and wait for an hour or two for the water to penetrate. Then, in an empty section of the bed along the irrigation system, use a trowel to dig a test hole down to the root zone to see how far the water has moved. Back off on the watering time if the soil seems quite wet or increase it if the water has not reached the root zone.

Handling Periods of Drought

Unlike gardeners in some parts of the continent, coastal PNW gardeners have little experience with growing crops under prolonged dry conditions. The serious regional drought in 2015, followed by a long dry season again in 2016, showed how important it is to know how to grow crops when weather patterns deliver a drought year.

Water Conservation

Ways to reduce the amount of water used for a garden and still get good harvests include:

- Plant deeper where the depth of soil permits. Started plants (not seeds) of tomatoes, peppers, potatoes, and corn can be planted deeper than you might think, putting roots in contact with deeper moisture zone. Set good-sized plants in 6- to 12-inch-deep holes (a posthole digger is useful) or set out plants or seed potatoes in trenches and fill in the soil as the plants grow up. Tomatoes and potatoes will root all along the buried part of their stem; not a technique for a cool summer or in shallow soils, but it works well in hot, dry years.
- **Change plant spacing.** If you have plenty of room for a garden, spacing plants widely (along with mulching well between them) allows a crop to grow with less water than might be taken up by high-density plantings.
- **Control weeds** so they don't compete for water. Immediately remove surplus crop plants or any plants past their prime that you won't be using so that you don't waste water on them (they make great mulch).
- Plant fruits trees and berry shrubs in the fall. Roots do grow and become established over the winter; therefore they won't need as much water in their first summer as they would if planted in the spring.

When Watering Restrictions Apply

To preserve community water supplies, municipalities impose water restrictions in dry seasons and drought years. As these become more stringent, garden watering may be limited to drip irrigation or hand watering. Some rural water districts cap the number of gallons each household can use in a month.

Watering restrictions that limit watering to two or three days a week should not be a hardship for vegetables if they are well-mulched with good levels of organic matter in the soil. Established trees and bushes need much less water than that: often a monthly soaking is plenty. For the few weeks that dwarf fruit trees and bushes are ripening a crop, however, they should be watered once a week, if possible.

If outdoor watering is banned, pile on the mulch and use household wastewater (e.g., from washing vegetables, rinsing dishes, running shower water until it warms) to keep plants going.

Mulching

A mulch is a material used to cover the surface of the soil. Mulches of organic material, such as leaves, straw, or crop waste, benefit gardens in many ways by:

- smothering weeds and preventing seeds from germinating;
- slowing evaporation of water from the soil surface in the summer (an estimated 10% to 15% of water loss);
- providing stable soil temperatures: cooler in summer and warmer in winter;
- adding organic matter and nutrients to the soil as they decompose;
- protecting the soil from erosion in heavy winter rain;
- making excellent habitat for ground beetles and other beneficial insects.

There are artificial mulches for sale, made from biodegradable paper or colored plastic. Some commercial growers use these products to control weeds and warm the soil in vegetable fields. Home gardeners can use these, too, but they increase the expense of gardening. Plus, the manufacturing and disposal of these materials is a burden on the environment. None of them improve the soil like an organic mulch does, and you certainly don't need them to enjoy an excellent harvest.

Mulching a Coastal Garden

Mulches are very beneficial in coastal gardens in summer, fall, and winter. The one time they have drawbacks is in spring because they keep the soil cool just when we want it to warm up for seeds. Therefore, a week or two before sowing seeds in a particular bed, I rake the remaining mulch off the bed into the pathway to let the soil warm up and make it easier to fork in amendments. There usually isn't much left of winter mulches; a surprising amount will have been digested into the soil.

Removing the mulch also removes shelter for slugs from the immediate vicinity of seedlings that are too small to tolerate damage. I find that slugs are not much of a problem under mulches around well-grown plants, probably because slugs are as likely to eat the mulch as the crop. Also, slug predators (ground beetles and rove beetles) live with their prey under the mulches. If you do have a problem with slugs, safe and effective ferric (iron) phosphate slug baits are now approved for organic growers, so you can use these to control slugs around seedbeds.

After a few weeks, when seedlings are well grown and the soil is warm (and before weeds get going), I move a light layer of mulch back onto the beds. I add more material as it gets warmer and drier, especially around vegetables such as peas and broccoli that like cooler soil. By late fall, when summer mulches are wearing thin, I start working in more mulch around winter crop plants and piling mulch on empty beds. In December, I top up the mulches to 6 inches (15 cm) around overwintering plants to keep their roots warmer and protect the shoulders of root crops from frost damage.

What to use for mulch depends on what you can get easily and cheaply. Most backyard gardeners don't have access to a truck or trailer to haul large amounts of bulky material, such as spoiled hay, but most urbanites have ready access to leaves in the fall.

Leaves: My favorite mulch is leaves. They are free, don't have weed seeds, and break down quickly because they start with a pretty good ratio of carbon to nitrogen. I use leaves as my main mulch on all beds for winter. I stockpile leaves in big plastic bags or bins covered with tarps so I have lots for the following summer.

4.8. True wealth! Leaves are free, so stockpile plenty for next summer's mulch.

4.9. After a winter in the rain, straw sticks together in thin sheets that are easy to peel off the bale like tiles for mulching.

Contrary to what you might have heard, all kinds of leaves are fine to use as a mulch, including big-leaf maple, oak, and arbutus (madrona) leaves. The only leaves to be wary of are black walnut, which contain a compound that inhibits growth of certain plants that are sensitive to it (see text box on p. 60).

You can shred big leaves or run a mower over them for use as a summer mulch, but it isn't necessary; for winter mulching, what we want is a fluffy insulating layer, so do not shred the leaves. I find that even big-leaf maple leaves used as winter mulch are well broken down by May.

Straw: My other favorite mulch is slightly decomposed straw. I buy a bale or two of straw in the fall when it is least expensive and leave it in the rain all winter, with the strings still in place. I turn the bale a couple of times over the winter to smother any seedlings that sprout from the sides. By the time I need it for early summer mulching, the straw is rotted enough to be pulled from the bale in thin, compact "sheets," almost like light sheets of cardboard.

Straw breaks down slowly as a surface mulch; I find it lasts for a year or two before it disappears.

Weeding

Spring is when weeding looms large in the minds of gardeners. If you have ever wondered where all those weeds come from so quickly, the answer is the "seed bank," the enormous collection of seeds that has been accumulating in the soil for decades. This is likely the biggest source of weeds in your garden. Many lie dormant until the soil is disturbed, which brings seeds to the surface, exposing them to light and warmth, which stimulates germination. Many are still able to sprout after ten to forty years or, in the case of curled dock, even eighty years. If you think of the soil as having been preplanted with weeds, you can see why it is a good idea to avoid cultivation methods that bring deep soil to the surface.

Here are some ways to minimize weeding chores:

- **Mulches:** Keep the soil in garden beds covered so that light doesn't reach weed seeds. I also keep pathways between beds well-mulched to control weeds. This is a good place to use long-lasting arbutus leaves, chipped tree branches, shredded bark, straw, or any other bulky organic materials you can lay hands on.
- **Dense planting:** Let the vegetables help with the job of controlling weeds. By planting vegetables close together, the crop shades the soil, which inhibits germination of seeds. By using small spaces intensively and all year-round, the weeds don't have a chance to get ahead.
- **Hand weeding:** If you do have to remove a few weeds here and there, do it while they are tiny and the soil is wet. This disturbs less soil than pulling large deep-rooted weeds, and it brings fewer seeds to the surface to germinate. For larger weeds, I recommend using an old-fashioned weed fork, which has a V-shaped notch at the end of a shank. Slide the shank into the soil beside the weed at an angle to cut the roots as deeply as possible. Instead of using the tool to pry out the weed, however, withdraw the fork in exactly the same path it went in so the soil is not disturbed. Then lift up the weed by the leaves. This leaves behind a small root-sized hole, rather than a larger disturbed area. If they haven't gone to seed yet, you can leave the weeds on the soil as a mulch.

Forget the Hoe, Bring on the Mulch

I can't think of a more tedious way to control weeds than hoeing, especially since it locks you into hoeing the same patch repeatedly. In contrast, a mulch just sits there all summer, passively keeping seeds from germinating. If you insist on hoeing, do it when weeds are tiny, use a sharp hoe, and just scuffle the surface enough to kill the seedlings. Chopping deeply injures the roots of crop plants and brings a new supply of weed seeds to the surface to germinate.

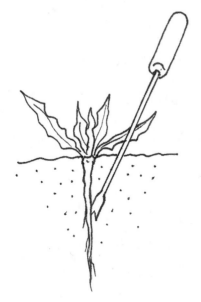

4.10. To use a weed fork effectively, just cut the root, but don't pry with the tool to disturb more soil.

- **Avoid bringing in seeds:** The more you can avoid adding seeds to your soil's seed bank, the better. I especially like leaves or straw for mulches and for composting because they carry few seeds. I am wary of horse manure and spoiled hay because they are full of seeds (hot composting these before using them helps). Cut off (literally) the supply of new seeds by cutting or mowing weedy areas around gardens before the first flowers open.

Staking and Trellising

Some crops really have to be staked or trellised onto some kind of support system: pole beans, indeterminate varieties of tomatoes, and most varieties of peas will produce well only if trellised. Trellising is optional for other vegetable such as cucumbers, melons, and winter squash, but these space hogs take up less space when trained onto a trellis.

Crop supports can be made of anything, from dead branches to fancy materials that match the decor of your home. You can use heavy twine (tied to a solid support), stakes of wood, bamboo, metal, plastic, tree branches, poles, wire mesh, or stucco wire. You might want to invest in tomato cages, which are useful for many years. You can also just hold plants up with strings tied to the garden fence. For annual vegetables, temporary supports, such as sticks and string, work fine. But for long-lived perennials such as grape vines, invest in well-built permanent supports.

Two rules apply here:

- Use supports strong enough to hold up the weight of the plants *and* to withstand wind. Plants in full production are heavy! A mature tomato vine loaded with fruit can easily weigh 45 pounds (20 kg). Now, add the force of the wind to that, and you can imagine how strong your support needs to be.
- Plan ahead. Assemble the materials and install the trellis or other supports *before* planting.

The following section describes some ways to support common crops.

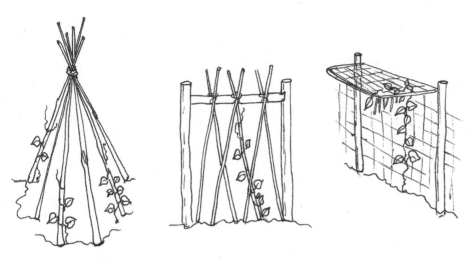

4.11. Variations on a bean trellis from the traditional bean tepee (*left*) to a fence with a shelf extension (*right*).

Pole beans: These beans will climb on most anything, from vertical strings to wooden poles to bamboo stakes.

For a traditional bean "tepee," take six to eight tall poles and securely bind the tips together with wire or string to form a tepee. Prop the base of the sticks far enough apart to make a stable structure. It is a good rule to make the width of the base at least one-third of the height. When covered with beans, such supports really catch the wind, so make sure it is anchored by pushing the legs into the soil as far as possible.

There are many variations on the bean tepee. Rather than all of the bean poles coming to one central point, you can lash them to a crossbar between two posts or tie them along a fence. Spacing out the poles makes it easier to pick the beans and allows the leaves to dry quickly after a rain. You can plant along a fence or at the base of a latticework trellis that has a right angle extension a couple of feet wide, like a shelf running the length of the section. The shelf (which can be made of latticework or stucco wire) allows the pods to hang straight down through it, making them easy to pick.

Peas: Peas vines climb best on string or wire: their tendrils don't get a good grip on smooth poles, such as bamboo stakes, or on supports wider than a pencil. Tall varieties need tall trellises, well anchored to withstand wind.

John's Handy Trellis

Here is how my neighbor built a handy folding trellis. He made two frames of scrap 2 × 4 wood, with one frame fitting just inside the other. With the small frame inside the large one, he drilled a hole through the frames on either side of the top end so he could tap a wooden dowel into the hole to act as a hinge. Stucco wire is stapled over both frames. To use it, just prop the frame open as wide as desired. It is heavy enough to stand solidly, yet easy to fold together for storage.

4.12. This folding trellis supports peas and provides a perfect spot for summer lettuce underneath.

Short varieties, such as dwarf sugar peas, can be supported sufficiently on small branches stuck into the ground along the row. Although the shortest varieties of peas can be left to sprawl, it is much easier to pick them when they are trellised.

Beware the soft woven string mesh sold for pea and bean supports! These are a nightmare to clean at the end of the crop when the vines are all tangled up in the netting. Stiff plastic mesh, wooden latticework, woven wire fencing, or sections of stucco wire work much better. You can support sections of rigid trellis materials by tying the ends to stakes securely driven into the ground. Bamboo garden stakes are also easy to thread vertically at intervals through stucco wire or plastic lattice to hold them up. Stucco wire is galvanized welded wire with a 2-inch square mesh, usually 4 feet wide; it is sold by the running foot at local lumber yards (or look for it at recycling depots). I am a great fan of stucco wire and have a collection of four- to six-foot-long sections that I have used for years for a variety of garden uses.

Tomatoes: All tomatoes are much easier to manage, take up less garden space, and are less prone to leaf disease if they are staked up off the ground. If you have the space and want to let them sprawl, try growing bush or determinate varieties because they do not have to be supported.

- **Stakes:** A strong wooden stake driven into the soil beside each plant is cheap and works fine. Keep tying the new growth to the stake as the plant grows.
- **Strings:** Very strong cord tied to a sturdy overhead support (such as an overhead strut in a greenhouse) can make a good tomato support. Tie the bottom end of the string around the stem at base of the plant (not too tightly; the stem needs a little room to grow). As the tomato grows, wind the top of the plant around the string so that it spirals upward. For greenhouse tomatoes that grow very tall, leave a long tail on the top end of the string so you can periodically untie it from the overhead support to let down another length of string. This lowers the section of the plant where tomatoes are currently ripening, making them easy to pick.
- **Tomato cages:** These come in several sizes and designs, are sturdy and stable, and last for years. You don't need to tie plants to the cage, but for taller varieties, add longer supporting stakes to extend above the cage height. They can be used for tomatoes grown in containers, too.
- **Tomato spirals:** If you have really deep soil without stones and can twist the spiral deeply into the ground, it is possible these might work for you. Around here, they are good at tipping over once plants have a full load of fruit.

Handling Extreme Temperatures

Gardeners on the coast of British Columbia and Washington have always had to cope with changeable weather and occasional blasts of Arctic air in the winter. As the climate continues to change, you must be prepared to act in time to protect plants during periods of even more unusual heat or cold.

Hot Weather Protection

Extreme hot spells are the summer equivalent of winter Arctic outbreaks: they usually don't last long, but can kill plants if you don't take immediate steps to protect them until temperatures moderate. Be especially alert to shading seedbeds and young plants on the hottest days, when temperatures go over 80°F (27°C). Tender leaves and young roots close to the surface are quickly burned at temperatures that wouldn't be a problem when roots are deeper and leaves are used to the heat.

For a day or two, in an emergency, use newspapers, curtains from the thrift shop, or old bed sheets (supported above the plants) as temporary covers. The essential thing is to prevent tender leaves and roots close to the surface from burning. Unlike shade cloth, these materials don't let in enough light to be left on beds for long periods. A good way to manage such covers is to deploy them in midmorning and remove them in late afternoon so plants can get some sunshine when air temperatures are lower.

For long-term use, you might want to invest in horticultural shade cloth. It is durable, lightweight, and lets in enough light that it can be left in place for the duration of a heat wave. For vegetables, choose a product blocking 30% to 50% of light, but no more. Some shade cloth blocks up to 80% light, which is much too dark for vegetables and more suitable for something like an orchid greenhouse.

There are two main kinds of shade cloth products:

- **Knitted polyethylene:** By far the best choice for vegetables, it is lightweight with an open stitch that lets out more heat; it is supposed to last longer than the woven products. The cut edges don't unravel. I find it easy to throw over seedling beds, supported on a few stakes; it is light enough to rest directly on mature plants, such as broccoli and cauliflower.

4.13. Knitted polyethylene 50% shade cloth works well to cool vegetable beds.

- **Woven polypropylene:** This is heavier, with a denser weave, and holds in more heat than the knitted products. It seems to be mainly intended for shading patios or greenhouses with plants that need dense shade, rather than for shading garden vegetables. Cut edges unravel, leaving little fragments of plastic around the garden, and the products I tested burned leaves where the fabric touched them on extremely hot days.

Don't try to use floating row cover fabric to shade beds: it was designed to keep *in* heat, so it can make overheating worse. For beds of carrots, parsnips, radishes, etc. covered with floating row cover or insect netting to keep out insects, lay the shade cloth on top of the insect cover to cool the plants in a heat wave.

Cold Weather Protection

Plants need protection from low temperatures whether a late spring cold snap or a winter outbreak of Arctic air. Most hardy vegetables need little, if any, protection to survive a typical mild coastal winter, and root crops are always safe in the soil, but be prepared to cover other overwintering crops during unusual cold periods (below 23°F/–5°C). Covers can be temporary, in place just for the cold days, or they can be used all winter, which allows overwintering plants to grow a bit more than they would if not protected.

In the spring, with a year-round planting schedule working for you, there usually isn't a need for season extension covers. Lettuce, spinach, other leafy greens, root crops, cauliflower, broccoli, and cabbage overwinter and start producing from February or March to early summer. However, you might want some type of tunnel or cold frame to protect warmth lovers, such as tomatoes or cucumbers, to speed up growth rate in the spring, to hasten a particular delicacy to the table, to get an early start when you don't have overwintered crops, or to protect against unusually cold spring weather.

Covers can range from a simple sheet of plastic to a high-tech greenhouse. There is considerable overlap in designs for extending the season for warmth-loving crops and for protecting overwintering crops. This section discusses designs for both uses, with the emphasis on the simpler low-cost methods. As cold frames are most useful for hardening off seedlings in the spring (though they can be used for season extension), they are described in Chapter 5.

Your choice of materials and design depends on the crops being protected, the time of year, and the amount you want to invest.

Floating row covers: Invented over 35 years ago, floating row covers are spun-bonded polyester or polypropylene fabrics, very lightweight and porous. They let in sunlight and rain and keep in some heat. Because they are feather-light, you can lay the fabric right on top of seedbeds and young plants without supporting hoops or frames. Weigh the edges down with stones, boards, or pegs to keep them in place.

Row covers are most useful in the spring to keep plants warmer during the day and to protect against a few degrees of frost at night. They are not sturdy enough for overwinter use.

The fabric is sold by the yard at garden centers and by mail order suppliers. It usually comes in 6- or 10-foot widths, and light and heavier weights. The lighter fabric holds in less heat and can also be used as a barrier to prevent insects from reaching crops during the growing season. The heavier fabric holds in more heat and lasts several years if handled carefully. Kits are available that include wire hoops, clips, and the fabric cut to size, with drawstring closures on the ends. When you are done with the row covers for the season, rinse out the fabric and hang it to dry before storing it.

Plastic sheets: Clear plastic is the cheapest way to cover plants for season extension, frost protection, or winter cold snaps. For winter use, it has the added bonus of keeping rain off the plants, which is much appreciated by lettuce,

4.14. An elegant plastic cover to protect spring lettuce.

spinach, and other greens with delicate leaves. You can use any clear plastic sheeting you have on hand. If you are buying it, 4 or 6 ml plastic is thick enough for the purpose and lasts for years if it is stored out of the summer sun. For the longest-wearing plastic, look for UV-stabilized plastic film sold specially for tunnels and greenhouses.

4.15 The sheet of plastic folded to the side was laid over this bed of Swiss chard to protect it during an Arctic outbreak of unusually cold air.

- **For spring seedlings:** Because the weight of plastic film is too much for seedlings, support it above the seedbed on hoops or frames. If you have a length of chicken wire or stucco wire, make a temporary support by arching a section over the bed and laying the plastic on top of that. Hold down the edges of the plastic with rocks or boards. (For more elaborate tunnels, see below.)
- **For winter crops:** Mature plants can hold up the plastic, so you don't necessarily need supports. In a cold snap, just drape the plastic temporarily over plants, weighing down the edges to hold the plastic in winter winds. Try to keep water or snow from building up too much on the plastic and crushing the plants. Even if they are flattened, however, most leafy greens will straighten up again once the weight is removed.

Perforated transparent film (Gro-Therm): This is a very thin, transparent plastic film designed to keep seedlings warm in the spring. It has three hundred tiny holes per square yard for ventilation, so it doesn't have to be removed on sunny spring days. The manufacturer promises temperatures up to 10 degrees (Fahrenheit) higher than under floating row covers and better light intensity. The evenly spaced holes allow for consistent growing conditions for heat-loving crops. Remove the cover for the summer because plants can overheat under it (unless you are on the cold and foggy outer coast). This material is not designed for winter crop protection.

Cloches: Traditionally, bell-shaped glass cloches were used to cover individual plants. But these are not tools for a busy person heading out the door every morning to work! They are so efficient at trapping the sun's heat that they must be carefully managed to avoid frying seedlings in the sun. Tip them up or remove them entirely as soon as the sun comes out.

Variations on this idea range from dome-shaped plastic cloches designed with an adjustable opening in the top to recycled milk jugs with the bottom cut out. I find that one-gallon plastic milk jug cloches work perfectly well. Cut the bottom out of the jug, set it over the plant, and push a stick through the handle of the jug to keep it in place. Put the lid or a flat stone on the mouth of the jug at night to keep the heat in; take it off for the day to allow ventilation or just leave it off entirely. Remove the cloche as soon as the weather warms.

Cloches that extend along a whole row can be made from pairs of glass panes, pieces of rigid plastic, or corrugated fiberglass. Join the rigid materials together at the top to make an A-frame cover running the length of a row. You can buy special clips to hold glass or plastic sheets together at the top edge, or make homemade supports or wooden blocks to hold the glass. Strips of corru-

4.16 Milk jugs make cheap and easy cloches. Don't forget to stake them down so they won't blow away.

gated fiberglass are flexible enough to be simply bent over to make row covers with rounded tops (but stake them down in case of wind). Leave ends open during the day for ventilation; at night, cover the ends with a board or plastic.

Tunnels: There are many variations on the plastic tunnel, but most are constructed of some kind of wooden frame or hoop supports (plastic plumbing pipe, heavy wire) covered with plastic. Some are temporary and designed to be moved to different beds, others are permanent and remain in place, like a traditional cold frame.

Tunnels are useful for season extension and for winter cold protection, especially when you want to cover a garden bed. In winter they protect plants from rain, so lettuce, spinach, and chard do well under them. If there is any weak sunlight at all, daytime temperatures will be higher inside than outside. However, temperatures overnight are about the same as outdoors. In a cold snap with snow on the ground, plants outside the tunnel are often warmer than the plants inside that don't have snow cover. So be prepared to throw tarps over top of the tunnel during a cold snap.

4.17 A sturdy tunnel–cold frame design that gives easy access to plants.

For use in the winter, keep tunnels or covers as low as possible and anchor them really well to resist wind. Heavy wire hoops for small tunnels are easy to force into the ground to a secure depth, but such tunnels collapse easily if there is heavy wet snow. In some soils, the ends of plastic pipe can be driven far enough into the ground to secure the tunnel (cut the pipe ends at a sharp angle). You can use pipe brackets to screw the bottom end of the pipe hoops to the sides of raised beds with wooden sides. Another option is to drive short sections of rebar into the ground as anchors, leaving a foot or so above ground. Slide the ends of plastic pipe hoops down over the rebar anchors. Space the hoops about 2 to 3 feet apart along the length of the tunnel.

Covers for tunnels can be standard 4 or 6 ml plastic or special plastic film designed for greenhouses. Secure plastic sheeting to pipe hoops with commercially available clips or make your own from short pieces of the same plastic pipe used for the hoop. Slit them down one side and soften in hot water to make them easier to snap over the plastic on the pipe. If using wooden frames, staple the plastic securely all along the frame.

4.18. A tunnel temporarily turns a garden bed into a greenhouse.

Ventilate and cool plastic tunnels during the day by opening the ends or rolling up the sides to allow air to flow. If a tunnel is going to be used all summer for tomatoes, it is essential to be able to ventilate from sides as well as ends to prevent condensation from forming and dripping onto the leaves; wet leaves promote late blight infections.

If you have the time and skill to build a more elaborate structure, there are many plans available. Kits are also sold at garden centers and through mail order catalogs.

Things to consider in tunnel design:

- Do you want something that is easy to move to different beds, or a more permanent tunnel that stays in one place?
- Is it designed for excellent ventilation? Avoiding overheating when the sun comes out is essential.

One last thing to consider—actually, it should be the first thing to consider: Do you really need a tunnel? It is very nice to have one in midwinter to speed up the growth of leafy greens, but if you keep some plastic sheets on hand to throw over leafy greens in case of winter cold snaps, you don't have to have a more elaborate structure to achieve a good harvest in our year-round climate.

CHAPTER 5

Starting Seedlings and Saving Seeds

This chapter covers how to start your own seedlings indoors for transplanting to the garden later. It also describes basic seed-saving methods for anyone interested in trying this rewarding aspect of gardening.

Starting Seedlings Indoors

There are several reasons for starting vegetables several weeks to months before they can go out in the garden:

- Heat-loving plants, such as tomatoes, peppers, winter squash, and cucumbers, take too long to ripen in the cool coastal climate. There really isn't enough time to sow them directly in the garden and have much of a crop.
- Some cool-season plants, such as leeks, Spanish onions, celery, and celeriac, also need an especially long growing season. These are usually started indoors in February to early March.
- Summer varieties of cabbage, broccoli, and cauliflower are ready to harvest much earlier if they go into the garden as transplants.
- Plants with large starchy seeds (mainly peas and beans) are attractive to pests and prone to disease in cool soil. Pre-sprouting them indoors cuts down considerably on losses.

The most compelling reason to start your own seedlings is to have the widest choice of varieties. If you are a tomato enthusiast, for example, there are many more varieties to choose from as seeds than as transplants. Given the high cost of seeds, however, if you only want one or two plants of many different tomato varieties, it might make more sense to buy plants, if you can get the kinds you

Should You Start Your Own Seedlings?

For beginning gardeners, I recommend starting off with transplants from garden centers or farmers markets (see Buying Transplants in Chapter 4 for what to look for). These local sources usually sell robust varieties known to do well in a range of conditions. While there are many reasons for growing your own transplants, to be successful, you have to provide good growing conditions and be prepared to give them daily care for five to ten weeks. This is definitely for the advanced class.

want. Although most garden centers carry a large selection of tomatoes, they rarely have more than a couple of varieties of other crops. Some vegetables may only be labeled by the crop name (e.g., "leeks" or "celeriac"). Without knowing the variety, you won't know which one to look for, or to avoid, the following year. This is particularly annoying for leeks because some varieties are much less cold-hardy than others. I hate to think of an unsuspecting gardener deprived of the joy of harvesting a fine fat leek in February!

Other reasons for starting your own seedlings: to make sure they are grown organically and to avoid bringing pests from nurseries to your garden (this is usually a low risk). Starting seedlings can also save cash if you need a large number of transplants, but it will cost you in terms of labor.

Requirements for Starting Seeds Indoors

The better the light, temperature, and moisture conditions you provide, the healthier your seedlings will be. Providing sufficient light is usually the most challenging of the three, and it is the most critical.

5.1. Bean seedlings started in vermiculite avoid the hazards of birds, pillbugs, and damping off. Every one of these seedlings grew into a sturdy plant (see Figure 2.12, p. 41).

Sprouting Large Seeds

Unlike starting transplants, sprouting peas and beans is easy, and a way to get around the fact that these big starchy seeds are highly attractive to pests. Birds and rodents love to dig up them up, and pillbugs, wireworms, slugs, climbing cutworms, and soil fungi attack them too. In typical spring weather, it is often very hard to achieve a good stand of seedlings. Rather than losing time replanting over and over, I think it is well worth the effort to sprout these indoors.

Both peas and beans can be started in trays of vermiculite indoors: peas from March onward, beans starting in early May. Every seed seems to germinate, and there is little risk of root rot as the vermiculite doesn't hold excess water. The seedlings can grow for two to three weeks (until they are a couple of inches high) on the food stored in the seed, so they don't need soil.

How to sprout seeds: I cram thirty seeds (enough for a 10-foot row or one bean tepee) into a container made from a 1-quart (liter) milk carton.

• Lay the carton on one side, cut out the top side, and punch drainage holes in the bottom. Fill with vermiculite, and poke the seeds about an inch deep.

• Set the container somewhere warm and keep the vermiculite moist. As soon as tips of sprouts show, move the carton to a windowsill with good light and grow them for two more weeks. For better light, you could put them in a cold frame during the day and bring them in at night.

• At planting time, gently disentangle the roots in the loose vermiculite and set them out. Plant bean seedlings so the shriveled seed leaves remain above the soil surface. These are the starchy remnants from the seed, which are so attractive to pillbugs and other pests.

5.2. Seedlings grown with plenty of light (*left*) have short, stocky stems, while those without enough light (*right*) are elongated and weak.

Are Your Seedlings Getting Enough Light?

Compare the stocky seedlings that come up outdoors with seedlings grown indoors. The outdoor plants have hardly any distance between the soil surface and the first pair of leaves. Indoor seedlings that grow tall, lean toward the light and have long pale stems below the first pair of leaves are not getting enough light. They are also very susceptible to damping off because of the weak stem. Depending on how elongated the stem has become, they may or may not be salvageable. Try to get them into better light as soon as possible.

Light: To grow good seedlings indoors requires the highest light levels you can manage. If you do not have an indoor grow-light setup, you will need a greenhouse, sunroom, or south-facing window that receives full sun. If you are making do with a south window, place the individual pots or flats in a single row along the windowsill because only the seedlings right up against the window will receive adequate light. As soon as the weather permits, move trays outside for the day to a cold frame or unheated greenhouse so they receive full, bright light.

If you don't have good window light and really want to grow seedlings, you will need to set up grow lights. Buy special full-spectrum grow lights, or use four 40-watt fluorescent tubes supplemented with one or two incandescent light bulbs to balance the light spectrum. To achieve the high light intensity required, the tubes must be less than 6 inches (15 cm) away from the top leaves of the seedlings. If you rig the light fixture on a pair of chains, it is easy to raise it as the seedlings grow taller. This light setup is not a perfect substitute for sunlight, so as soon as possible, move the seedlings to a cold frame or greenhouse during the day.

Temperature: Most vegetable seeds germinate well at 70° to 86°F (21° to 30°C) (see Table 4.1, p. 91). The top of the refrigerator or hot water heater used to be a good place to germinate seeds, but not in this day of energy-efficient appliances. If you don't have a warm place to set seedling trays, investing in a bottom-heat unit for seedlings is well worth it. Because bottom heat is only needed for the germination period, you can cycle a lot of seedlings through one unit the size of a standard seedling tray (about 10 × 20 inches/25 × 50 cm).

Good air circulation over the surface is essential, so do not cover the seed trays with those plastic covers that often come with the bottom-heat units. After the seeds sprout, move the trays to cooler, bright conditions. The best temperature for growth is 60° to 68°F (16° to 20°C), which is about 10 degrees lower than germination temperatures.

Moisture: The soil should be moist, but not wet. Many seeds can germinate in barely damp soil because they are able to take up enough water from the humid air between soil particles (corn, cabbage family, and squash family seeds do this). More people go wrong *overwatering* rather than with *underwatering* seeds. They often lose their seedlings to damping off, which thrives in wet soil.

So, water seed trays sparingly. I soak the soil mix before sowing seeds and then don't usually have to water for a couple of days. When the surface starts to dry out, water trays from the bottom by setting them in a shallow pan of water for a short time (ten minutes or so). Don't leave them so long that the soil surface becomes waterlogged.

Once the seedlings are a couple of inches tall, they take up water at an increasing rate and should be checked daily. It is fine to water sturdy well-grown seedlings from above because they are past the high-risk stage for damping off. If the soil is allowed to dry out, it kills fine root hairs and stunts future growth, but you don't want the roots to sit in waterlogged soil either.

Containers: You can use any kind of clean container for seedlings: egg cartons, milk cartons, cottage cheese containers, fast food clamshells, etc. Just be sure to punch two or three holes in the bottom to allow water to drain.

It doesn't take long for gardeners to end up with a collection of pots and seedling trays that just need to be cleaned before reusing. Soak the pots in a bucket of water to loosen the soil, then scrub with a brush. Optional step (but I highly recommend it): soak the pots for fifteen minutes

5.3. Seedlings grown in individual cells will be easy to transplant later.

in a bleach solution, 10 parts water to 1 part hydrogen peroxide bleach (better for the environment than chlorine bleach), then rinse well. For best results, pots should be clean when you put them into the bleach.

New seedling trays made of recycled plastic are also available. They are inexpensive and with care last for several uses. Those with individual cells for seedlings produce good results because roots suffer less disturbance during transplanting.

Peat pots and pellets are still sold, and since they have been on the market for decades, I guess they must work for someone. I found that seedlings didn't get their roots through the pot, they dried out easily, and I ended up ripping off hardened remnants of the pots to plant the seedling anyway. Recycled plastic containers for me!

Soil mixes: Back when you couldn't buy commercial organic soil mixes for seedlings, I used to make my own mix (see Table 5.1). Now, I am happy to buy a bag of commercial mix, certified by OMRI (Organic Materials Review Institute) for use by organic growers, as it saves a lot of time and effort and gives consistent results.

Look for products, such as Sunshine® Organic Planting Mix or Seasoil™ Potting Mix, that state they are for seedling production. Check the labels of other commercial "potting soil" products before you buy. Some are intended as

Table 5.1. Basic homemade seedling mix.

	Ingredient	Notes
1 part	Finished homemade compost or commercial compost	Screen it to remove large particles.
1 part	Vermiculite or perlite	Coarse sand can be substituted.
1 part	Coconut coir or peat moss	Coir is more environmentally sustainable than peat.
1 part	Good garden soil	Use the best you have.
For each gallon of mix, add:	1 Tbsp agricultural lime	For acid soils; not necessary if soil is near neutral pH.

Note: All proportions are approximate and should be adjusted according to conditions: e.g., if the soil is heavy clay, use less soil and more vermiculite and coir.

soil substitutes for use in containers and don't have nutrients. Seeds germinate in these mixes but stop growing as soon as they run out of the food stored in the seed itself. Seedlings in such mixes need regular applications of liquid fertilizer or should be transplanted into a fertile soil mix as soon as they have two leaves.

A good reason for making your own seedling mix is to avoid the use of peat moss, which is a non-renewable resource mined from peat bogs. Despite being a natural product, it isn't renewable on any realistic time scale because bogs would take centuries to recover and such degraded bogs no longer help hold carbon. Soil mixes made with coir (coconut fiber), composted bark, or other ingredients in place of peat work just fine, however, and have the advantage of using waste products.

Is It Necessary to Pasteurize Soil Mix?

The purpose of heating soil to 140°F (60°C) is to kill soilborne diseases (mainly damping off). A soil mix made with finished compost, however, contains beneficial soil fungi that help suppress damping off, and these are also killed when the soil is heated. When I used to make seedling mixes, I actually had better results when I stopped pasteurizing the soil and concentrated instead on providing warm germination temperatures and avoiding overwatering (certainly easier than trying to heat a soil mix evenly in a kitchen oven!).

Steps for Starting Seeds Indoors

1. Fill containers with potting mix, lightly pressed down to firm the mix. I like to soak the soil mix at this point, before seeding.

2. Sow the seeds. Using a pointed tool, such as a chopstick, open a little hole in the mix and drop in the seed and close it up. Or don't quite fill the container with soil mix, place the seeds on the soil, and cover with another layer of soil. If you are using a denser mix, such as the homemade soil mix described in Table 5.1, for good results, cover the seeds with vermiculite instead of soil mix. Sow two or three seeds in individual pots or in each cell of a seedling tray. Sow eight to ten seeds in small flats where you intend to grow four to six seedlings.

3. Set the containers on bottom heat or in a warm spot, aiming for 70° to 86°F (21° to 30°C). Don't cover the containers. Water from below when the top of the soil dries out, by setting seedling containers in a larger tray of water. Lift them out of the water when they feel heavier from taking up water, but don't wait until the surface is soggy.

4. As soon as any seedlings show the tip of a shoot above the soil surface, move the pots to high-intensity light and cooler temperatures (60° to 68°F/ 16° to 20°C).

5. When seedlings are about an inch high, choose the best ones and pull out or clip off the extras.

6. Grow on the seedlings. If possible, put them in a cold frame or greenhouse on sunny days. Bring them indoors at night until the minimum temperature stays above 54°F (12°C).

7. If seedlings are growing too large for their pots and it is still too cold to put them out, repot them in bigger containers and keep them growing vigorously.

Hardening Off Seedlings

Seedlings that are grown under lights, in greenhouses, or on windowsills will have soft stems and tender leaves with thin cuticles (the thin waxy coating on leaf surfaces). They have to gradually get used to direct sun, wind, and cooler nights before they are sent out into the world. Through this process of hardening off, their growth slows a little as food reserves build up in the roots, and the cuticle on the leaves thickens up to protect them from sunburn.

The hardening off process is simple: get seedlings used to outdoor conditions gradually, starting with an hour in the sun the first day (or longer in cloudy weather). Move them back under glass or into light shade for the rest of the day. Over about a week, expose them to direct sun for longer periods, until they are outside all day.

For hardy plants, such as onions, leafy greens, and cabbage, hardening off also gets seedlings used to cooler temperatures. Small seedlings (for example, cabbage with fewer than five leaves) can get used to quite low

5.4. Sunburn damage on cucumbers and squash appears as biscuit-colored spots and blotches on leaves and stems.

temperatures. For seedlings larger than that, however, exposure to temperatures under 40° to 50°F (4° to 10°C) for a couple of weeks may cause them go to seed in midsummer (see Vernalization in Chapter 1, p. 12).

Hardening off tender crops, such as tomatoes, peppers, cucumber, squash, and melons, mainly means getting them used to direct sun. Cucumbers, for example, can be seriously set back or even die from sunburn if they are abruptly moved from indoors into full sun for a whole day.

Cold frames are excellent tools for hardening off plants. As the weather warms, plants gradually become used to the sun as the frames are opened a little

5.5. The clear sides of this cold frame provide maximum light to seedlings.

Cold Frames

A traditional cold frame is handy to have for producing good-quality seedlings if you don't have a greenhouse or plastic tunnel. Make a simple cold frame from four boards for sides and an old window (or clear plastic) as the cover. Set it so that the glass faces south and is slanted downward at the front to allow in light. Use a stick to prop up the window to ventilate the frame during the day, because it quickly overheats inside when the sun shines. You can build or buy much more elaborate designs, including frames made entirely of rigid clear plastic and frames with automatic openers to lift the covers. When I lived in eastern Canada, I used an extensive collection of cold frames to give seedlings a good start and to extend the growing season for various plants. When I moved to the West Coast, however, I soon found that one small cold frame was all I needed.

How to Tell if Plants Are Root-Bound

Lift the pot and look for roots coming out of the drainage holes. A few roots showing is okay, but a straggly beard of roots trailing out of each hole is a bad sign. Another way to check is to gently slide a seedling slightly out of the container: the more roots you can see wrapping around the sides of the root ball, the more root-bound the plants are. If you can't get the root ball to slide out easily, it is probably extremely root-bound.

more each day for ventilation. By the time plants are ready to be set out, they are used to the sun and outdoor conditions and don't need any more special treatment.

The tricky thing is that *overhardening* plants can slow their growth so much that they may never recover, delaying and reducing the total harvest. Transplants become overhardened if they are held too long in pots and become root-bound, or are stressed by uneven watering or lack of nutrients. Transplants for sale have usually been hardened off enough by the time they reach the market. They risk becoming overhardened if kept too much longer in their pots.

Ideally, you have timed seeding dates so transplants are the perfect size to plant out when the weather is right. Given the difficulty of predicting spring weather on the coast, however, that doesn't always happen. Be prepared to move seedling into larger pots to avoid overhardening if it isn't warm enough to put them out.

Seed Saving

I think everyone should know how to save seeds, at least the easy ones. When it comes to seed saving, coastal gardeners have an enormous advantage because many vegetables are biennials and have to be kept over the winter before they will flower. This takes special management where winters are cold, but on the coast, most biennials are hardy enough to stay in the garden all winter. It is just a matter of waiting until the next summer and letting them get on with flowering and setting seeds.

5.6. Saving bean seeds is dead easy. Just leave the pods on the plant until seeds harden and dry thoroughly, then pop them out of the pods.

Saving seed cuts down on costs, of course, and with plenty of seeds on hand, you can sow extra to ensure a good stand despite pests. It also gives

Only Save Seeds from Open-Pollinated Varieties

Don't save seed from hybrids (if a variety name has "F1" after it, it is a hybrid), if you want plants that are the same as the ones you grew originally. Unlike hybrids, open-pollinated (OP) varieties come true from seed because both parents are the same variety. Of course, most hybrid plants can produce seeds, and you could grow them out to see what appears. You might even experiment with natural hybrids by letting several varieties of kale or other groups of related plants flower at the same time and see what results when bees cross-pollinate the flowers.

you surpluses to trade with other gardeners. And, when you find a variety you really like, you might be able to keep it going yourself, long after it disappears from seed catalogs.

Most seeds keep for years if stored properly (see below), so you only need to save seeds from a few different vegetables each year to end up with a good collection of varieties. Aside from remembering not to save seeds from hybrid varieties, the main issue to be aware of is the risk of flowers being cross-pollinated by a different variety (or in some cases by related weeds).

Basic Seed-Saving Methods

Notes specific to each type of vegetable are included under their entry in the A to Z Vegetables section in Chapter 10.

Isolate blooming plants in space or time: That sounds like science fiction, but all it means is this: if you want to save seeds, either put a lot of space between varieties or don't allow different varieties of the same vegetable to bloom at the same time in your garden. There is also a third alternative for plants that are self-fertile, such as peppers and eggplants: cover plants with a floating row cover or screen cage to keep out bees and other pollinators (you will have to pollinate these flowers by hand).

Most vegetables have a high risk of cross-pollination (see Table 5.2). Seeds of most are quite easy to save, but you do need to make sure the flowers don't receive pollen from other plants in your garden or nearby gardens. The best way to do this is to save only one variety at a time, and ensure no other closely related plants are flowering in the garden at the same time. Cut down flower stalks of other plants before the flowers open or remove the plants altogether so there is no stray pollen for wind or bees to move around. Gardeners in community gardens might not be able to save pure varieties because there may be cross-pollination from plants in other plots. Very light pollen (such as spinach or corn) that blows on the wind can cross-pollinate from gardens over half a mile away (one kilometer), though the risk of that happening is pretty remote.

Vegetables that are self-fertile and have a low risk of cross-pollination (see Table 5.2) are unlikely to cross if they are grown a short distance (30 feet/ 10 meters) from related plants in bloom at the same time. In home gardens, however, where plants grow closer together, wind or bees can move pollen between them, so it is still best to grow out only one variety at a time, and remove flowers of related plants during the blooming period.

Saving seeds of a few vegetables is definitely for the advanced class:

- **Squash, cucumber, and melon:** Both male and female flowers have to be bagged or taped shut so they can be hand pollinated. Squash crosses produce notoriously inferior fruit.

Table 5.2. Risk of cross-pollination.

Cross-Pollination Risk	Target Separation Distance between Varieties When in Bloom	Vegetables
Low Risk	25–35 feet (8–10 m)	Beans (except scarlet runner beans), peas, lettuce, endive, most tomatoes
Intermediate Risk	150 feet (45 m)	Heritage tomatoes with broad leaves (their flowers are more open to pollinating insects)
High Risk	500 feet (150 m)	Scarlet runner beans, broccoli, cabbage, Brussels sprouts, Chinese cabbage, kale, mustard, radishes, beets, Swiss chard, carrots, celery, celeriac, leeks, onions, parsnips, turnips, peppers
Extreme Risk	1 mile (1–2 km)	Spinach, sweet corn

Note: The separation distance applies only when varieties are in bloom at the same time.

- **Sweet corn:** It takes special methods to ensure there is no chance of unwanted wind-borne pollen reaching the silks.
- **Cauliflower:** Heads of summer cauliflower have to be maintained through the winter (usually in a greenhouse) so flowers can develop the following spring.

If you are interested in learning how to save seeds from these plants, see the Resources section for sources of more detailed instructions.

Decide which plants to use for seed: Choose parent plants based on whether they are showing the characteristics you want. It might seem logical to save seeds from the first plants that produce seed, but for some vegetables, those are the very ones you don't want to keep. For example, late seed production is a good thing in leafy greens that you want to harvest over a long period. The same goes for radishes, leeks, and onions. On the other hand, you might want to save seed from bean and pea plants that produce pods earliest. Watch for plants that have other characteristics that you like, such as taste, size, vigor, or color.

Save seeds from as many different plants of each variety as you can, as long as they have the desired characteristics. Try to save seeds from at least three different plants at one time—from six to ten plants is even better—so you maintain a pretty good level of genetic diversity within the variety.

Label everything! Mark the parent plants when they are planted, and label seed heads the moment they are harvested. Tie labels onto the stalks or label the container. Don't wait until later because, believe me, seed pods of many plants look identical when they dry.

Allow seeds to mature on the plant: Seeds of most plants do not mature at the same time, so keep checking the plants or pods. It can take most of the summer for some to ripen. You can open a test seed pod every week or two to check when seeds lose their green color and harden up. When seeds are easy to shell out of pods and look hard and dry, they are ready to harvest. Collect just the ripest pods or heads, leaving later seed to ripen on the plant. Practically,

5.7. Swiss chard blooms after spending the winter in the garden.

5.8. Leek flowers take the whole summer to ripen their seeds.

however, if you want to cut seed stalks only once, harvest them when the earliest third of seed pods have thoroughly matured. Much of the later-forming seed will still mature after the stalks are cut. Here is when to expect seed heads to form:

- Annuals form seed their first year. Arugula, beans, summer broccoli, lettuce, peas, spinach, mustard greens, corn salad, Chinese cabbage, summer radishes, dill, and cilantro are annuals. Tomatoes and peppers are perennials, but for seed-saving purposes are treated as annuals because they produce seeds the first year.

- Biennials don't form seed until the following summer. Kale, Swiss chard, winter broccoli, Brussels sprouts, cabbage, celery, endive, parsley, leeks, sweet onions, carrots, beets, parsnips, winter radishes, and turnips are some of the biennials that overwinter successfully on the coast.

Dry the seeds: You can do this in a garage, basement, back porch, shed, back room, top of refrigerator, etc. The seed stalks (or entire plants of some vegetables) can be cut and hung upside down to finish drying. I hang plants inside paper bags (with holes cut in the upper part of the bag for ventilation) to catch seeds. You can also pick seed heads and pods and spread them on trays to dry. Corn salad

5.9. One way to dry seeds and keep them from getting lost.

5.10. Using a pestle to crack open kale seed pods.

seeds, for example, shatter out of the seed head very easily, so they should be dried on trays to avoid losing them. Never use a heat source over 90°F (32°C) to dry seed.

Shell out seeds: When seeds are thoroughly dry, rub dry pods between your fingers to crack off shells, or pound them in a bowl with a pestle to free the seeds. Shake them through a colander or a mesh screen to separate them from chaff. To remove finer chaff, winnow them gently in a breeze or roll the seeds down a piece of flannel, which catches the chaff. Some seeds are very easy to pop out of hulls, while others, such as

5.11. Cabbage family seeds are easy to separate from the pods once they are pounded loose.

5.12. Rubbing lettuce seeds through a sieve to clean off fluff.

5.13 Winnowing lettuce seeds in a breeze to blow away chaff.

leeks, are tough to separate. You do not need perfectly cleaned seed, so don't spend a lot of time getting out every particle of chaff.

How to Store Seeds

Seeds stay viable (able to germinate) longest when they are kept cool and dry. Moisture is the enemy of seeds. As soon as a seed begins to absorb moisture, it begins to wake up from dormancy.

When seeds become too old, they won't germinate. How long this takes depends on the kind of seed and how well they have been stored. Typical storage times for seeds are given in Table 5.3. If in doubt, you can always do a simple germination test to find out if the seed is still good (see below).

With seeds now costing $3 to $5 per packet, it is well worth taking good care of your investment. If stored properly, even seeds with a short storage life can be kept a couple of years longer than the figures given in Table 5.3. Here's how:

Keep the air out: Put thoroughly dry seeds in labeled envelopes. Small paper envelopes work fine, but store them in airtight containers, such as jars or plastic containers with tight seals or heavy plastic ziplock bags.

Store seed containers in a dark, cool, dry place. The ideal spot for your seeds might be in a cool cupboard in the basement or unheated back room or other place away from heat. You can store them in the freezer, but *only* do this if you are careful to let the contents return to room temperature before opening the container. If it is opened while the contents are still cold, moisture in the air immediately condenses on the seed packages. This undoes the care you took to provide dry conditions. I store large quantities of seed in my freezer, but hold the quantities I want for planting this season in a cool cupboard.

The small desiccant packets that come in pill bottles, shoe boxes, etc., hold silica gel that keeps the contents of the container dry. You can

5.14. The perfect seed container: What will we do now that film canisters are a thing of the past?

Table 5.3. Approximate number of years that seed stored under cool dry conditions should still give a high germination rate. Under the best storage conditions, seeds keep even longer.

Seed	Years	Seed	Years	Seed	Years
Bean	3	Cucumber	5	Pea	3
Beet	3	Eggplant	5	Pepper	4
Broccoli	4	Endive	5	Pumpkin	4
Brussels sprouts	5	Fennel	4	Radish	5
Cabbage	5	Kale	5	Rutabaga	5
Carrot	3	Kohlrabi	5	Salsify	2
Cauliflower	5	Leek	3	Sea kale	1–2
Celeriac	5	Lettuce	5	Spinach	5
Celery	5	Muskmelon	5	Squash	5
Chicory	5	Mustard, leaf	4	Swiss chard	4
Chinese cabbage	5	New Zealand spinach	5	Tomato	4
Collards	5	Onion	1–2	Turnip	5
Corn	1–2	Parsley	2	Watermelon	5
Corn salad	5	Parsnip	1–2		

Source: Knott, J.E., *Handbook for Vegetable Growers*, John Wiley & Sons, 1957.

A Simple Germination Test

When in doubt about the viability of old seeds, it is easy to do a quick germination test. If you do this in January, you will have time to buy fresh seed if necessary. Here's how:

• Count out twenty seeds if you have a good supply, five to ten seeds if you only have a few.

• Spread the seeds on the bottom half of a wet paper towel and cover with the top half to keep them moist. If you are checking several different kinds of seeds, place them in groups on the same paper towel, making sure to label each group. Before wetting it, you can write on the paper towel with a waterproof pen or pencil. Put the moist towel with the seeds in a plastic container or bag, label, and cover or close loosely (don't seal it).

• Put the container in a warm spot and check daily to make sure the paper towel doesn't dry out. Most seeds will germinate within three to five days (carrots, parsnips, and parsley take longer).

• Count how many seeds show a tiny little root sprout and calculate the percentage of viable seeds. For example, if fifteen out of twenty seeds germinate, that is a 75% germination rate. A germination rate above 75% is fine. If the percentage is lower, sow those seeds more thickly to make up for it. If fewer than half germinate, it is time to buy new seed or grow out a planting to save fresh seed.

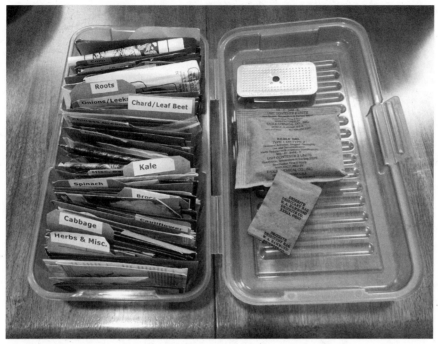

5.15. Storing seeds with desiccant packs will add years to their life.

reuse these or buy larger desiccant packs to put in seed containers. They are well worth the cost because it adds considerably to the life of the stored seeds. Sometimes seed suppliers include desiccant packs with seed orders or sell them separately. Lee Valley Tools (leevalley.com) sells reusable silica gel desiccant in a metal case (look up "dehumidifiers" in their catalog). The small one (40 g) is sufficient to dehumidify the interior of something the size of a tool box, making it ideal for a big plastic container of seed packets. You can reuse these dehumidifiers for many years by heating them for a couple of hours in the oven to dry out the silica gel granules.

CHAPTER 6

Basic Methods for Growing Fruit

There are few things more delightful than sweet juicy plums or crisp fall apples from your own tree, unless it a perfectly ripe fig or a sun-warmed bunch of grapes. And don't get me started on the delights of the many berries that grow so well here! Tree fruit can be a hit-or-miss crop on the coast because trees bloom early in the year, when rainy spring weather can keep bees from pollinating the flowers. Figs, grapes, and berries don't have this problem. Even if you don't have room for fruit trees in a very small garden, you might fit in strawberries or perhaps a table grape along a fence.

The Right Size of Fruit Tree

Standard fruit trees can grow 20 feet tall or more, which is way too big for home gardens. They are a lot of work to prune, and when there is a crop, there is an avalanche of fruit to deal with. If you are planting new trees in a home garden, I recommend dwarf fruit trees, which don't need much pruning and allow you to reach fruit without climbing a ladder. Best of all, they start producing fruit in as little as three years. They can also be planted along fences or walls and kept pruned to fit small spaces.

Dwarf trees need more fertile soil and irrigation than standard trees, which actually makes them an *excellent* fit for a backyard garden because their needs are similar to vegetables.

Nurseries sell dwarf apples, pears, peaches, plums, and sweet cherries. Most dwarf fruit trees can be kept under 10 to 12 feet tall. When mature, they can easily be as wide as they are tall, so allow enough space to work around the tree for pruning and picking. If you can get apple trees grafted onto the more dwarfing M27 rootstock, these delightful little trees are easy to keep to 6 to 8 feet tall; they can be planted 3 to 4 feet apart to suit a small yard.

Semi-dwarf trees (grown on a rootstock that produces a somewhat larger tree) are also available, but these do get up to 15 feet high and wide. Keep this

Grafted vs. Genetic Dwarf Fruit Trees

Most dwarf trees are made by grafting tops from known varieties onto special dwarfing rootstocks, which constrains the tree from growing to full size, yet it produces normal-sized fruit. Genetic dwarf trees are not grafted to keep them small; they are just naturally very tiny trees. There are genetic dwarf varieties of peaches and nectarines, and also Meyer lemons. Most reach only 3 to 6 feet high and are well-suited to growing in containers.

6.1. The August bounty in a warm summer: plums, figs, and strawberries.

in mind when planning. The impact of a tree on your garden is not just how much shade it casts, but also competition from its roots for water and nutrients. A tree's roots reach well beyond the dripline, or ends of the branches.

Multi-graft trees: Dwarf multi-graft trees are great for small home gardens. Most people only have room for a couple of small fruit trees at most, which doesn't allow a wide selection of varieties. Multi-graft trees have three, four, or five varieties grafted onto a single central trunk. Not only does this give you more varieties to enjoy, but it can spread out the harvest. For example, my three-way plum tree has an early ripening plum (Opal), a midseason plum (Victoria), and a later variety (Italian Prune). It provides fresh plums from early August through September, much longer than a tree with one variety could. With several varieties on one tree it is also more likely that flowers will be pollinated.

Pruning multi-graft dwarf trees can be tricky, however, because the branches of the different varieties don't always grow at the same rate. The general shape of the tree is usually already determined by how the grafted branches have been placed on the trunk. The difficulty is in keeping each of the varieties balanced with the others in size and vigor. Sometimes one of the grafted branches fades away. Because this seems to happen more on trees with four or five varieties, I recommend trees grafted with three varieties.

Choosing Varieties

Fruit trees and bushes are a long-term investment, not only because they live for so long, but because most take several years before you see a crop. So choosing the variety most likely to produce a successful crop is important. Here are some traits to consider when choosing fruit varieties:

Disease resistance: The coast region is a challenging one for growing tree fruit because fungus diseases thrive in the moist climate. Apple scab infections (see Chapter 9), for example, are often severe in a wet spring. You can spray sulfur (but you need to spray quite a lot!) to control apple scab, or you can sit in your lawn chair instead, enjoying the view of your *scab-resistant* apples not being infected. There are apples and grapes resistant to powdery mildew, peaches resistant to peach leaf curl, and pears resistant to pear scab and other diseases.

6.2. Apple varieties resistant to apple scab never end up like this after a wet summer.

6.3. This Spartan apple is still crisp on October 1, even though it was harvested in October *last* year.

Early or late fruit: A mix of varieties that bear fruit early, midseason, and late will extend the length of the harvest from fruit trees and blueberries. For example, there is nearly a five-month spread in harvest dates between July apples, such as Yellow Transparent, and the many others that ripen into late fall.

Storage ability: You are probably familiar with long-keeping varieties of apples (such as what you see in the grocery store), but you may not know that winter pears and kiwi fruit also keep well. Winter varieties, such as Bosc or Anjou, and kiwi fruit are picked in the fall before they ripen and can be held in cold storage for three to four months.

Cross-pollination: Flowers of apples, pears, and some varieties of plums and cherries must receive pollen from another tree of a different variety for successful fertilization of the flowers. Do a little research or ask at the nursery whether the trees you are planning to buy require cross-pollination.

For successful cross-pollination, you need two varieties with compatible pollen. A few apples (e.g., Gravenstein, Mutsu, Jonagold, Winesap) have pollen that won't fertilize other varieties, yet they still need a cross-pollinator; if you grow these, you would need three varieties to ensure fruit from each tree.

Part of assuring pollination in apples is making sure that the varieties you choose also bloom at the same time. There can be a 2- to 3-week difference between the flowering period of early bloomers (e.g., Gravenstein) and late bloomers (e.g., Braeburn). Multi-graft fruit trees have varieties chosen by the nursery that grafted them for pollen compatibility and similar bloom periods.

Long production period: This mainly applies to strawberries. If you grow everbearing or day-neutral strawberries, the harvest extends from June to October. Everbearing raspberries don't actually produce evenly all season, but they do have two fruiting periods, midsummer and early fall, on the same plants.

Planting Fruit Trees and Bushes

Fruit trees and bushes need well-drained soil that has good fertility but is not overly high in nitrogen. Soil that has been previously cultivated for a vegetable garden is ideal for dwarf fruit trees and may not need much in the way of amendments if it has been used as a garden for a few years (see Chapter 3 for managing soil). Blueberries must grow in acid soil, so do not add lime and avoid other amendments that raise the pH, such as bone meal and wood ashes.

Spring planting is traditional and is when nurseries usually have the largest choice of varieties, but November is an excellent time to plant trees and bushes on the coast. They have all winter to establish their roots, therefore will need less water the following summer.

When you buy fruit trees, their roots will either be in soil in a large pot or a burlap-wrapped ball, or the roots will be bare. Bare-root trees look pitiful because they don't have many fine roots, but these will grow after planting. At the nursery, they may simply pull the tree out of the sawdust it was standing in and give it to you in a plastic bag. Such trees must be planted immediately. If the final planting site isn't ready, you should "heel them in" the same day you get them: in a shady place with loose soil, dig enough of a shallow trench to hold the roots, lay the tree at an angle with the roots in the trench, and cover them with moist soil. But this should only be a very temporary measure. Plant as soon as possible.

Steps for planting a fruit tree:

- Dig out the topsoil (the darkest layer) and set it aside on a tarp. Then dig out the soil a couple of feet wider in all directions than the root ball of the tree. For a bare-root tree, make the excavation about 3 feet across. The hole should just be deep enough to hold the full length of the tree roots without bending them, but it doesn't have to be deeper. Pile the subsoil separately from the topsoil.

- In acid soils, dig ½ cup of agricultural lime into the bottom and sides of the hole and mix a little lime into the soil that has been removed (do not do this for blueberries).
- Depending on how fertile the soil is, dig in ½ cup of bone meal in the bottom and sides of the hole, or mix in a complete organic fertilizer. If the soil is poor, also mix in a couple of gallons of compost, but avoid using manure or fertilizers high in nitrogen.
- If the tree is in soil, remove the pot or burlap and gently wash off the soil around the roots. Straighten out any bent roots and fan out the root system to prevent encircling roots from strangling the root ball in future.
- Set the tree upright in the hole. Get a helper to hold it straight, or brace it temporarily. Set grafted fruit trees so that the graft union (an obvious bulge at the base of the trunk) is an inch above the soil to prevent sprouts from coming up from the rootstock. Trees that aren't grafted should sit at the same level the soil was in the container.
- Shovel the amended topsoil around the roots, keeping them spread out. Work the soil into air pockets and firm well as you go. Once the topsoil mix is used up around the roots, use the subsoil that was set aside, mixed with complete organic fertilizer and compost, plus lime if required, and finish filling in the hole.
- Build up a low mound of soil in a ring about a foot out from the trunk to make a shallow basin to hold irrigation water.
- Water well. Continue to give the tree 2 gallons of water per week until it is well-established. This will take all summer for a bare-rooted fruit tree planted in the spring; fall-planted trees usually only need weekly water during the summer drought.
- Drive in a sturdy stake about a foot away from the trunk to support the tree until the roots are well-anchored. Tie the young tree to the stake with cloth strips or other soft plant ties.
- In a year or two, install permanent posts to support dwarf fruit trees. Their root systems are not large, and trees loaded with fruit are easily tipped in

windstorms. As the branches spread, you may need to add temporary supports to keep branches from breaking when loaded with fruit. For a really good bracing job, space three posts around the tree about 2 to 3 feet away from the trunk. Make permanent ties for trees out of heavy wire, threaded through a section of old garden hose to cushion the wire where it wraps around the trunk.

Follow the same steps to plant a fruit bush, though the planting holes would be smaller. Set the plants the same level they were in the nursery or container and be sure to omit using amendments that would raise pH when planting blueberry bushes (use leaf mold as an amendment if you have it). Because grapes have deeper root systems than other fruit, holes for them should be dug deeper.

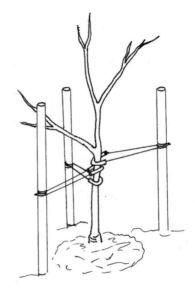

6.4. Anchoring a dwarf fruit tree securely with three posts is well worth the effort. Pad the wires with pieces of old hose to protect the tender bark.

Annual Care

In following years, fruit trees and bushes need moderate amounts of fertilizer in the spring, lime in the fall (for acid soils), and irrigation in summer dry weather. They require at least some pruning (covered in detail, below).

Fertility: Dwarf fruit trees should be fertilized annually, but not with fertilizers high in nitrogen. Compost is an ideal fertilizer, which you might supplement with a complete organic fertilizer sprinkled over the soil and scratched in lightly for the first few years. For acidic soil, spreading lime in the fall (see Chapter 3) is a good idea because it is carried downward in the soil by fall rains; you can also spread lime in the spring. I find that since I use leaves as a mulch to keep down weeds, my established trees now don't need much else for good growth, other than lime and a little balanced organic fertilizer spread on the soil.

Irrigation: The heavier the crop, the more water a fruit tree can use in the summer. Infrequent deep soaking is best, therefore, established trees carrying a crop should be irrigated every ten to fourteen days in dry weather, although it varies depending on your soil type and drainage (see Chapter 4). Fruit bushes and strawberries have much smaller root systems, so they should be watered weekly, along with the vegetable garden.

If you don't water fruit trees much over the summer to conserve water, do try to increase the irrigation as the fruit matures. Otherwise, a late summer or early fall rainstorm can cause fruit to split when trees that were kept short of water suddenly take up a lot. This is most likely to happen to soft fruit, such as plums and cherries, but can happen to apples as well. Keeping fruit trees too short on water can impair the development of next year's fruit buds and result in a poor crop the following year.

Pruning Demystified

This section covers the simplest pruning methods for fruit trees and vines. That's all most home gardeners need. Commercial orchardists need a lot of knowledge and skill to balance fruit production with plant growth for maximum yield. But for a home garden, considerations are different: it is perfectly possible to have healthy, productive plants by applying a few simple pruning methods.

There are several ways to train fruiting plants, but what you choose to do depends on available space and how you want the landscape to look. For example, tightly controlled wine grapes on a three-wire trellis look completely different from a table grape growing picturesquely over an arbor.

The following section covers common fruit trees, including figs, table grapes, and kiwi vines. Specific information on pruning berries and other fruit is included with their entries in the A to Z Fruit section in Chapter 11. More detailed information is available online. Local garden centers, nurseries, and garden clubs may also provide pruning workshops or demonstrations.

Pruning Tree Fruit

This section applies to apples, pears, cherries, plums, peaches, and related trees, but not to figs, which are covered on page 159. There are only a few principles to follow, and they are most important when a tree is young, because that is when you establish its shape. With dwarf trees, there is not much pruning to do after the framework of the tree is established. Trees can be pruned either when they are dormant (in midwinter) or in the summer or both.

Fruit trees are pruned for the following reasons:

- allow air circulation around leaves and permit sunlight to reach the center of the tree,
- select stronger branches that are less likely to break under heavy fruit loads or wind,
- keep fruit within reach and of a good size and quality,
- maintain the dimensions so the tree fits into the space available.

If the shape of your fruit tree doesn't come out looking like a book illustration, just enjoy its idiosyncrasies and keep up the annual maintenance pruning—your tree will reward you with perfectly fine fruit.

Dormant Pruning

Pruning in the winter tends to stimulate more vigorous growth. For a tree that is hardly growing, dormant pruning pushes it into a higher rate of growth. However, it also encourages a rapidly growing tree, such as a rampant peach or cherry, to grow even faster during the summer, making it even harder to maintain the desired size.

As a rule, if you keep up with pruning every year, you should not need to remove more than 15% of the branches (usually much less) on an established dwarf fruit tree. Excessive pruning makes a tree produce soft vertical shoots, or watersprouts, in the summer. Extreme pruning (removing more than a third of the branches at one time) can shock a tree badly and cause it to send up a lot of weak watersprouts. If you have a neglected tree that you want to bring back into production, reshape it gradually over three or more years, rather than doing it all at once.

Summer Pruning

Pruning in the growing season (after the end of July) tends to have the opposite effect from dormant pruning. It slows tree growth because it removes leaf area and reduces the amount of food stored in the roots. For that rampant peach, this is exactly what is needed. How much you cut back the ends of branches depends on how tightly you need to control the tree's size to fit the space, but generally you can prune back half the length of branches. This is the time to remove crossed and poorly angled or weak branches if it wasn't

6.5. These upright watersprouts have been growing all summer. I should have pruned them off much earlier.

done in the winter. In apples and pears, summer pruning can force leaf buds to convert to flower buds next year, increasing future fruit production.

Also watch for watersprouts developing in June; prune them or rub them off with your fingers while they are still small.

Pruning Techniques

Shortening branches: When you cut off the end of a branch, growth will concentrate on the last bud, so choose a bud that will make a future branch pointing in the direction you want it to grow. The ideal bud is usually on the underside of the branch, with its tip pointing away from the center of the tree. When a shoot develops, it will go outward and somewhat upward, away from the center. If the bud is on the top side of the branch, with the tip pointing up, the new shoots will grow straight up, becoming a dominant and overly vigorous branch. If the bud is on the side of the branch, the shoot may grow at a right angle from the main branch and probably cross another beside it.

Make the cut just past the bud you want to keep, at a slight slant, far enough from the bud to make sure it isn't injured, but close enough to avoid leaving a dead stub sticking out past it. A cut a quarter of an inch past the bud is fine, half an inch (1 cm) is a bit too much, but it is better to err on the side of leaving a stub than to risk injuring the bud you intended to keep.

Removing branches: The best branches to keep for fruit production come out and upward from the trunk at about a 45-degree angle. Remove those bending too far downward, which are more prone to sending up watersprouts, and any branches pointing upward at a narrow angle with the trunk. Those make weak crotches that are liable to break under a full load of fruit.

Two Techniques to Avoid

Old gardening books advise cutting off branches flush with the trunk and applying pruning paint to the wounds. Research has shown that neither is good for the tree. We now know that cuts exactly flush with the branch or trunk disrupt the natural "wound collar" at the base of each branch. Wounds heal faster if cuts are made just slightly away from the trunk (see Figure 6.9), but not far enough away to leave a stub. Large wounds have been found to heal better when they are *not* covered with pruning paint. There is also less risk of sealing in disease organisms when the wound is left open to heal naturally.

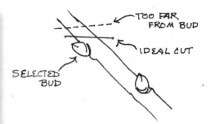

6.6. Where to cut in relation to the bud you have selected.

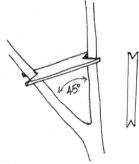

6.7. Use a simple spreader made from a notched piece of wood to hold a young branch at a 45-degree angle from the trunk.

Training branches: Some trees, such as pears, naturally have narrow crotches, but when the branches are young and flexible, you can use spreaders to push them apart to the 45-degree angle. They temporarily hold the branches at the wider angle until they become established. You can make spreaders from 1- or 2-inch-wide lath or scrap wood, cut just long enough to achieve the desired spread, with a notch cut at either end to hold the branch. Heavy wire plant ties with a thick rubber coating (see below) are also very easy to adjust and don't scrape the bark. Gently force the young branch to the wider angle and leave the spreader in place for a year.

6.9. The arrow points to the curve of the natural wound collar around the base of a branch. Pruning cuts should be just outside this.

6.8. Thick coated wire can make a spreader for young branches.

Establishing Fruit Tree Shapes

Fruit trees are usually pruned into one of two main shapes (open center or central leader), but you can prune them to any shape that fits your yard. They can also be trained to fit a trellis by tying young branches to the desired position while they are still flexible. After a year tied in position, the branches will stay there.

Central leader: Mainly used for apples and pears, central leader trees have an obvious central trunk with a series of strong, well-spaced side branches along the trunk. To maintain this shape, keep the side branches pruned back enough so that the tip of the central trunk is always a little taller than the tips of side branches. This makes a sturdy tree, but the branch arrangement isn't suited to multi-graft trees (prune those to an open center form, described below).

To start a young tree: If the tree is a one-year-old whip without side branches, cut it back at planting time to about 32 inches (80 cm) tall. If the tree is older, with several side branches, cut back the central trunk (which will be the leader) to about 8 inches (20 cm) above the topmost side branch; also remove any branches close to the ground. As the tree grows, choose branches that are more or less evenly spaced apart vertically along the trunk and around the trunk to become the main branches; remove the others. The ideal tree has a spiral of well-placed branches with no one branch directly above another.

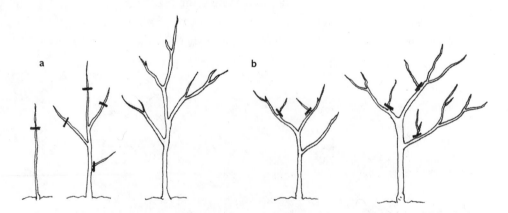

6.10. (a) Central leader tree in its first year, one year later, and as an older tree, showing location of pruning cuts. (b) Open center tree or multi-graft tree in its first year and one or two years later, showing location of pruning cuts.

Open center: Trees pruned to this shape have several strong main branches reaching upward and outward, spaced along the main trunk, leaving its center open. This allows air circulation and sunlight into the center of the tree. It particularly suits multi-graft trees because it is easier to keep the different varieties equal in size.

To start a young tree: For a single-trunk one-year-old tree, if it wasn't done at the nursery, cut back the top third of the trunk. Let the side buds develop into branches. When the buds break along the trunk, select three or four that are well-spaced around and up the trunk and rub off the others. Older trees sold at nurseries may already have established branches, but you should still prune back the ends of branches and the main trunk by one third; keep branches that are well-placed and remove any that aren't.

On multi-graft trees, the placement of the main scaffold branches has already been determined by the position of the grafted branches. For these trees, aim to keep all of the grafted branches equal in size, with the tips of the branches equal in height as well, to prevent any one variety from becoming too large and overtaking the neighboring ones.

Other shapes: You can prune a tree to any shape, including flat against a wall, or espaliered, to save space. To fit it into such a restricted shape, though, you really need to be vigilant for the first couple of years to select buds in the right place to become future branches. While branches are still flexible, tie them into place onto a trellis. You can buy special tape for this purpose, but Velcro plant ties work very well, as do strips of cloth.

It is essential to check espaliered trees regularly to make sure that the bark of branches and trunks does not rub on wires. This type of injury provides an entry point for diseases, such as European canker (in apples, pears) or bacterial canker (in cherries, peaches), which are very common in the damp coastal climate.

Some trees, such as peaches and figs, do well grown as big bushes, which keeps the fruit low and easier to reach. At planting time, cut the trunk of a young tree back to 1 to 2 feet above the ground. New buds stimulated to grow from this short trunk become the lowest tier of branches. After that, shape and prune as for a regular height tree. There are other, more complicated pruning systems, including step-over (horizontal cordon) trees, popular in British

6.11. An espaliered apple tree saves space and benefits from a warm wall to ripen fruit.

gardens. These have the main trunk bent parallel to the ground with branches growing upward trained on wires. Training such trees takes skill and the right varieties, best left to more expert growers.

Annual Pruning

After the main shape is established, a little annual pruning is necessary to keep trees in good shape. Here is what to look for:

- Remove broken and crossed branches. Decide which of two crossed branches is best placed and looks like it will have space all around it in future; prune out the other.
- Thin crowded branches. Look for places where a branch should be removed to open up air circulation and allow sun into the tree. For open center trees,

remove any branches and young shoots pointing backward, into the center of the tree.

- Head back long branches. Prune back their tips to keep the tree within the space or to balance the size of one grafted variety with others on the same tree.

- For multi-graft trees, try to keep more vigorous grafts pruned back so they stay about the same size as less vigorous grafts. If one branch isn't doing as well as the others, try to keep the tips of the other branches pruned back to the same height or slightly lower than the tip of the weaker branch. This gives a weak branch a more dominant position on the tree, which means it receives a bigger share of internal growth hormones and grows more vigorously. Be prepared for the fact that sometimes one weaker variety just gets voted off the tree by the other grafts.

Hand Pollinating Fruit Flowers

In some years, there is bright warm weather during the fruit bloom period, but, of course, it can also rain. Cool, wet spring weather interferes with pollination, both because emergence of pollinating insects is delayed and because insects won't fly in cold or rain. Generally, due to the loss of native plants and natural habitat, the number of bees and other pollinators flying around our gardens is also lower than it used to be. In some weeks, when more attractive plants are in bloom (such as maple trees), bees go there rather than to fruit blossoms.

To improve fruit set, you might want to try hand pollinating. Tedious, yes, but remember: if the weather is poor during the week or two that the tree blooms, it can mean little or no crop for the year. The effort is worth it, although it doesn't take long fiddling around with a little paintbrush to appreciate the immense value of pollinators (and the tragedy of their loss!). In some years, the only branches of my fruit trees with a good crop are those I could reach to hand pollinate.

Here's how: In the driest, warmest period during the day, gently dust pollen from flower to flower with a small soft paintbrush (get the cheapest, no need for artists' quality). Gently tap the brush in the center of each flower or, even better, use a slight combing motion from the anthers (taller pollen bearing structures arranged in a ring around the center) toward the single central pistil (female structure). The more times a flower is touched, the better the chances

6.12. Hand pollination using a small paintbrush to transfer pollen between fruit flowers.

of fertilization. The pollen is hard to see, but after a while, enough builds up on the brush to be visible.

For peaches, nectarines, and self-fertile varieties of cherries and plums, just keep moving from flower to flower within the tree. For trees that need cross-pollination (apples, pears, and some cherries and plums), you must go back and forth between flowers of different varieties. If you can cut some clusters of flowers or whole flowering branches from compatible trees, carry them to the tree you want to fertilize. With multi-graft trees, it is easy to reach back and forth between the different varieties on the same tree.

Thinning Fruit

As painful as it may seem when you are looking at a tree loaded with lots of fruit, you must thin them. You will harvest fewer but much larger fruit, and the tree won't exhaust itself over-producing, which can reduce the next year's crop. Some apples varieties, such as Gravensteins, are prone to biennial bearing: if left to their own devices, they tend to have a big crop one year and hardly any apples the next year. By stringently thinning out the apples in the heavy year, you can keep the tree producing a moderate crop every year.

Do your thinning after what is called the June drop (which may actually take until early July on the coast), a natural thinning process that causes trees to shed some of their immature fruit, including fruit that was not completely fertilized. It reduces the fruit load when the tree has set more fruit than it can handle, but it may also be caused by less-than-ideal growing conditions. In some trees, excessive fruit drop may be related to soil moisture (either too dry or too wet—you can't win!). In any case, wait until after the tree has dropped what it wants to, because you may not need to thin much more.

When you start thinning, remove damaged or deformed fruit first and then see what is left to do. Some guidelines for thinning:

6.13. The tree is going to drop the two smallest apples at the bottom during the June drop.

- **Apples and pears:** If every flower cluster along the branches has set fruit, leave just one fruit per cluster and remove the others; leave two fruits per cluster if the branch has a light load.
- **Peaches:** Final spacing should be 6 to 8 inches (15 to 20 cm) between fruit.
- **Plums:** Space fruit so they have room to develop without touching; there should be about 3 inches (6 to 8 cm) between each plum.

Pruning and Training Figs

Figs are very different from the other fruit trees described above: they are self-fertile with closed fruit (no flowers are visible) so that no fertilization needs to be done by pollinators. The fruit develops singly so there is no need for thinning. Pruning figs in the PNW also differs from how it is done in hot climates and from how others kinds of fruit trees are pruned.

Figs produce two crops of fruit per year, but only the first (called the breba crop) ripens reliably in the PNW (in hot regions, the second crop is considered the main crop). Pruning has to be done in such a way to maximize the breba crop, which is produced on the new growth from last summer. This means *not* cutting back the ends of branches while the tree is dormant. The trees still need to pruned, however, because otherwise they become huge trees with unreachable fruit.

Start shaping the tree at planting time by cutting the main trunk back to the height you want the first branches to form. If desired, you can cut it back to a foot above the ground to force branches to start so low that it grows as a bush. Later in the summer, after new branches have sprouted, decide which three or four branches are best placed and strongest. Keep these for the main framework and remove the others. If the young tree already has branches when you bought it, you can still cut back the trunk, or you can leave the existing branches to become the first set of main branches.

In March of the second year, cut back the main branches to 2 feet long, which forces more side branches to grow. Repeat the following year, so the tree will have even more branches and an open center shape (see p. 155). It

6.14. Early pruning on this fig established an open center with many branches.

should start producing figs in year three or four. Thereafter, the goal is to keep as much of the mature new wood from last year as possible, while keeping the tree to a manageable size. The annual pruning program for a fruiting tree recommended by Bob Duncan of Fruit Trees and More (fruittreesandmore.com) is this: in early March, prune back every branch that bore fruit the previous summer. Rather than cutting back to the main branch, however, leave a stub of an inch or two, which allows a couple of new shoots to develop from the stub in the current growing season. These shoots will bear the breba crop the following year. Thin branches out of the center of the tree if it gets too crowded, but try to leave as much new wood as possible and don't cut back the tips of one-year-old branches.

Another approach that is less organized, but also works, is to remove a few of the tallest branches every year, leaving a stub at the base to sprout new shoots. This keeps the average height down, while preserving one-year-old wood on the other branches to produce the breba crop. You can cut back whole large branches or even main trunks quite drastically on trees that have become too tall. I cut down the main trunk of an 18-year-old tree to allow the shoots from the base to take over, and the tree is now a big shrub with figs in easy picking range.

Summer pruning to shape trees, such as those in containers that must be kept small, should be limited to pinching back just the tips of branches during the growing season. Do this after five or six leaves have appeared on this season's new growth, where next year's fruit will be.

Pruning Grapes

Grapes have to be supported on something sturdy enough to hold a heavy vine full of ripe fruit. Commercial grapes are usually trained onto a system of two or three horizontal wires strung between strongly braced posts, but you can train grapes to go anywhere: along the backyard fence, up a wall, over an arbor, or onto a trellis. The vines drop their leaves in the winter, so grow them where you want summer shade but don't want leaves blocking light in winter. Grape vines are also very forgiving; if you don't like their form, you can reshape the vine entirely in the future.

There is one simple rule for grape pruning: prune hard. The most common reason for a poor crop is that vines were not pruned enough. You should

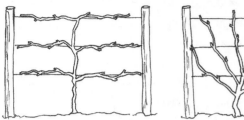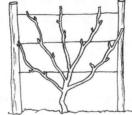

6.15. Basic shapes for grape vines: Parallel wires (*left*) or fan-shaped (*right*).

remove 90% of the wood during dormant pruning (I did say prune hard!). The following is a simplified method that suits most table grapes.

In its first year, allow the young vine to grow without pruning. Tie it to a stake to support it temporarily.

In its second year, decide which side branches to keep and which to remove, so the vine will have the desired shape. Depending on how well the plant grew, there may be three to six good side branches. Keep the ones that are spaced about one to two feet apart if you are following a system like the one shown in Figure 6.15. Keep up to four if they are where you want them; you can select more side branches next year if the vine isn't tall enough yet to reach the top wires of the trellis. These side branches will become the main "arms," or framework, of the vines. The shoots that develop all along the length of these arms are the fruiting canes that will carry this season's crop.

6.16. A table grape vine with a confused shape halfway between a fan and parallel arms. No matter! It ripened twenty-eight large bunches of perfect grapes last year.

If the vine produces flowers this year, snip them off to allow the plant to put its energy into growth.

Table grapes can be trained along, up, over, or around any structure and to fit any space, as long as the space between the arms allows the fruiting canes to develop and get full sun. While grapes over an arbor really are lovely to sit under, give some thought to making it easy to reach the vines regularly for summer pruning.

Possible shapes for grapes:

- Vines along a fence can be grown with a single arm in each direction or two or three parallel arms extending at right angles from the main trunk. These can extend from both sides or from just one side to fit the location.
- Vines can be fanned out with the main arms in a V-shape on a trellis.
- Vines can be trained over an arbor by allowing them to grow longer vertically (this could take two years) before selecting arms to fan out over the arbor.

In the third year and thereafter, pruning is pretty straightforward because the shape of the vine is established. You can let the vines carry a small crop of grapes in their third summer if they are growing well. Shoots that are as big around at the base as your little finger can be allowed to develop one bunch. Thinner shoots shouldn't carry fruit this year.

Dormant pruning: In March cut back each of the side shoots that grew from the arms, leaving two buds at each joint. The first bud grows right at the base where the side shoot is attached to the arm; the second bud grows at the next obvious joint. Leaving both of these buds to grow gives you a choice of which to keep once they have started to develop.

Summer pruning: After the buds have sprouted and the shoots have grown an inch or two, choose the strongest or best-placed shoot at each joint. Rub off the rest. Also, remove any buds that sprout on the main trunk if they are not where you want a new branch. To simplify pruning, you can prune to one bud instead of two in March. Most will sprout just one shoot, so you won't need to revisit them, but check vines later to rub off extra shoots because sometimes a couple of buds "break" on more vigorous varieties.

6.17. Now that the buds have sprouted, it is time to choose the strongest and rub off the smaller ones on the left.

6.18. If you catch the developing shoots and tips of branches while they are soft, they are easy to snap off with your fingers.

In late June, after the grape clusters have started to develop, keep the best one on each cane (usually, but not always, the first one) and snip off the rest. On vines over five years old, I sometimes leave a second cluster to develop if the shoot is particularly vigorous. As the shoots continue to grow, snap off the tips at the third to fifth leaf past the forming cluster of grapes. Also cut back the tips of any shoots without fruit. All summer, regularly pinch out new shoots that develop at the joints of the branches.

You do have to keep on top of the summer pruning: check your vines every week or two, or they will become a tangled mass that is very hard to deal with. If the grapes are trained over an arbor for shade, you might want to allow the vines to grow a little longer, but do remove excess bunches and head back shoots with no fruit. If you aren't happy with the harvest once the vine is five years old, prune it more heavily the next year.

Protecting Grapes

Birds, raccoons, squirrels, sugar-crazy wasps, and city rats love ripe grapes. There are several approaches to keeping them away (for details of these methods, see Chapter 9):

Netting: I used to recommend covering vines with a bird netting or a specially designed mesh for grape growers. With clips to secure the netting to the trellis and close gaps, it keeps out birds, rats, and raccoons. Since the invasion of a new fruit pest, the spotted wing Drosophila (see p. 244), however, which has become widely established in the PNW since 2012, I have been recommending that grape growers use insect netting instead of bird netting to keep out fruit flies as well as birds (see p. 218). Netting works okay for well-pruned grapes on easy-to-reach trellises. However, it is next to impossible to securely cover vines growing on walls or other non-standard trellises.

Bags: Covering individual bunches of grapes with bags prevents damage from birds, rats, squirrels as well as insects, including the dreaded spotted wing Drosophila. Slip a lightweight bag (made of insect netting, organza, sheer curtain material, etc.) over each developing bunch of grapes, cinch up the drawstring, and leave it until time to pick (instructions for making the bags are given under Vertebrates in Chapter 9, p. 279). The bags don't interfere with summer pruning, and they work for vines that are impossible to cover with netting. The bags also keep direct sun off the fruit, which is desirable (the leaves need the sun, not the fruit), and the grapes develop without blemishes. If made of sturdy fabric with strong drawstrings, bags also foil raccoons.

Motion-activated animal repellents: Sensors in these devices pick up the movement of animals and trigger a short but startling burst of water to frighten them away. They work very well as a temporary frightener for raccoons while grapes are ripening. Doesn't scare the fruit flies, though.

Pruning Kiwi Fruit

To grow fuzzy kiwi (the egg-sized, grocery store kind), you need both a male and a female plant. Male plants can be kept much smaller than the female, so the two can be trellised together on a large trellis or separately, beside each other. The shape and size of the support can be much like that for grapes: sturdy, permanent, and shaped to fit whatever space you have.

Hardy kiwi is a different species with smaller fruit (for more information, see Chapter 11); some varieties are self-fertile, so you only need one plant. They are less vigorous than fuzzy kiwi, but generally follow the same pruning pattern, described below:

First year: Allow the vines to grow as tall as possible. The main stem of this new growth will eventually become the main trunk, so don't let the vines wind around the post. It will really, really want to do this, so keep it straight by tying it in place every foot or so as it grows.

Second year: Choose two or three well-spaced branches, which will become the main arms of the vine. Prune out the rest. The arms will run along wires or crosspieces on the trellis. Keep them from wrapping around the trellis wires by tying them straight.

Third year and thereafter: At this point, pruning instructions for the male and female vines diverge:

- **Male vines:** After the vines flower each year, you can cut the male plant back. Prune the flowering branches back to about 2 feet (60 cm) long and keep them pinched back if they become too long later. In the winter, continue to prune out crowded and tangled branches.

- **Female vines:** Choose side branches spaced about a foot (30 cm) apart on both sides of the main arms (or to fit the trellis). These side branches are where the flowers and fruit will grow.

After the female vine starts fruiting, keep any one fruiting branch for two or possibly three years, then prune it back to one or two buds at the base of the branch. When these buds send up shoots, rub off all but the strongest shoot, and let that one grow to become the next fruiting branch for a few years.

When the vine is dormant, prune out older branches to keep as much one-year-old wood (that's what grew the previous summer) as possible. Remove crossing and crowded shoots to leave next year's fruiting arms about a foot apart (30 cm).

6.19. One (!) mature female kiwi vine (the male is the small plant behind it) spreading on a long trellis.

During the growing season, starting in May, remove shoots that show no sign of flowers. Keep on top of removing watersprouts, which shoot upward from the main branches and are extremely vigorous. If you want to increase the fruiting branches for next year, cut the watersprouts back to two buds; when these sprout shoots, rub off the weakest one and keep the other. Also cut off the ends of shoots that are twisting around others and cut back any fruiting branches to fit the space.

Although this all sounds very organized, in reality, kiwi vines rapidly get out of hand, twist around each other and the trellis, and shoot vigorously off in all directions. Do the best you can to keep the vines to the basic form and remove excessive shoot growth to allow the plants to concentrate their energy in the developing fruit. A mature vine produces an awful lot of fruit no matter how it is managed.

The less vigorous hardy kiwis are easier to control. Simply prune all side shoots from the main branches to two buds as for grapes; later, choose the best buds and rub off others. Luckily, because kiwis are picked before they ripen, raccoons and other critters are not usually a problem.

Troubleshooting Fruit Problems

No flowers: The tree or vine may be too young to bear flowers. Dwarf trees start flowering early, usually by the time they are three years old, but varieties differ in how long they take to start bearing fruit. Female kiwi vines may not flower until they are six or seven years old (males usually flower earlier). If a tree is old enough to flower but still doesn't produce flowers, review the growing conditions: is it receiving enough sun? Too much nitrogen?

Lots of flowers, but little or no fruit: The flowers were not fertilized. Many varieties of fruit need pollen from another variety to successfully fertilize the flowers. You may have to plant another compatible tree or find someone to help you graft branches of a different variety onto your existing tree. It takes a couple of years for the new tree to flower, but in the meantime, if you can, cut some flowering branches from a friend's tree or an abandoned tree, put them in a bucket of water, and hang the bouquet in your tree.

If your tree is a self-fertile variety, but the flowers don't set fruit, it may be because there was too little pollinator activity when the flowers were open.

Although wild bees and other insects fly in cooler weather than honeybees, no insects fly in wet weather. It is not unusual to have a complete crop failure on fruit trees that had the bad luck to bloom during a cold or rainy period in the spring.

If your trees are not setting fruit due to bad weather or lack of pollinators, try hand pollinating the flowers. For how to pollinate fruit flowers, see page 157.

Lots of tiny fruit that fall off: If the tiny fruit don't grow at all and fall off a few weeks after the petals fall, they probably weren't fertilized successfully. If the fruit clearly grows a little and doesn't drop off until late June or early July, then the tree is naturally thinning the crop. This is the June drop. Unfortunately some varieties are prone to dropping a lot of fruit, but it can also be due to inadequate pollination or poor growing conditions. You should wait until after this occurs before you thin the remaining fruit.

CHAPTER 7

Food Crops in Greenhouses and Containers

Greenhouses

Sooner or later, keen gardeners end up investing in some type of greenhouse. In the cool, foggy zones near the ocean, greenhouses or tunnels are a necessity if you want to grow tomatoes, peppers, or other heat-loving crops in the summer. If you already have a greenhouse, you can use it to produce food through the winter. It is also the ideal place to overwinter tender herbs, potted citrus trees, and other plants.

A greenhouse can be anything from a simple plastic-covered frame to a custom-designed glass house. It can be freestanding or attached to other buildings, unheated or heated, and cost from a few dollars to thousands for a fully equipped glasshouse. I am not going into detail on all of these options, because as far as food production goes, a simple unheated plastic tunnel greenhouse provides enough protection for summer and winter crops in this climate. Here are three important design elements to consider:

Site in full sun: The warmth inside a greenhouse won't make up for a shortage of the sunlight that plants need for photosynthesis. If the greenhouse will be used in the summer for tomatoes and other warm-season crops, it should receive six to eight hours of direct sun during the growing season. For winter crops, it should be placed to receive as much direct sun as possible in the winter. An hour or two is adequate in December, but the more direct sun the greenhouse receives, the faster the crops will grow.

Whether the greenhouse ridge runs north–south or east–west isn't important unless it is attached to another building. In that case, the glazed (transparent) side should face south as much as possible.

Adequate ventilation: This is a very important feature! You will need to ventilate a greenhouse to cool it many more days of the year than might think.

- **Winter ventilation:** No matter how cold it is at night, an unheated greenhouse can easily reach temperatures over 95°F (35°C) on a sunny day in February. Such wide swings from day to night are very stressful to plants. When daytime temperatures are too high, leaves grow soft, making them more susceptible to freezing and diseases. Plants do much better if daytime temperatures rise no more than 25°F (15°C) above night temperatures.
- **Summer ventilation:** Without good ventilation, temperatures can easily exceed 104°F (40°C) on summer days, even with vents and doors open. Temperatures this high stress plants (which stop photosynthesizing) and also sterilize the pollen in tomato flowers, so they won't produce fruit.

The Problem with Shading

A traditional way to cool a greenhouse in the summer is to shade it using a blind or by spattering the glass with whitewash. These provide cooling all season and are fine for ornamentals that do well in low light, but when you reduce the light levels for tomatoes and other vegetables, you also reduce the size and quality of the crop (greenhouse growers say a 1% decrease in light levels causes a 1% drop in tomato harvest). Plan to cool your greenhouse mainly through improved ventilation, not by shading. However, for a heat wave, deploying temporary shading (horticultural shade cloth, curtain material, etc.) is a good way to avoid serious overheating. Covering the greenhouse with shade cloth has the best effect, but if that is not possible, laying shade cloth over the plants inside the greenhouse is still better than doing nothing.

How hot it gets inside in full sun depends on the covering material. Glass allows in the most infrared radiation, which is what heats up the interior. Greenhouse grades of fiberglass or plastics are not quite as transparent, so they don't heat up quite as much, but they still require excellent ventilation.

For adequate ventilation, the greenhouse should have at least two large openings, ideally at either end, with one lower and the other higher, so rising hot air draws in outside air through the lower vent. Venting along the top ridge is an efficient way to dump heat, especially if there are lower vents on either end to bring in cooler air from outside. If the openings are not big enough, you may have to use fans to move the air. Commercial greenhouse suppliers sell electric ventilation fans. Some models are operated on batteries charged by solar cells, though these do not have the power to move large volumes of air. If you design your greenhouse with large

Manual or Automatic Vents?

If someone is around to open manual vents every day *without fail*, you can get away with manually operated vents. But, if they aren't opened on just a single sunny spring day, it can mean serious damage or even death to the plants inside. For safety, I recommend installing at least one automatic vent that will open when temperatures inside reach a preset level. An economical solution is to use the heat-activated vent openers sold by garden and greenhouse suppliers. These are lifting arms that move mechanically as a wax or gas-filled cylinder heats up in the sun—no electricity needed. As the gas expands inside, it drives out a piston that lifts the vent cover. They can lift up to 15 pounds (7 kg) and are quite sturdy, lasting for years.

enough vents, you won't need fans. For folks who live on the foggy ocean coast, cooling the greenhouse is much less of a problem, but there should still be provisions to ventilate well.

Deep soil beds: It is much easier to grow vegetables in a bed with soil at least 18 inches (45 cm) deep than in pots or containers on benches. As well as providing more access to nutrients, deep soil doesn't heat up as much, change temperatures as rapidly, or dry out as quickly as soil in containers, all of which benefits plant roots.

The growing bed could be at ground level or raised. A dual-purpose greenhouse design has a deep in-ground or raised bed running along the south side and space for shelves or tables along the

7.1. This attached greenhouse has a deep soil bed along the front, space for potted plants along the back (sweet potatoes in this case), and shelves for smaller plants on the back wall.

north side. For a greenhouse attached to a building, the back wall is an ideal place for shelves, with the growing bed running along the glazed side.

Managing Greenhouse Crops

There are many more exhaustive sources of information on managing specific greenhouse crops, but the following basic tips should be sufficient for gardeners growing food crops in an unheated home greenhouse.

Soil fertility: Soils in a greenhouse are not exposed to heavy winter rainfall that acidify the soil and leach out nutrients, so it is a good idea to test the soil pH more often than for outdoor gardens. In any case, take care not to overuse lime or other materials that raise the pH (wood ashes or bone meal). With this caveat, manage the soil like any garden bed, with yearly additions of compost and other organic amendments to maintain fertility. Use liquid fertilizer on plants in the summer if growth slows.

7.2. In November, the last pepper and tomato plants remain from summer. I have just transplanted lettuce, Swiss chard, and other plants into the bed to fill it for winter.

Mulching: In the summer, plants in a greenhouse benefit greatly from an organic mulch on the soil even if they are in pots, rather than in a soil bed. It reduces water loss through evaporation and insulates the soil, keeping it cooler.

Watering: Soil in a deep bed stays moist for months in the winter, but it does have to be watered occasionally. Once the brighter and longer days of February arrive, plants grow more rapidly and start to take up more water from the soil. In the summer, watering may be required daily because plants really suck up a lot of water in hot conditions.

Cold protection: Crops in an unheated greenhouse will not have the benefit of snow cover to insulate them in a cold snap. Ironically, in the coldest weather, they may need more protection than plants growing outdoors that are covered with snow. Keep plastic sheets, old blankets, or tarps handy to throw over the beds at night to protect plants if temperatures threaten to go below 23°F (−5°C). It won't be appreciably warmer inside an unheated greenhouse over a long winter night than it is outside.

Keeping the space filled: The joy of a greenhouse in this climate is a longer harvest of heat-loving vegetables. While tomatoes and cucumbers produce pretty well outdoors in many coastal gardens, you can start picking them earlier and over a longer season in a greenhouse. Other crops that thrive in greenhouses include peppers, sweet basil, melons, and long English cucumbers and sweet potatoes (yams). Given their high heat requirements, you have a much better chance of harvesting large-fruited eggplants or watermelons if they are in a greenhouse (or a tunnel).

But this is only half of the equation: the other joy of having a greenhouse is that you can fill it with cool-season vegetables for the rest of the year. Unheated greenhouses are excellent for growing leafy greens (as opposed to root crops, which are better off outdoors, under mulch). I keep my small unheated greenhouse crammed with Swiss chard and salad plants (lettuce, kale, spinach, parsley, arugula, mizuna, and komatsuna) all winter after the tomatoes, peppers, and melons are done.

To fill the greenhouse with winter crops, sow lettuce and other leafy greens under the summer crops. If there isn't space to sow winter crops, you can lift entire plants from the garden and transplant them to the greenhouse. I keep the beds filled by moving good-sized plants of Swiss chard, kale, and other greens in to take over as the tomatoes and peppers finish.

Growing Food in Containers

Determined gardeners have found that it is possible to grow all kinds of crops in containers. Some food plants are more suited to container life than others, but you can grow pretty much anything if you really, really want to. Where late blight kills garden tomatoes too early for a crop, growing them in containers under the overhang of a roof (to keep the leaves dry and prevent infection) can be much more successful than planting them out in the garden.

7.3. Tomatoes and eggplant growing safely in pots under the overhang of the porch roof, where the leaves will stay dry, yet receive full sun.

Plants with small root systems and those that produce a crop over a long season are ideal for container culture. These include tomatoes, peppers, and eggplants; cut-and-come again greens such as Swiss chard, kale, and perennial arugula; parsley and other herbs; strawberries; pole beans; cucumbers; and bush varieties of squash. Lettuce and other annual greens do well in containers because they have relatively short roots. They are short-lived, however, and go to seed in a few months, so plan on sowing them several times over the season.

Containers

Almost anything that holds soil and has a hole in the bottom can be used as a container, from strong plastic bags to beautifully glazed ceramic pots to large self-watering containers.

Choose lightweight materials when the weight of the container is an issue, such as on an apartment balcony, a deck, or a roof. Plastic and fiberglass are the lightest; wood weighs a bit more, but is still considerably lighter than pottery. Where containers are sitting on the ground or a patio, the weight usually doesn't matter, so you have a wider choice of materials and designs.

Hanging containers should be the lightest weight. Most on the market are 1-gallon containers or smaller, best suited to small plants with small fruit, such as cherry tomatoes or hot peppers. For any type of hanging container, choose tomatoes with small fruit because the hanging vines often break under the weight of a crop of large fruited tomatoes. Make sure hanging containers are hooked to a strong support.

If you want to grow plants in outdoor containers over the winter, put them in frost-resistant pots of wood, plastic, or fiberglass. If unglazed pottery is left where it can freeze, water absorbed into the clay freezes and expands, which chips or breaks the pot. Glazed ceramic pots can be left outdoors in light frost because they don't absorb water, but if there is a prolonged cold snap and the soil mass freezes and expands, it can crack any ceramic pot.

The larger the container, the better: The larger the volume of soil, the more room there is for roots to take up nutrients. Roots are also more insulated from temperature changes, and plants need watering less often. When it is important to keep the weight of a container low, use lightweight containers and soil mixes rather than skimping on soil volume.

Guidelines for what to fit into a container:

- 1 gallon (3.8 L): four to five lettuce plants or one pepper plant
- 2 gallons (7.6 L): one cherry tomato, eggplant, or pepper plant
- 5 to 7 gallons (18.9–26.5 L): one large-fruited tomato plant

7.4. One sweet pepper growing beautifully in the right-sized pot.

Ensure good drainage: Every container needs drainage holes in the bottom, preferably more than one. To prevent the holes from getting clogged by roots, place a flat rock or a piece of broken pot over the drainage hole. Holes where the sides meet the bottom of the container are much less likely to clog than a single hole in the center of the bottom.

Use pot "feet" to raise pots off of the ground to ensure that surplus water flowing through the hole in the bottom can keep on flowing away. Three small blocks of wood or stones will do the same job as more ornamental pottery feet. Use a very large saucer under the container if water dripping from the pot could cause a problem (such as staining the surface it's on, or dripping onto a balcony below). You still need to use pot feet to elevate the bottom of the container above the saucer to ensure good drainage because the pot itself shouldn't ever be sitting in water.

Where to put containers: Lettuce and other greens need full sun for at least half a day; six to eight hours of sun is required for tomatoes, peppers, and other vegetables. One advantage of container growing is that it is often possible to reposition pots over the season to keep them in the best sun.

On balconies or flat roofs, set containers at least a foot away from walls or the edges of the roof to avoid stressing the flashing joint. The weight of a container pulls down on this flashing and can compromise the waterproofing at the joint and cause a leak. On decks, set heavy pots over support posts or beams. You can also spread the weight of pots over a wider area by setting them on pallets.

7.5. These cucumbers won't be let down. They are supported on strings secured to a solid frame outside their pots.

> ## Pot Liners Make Light Work
> I like to use plastic pots as liners inside large ceramic pots. It makes life much easier because you can lift out the plastic pot to fill or empty it or when moving the pot. The inner plastic pot can also safely stay outdoors over the winter while the ceramic pot is stored away where it won't crack.

Provide supports: Tall plants need some type of strong, stable support. If the pot is large and heavy enough, you can fit a stake or trellis inside it. A tomato cage, for example, works well to support tomato plants in a large pot because the three or four legs of the cage provide stability. Plants in small and lighter-weight pots can be supported on strings or trellises fastened to a wall, fence, or frame supported outside the pot.

Soil and Fertilizing

Soil for vegetables in containers must be very fertile because they have such a confined root zone. Suggested soil mixes:

- **Where weight of the container is not a concern:** Mix equal parts coir/peat moss, good garden soil, compost, and sand. Using perlite or vermiculite instead of the sand will improve the drainage and make the mix lighter in weight.
- **For containers on balconies and roofs:** To make the lightest weight mix, omit soil because it is too heavy. Mix in a generous amount of homemade or commercial compost, such as fish/wood-waste compost. You may be better off with a lightweight commercial organic planting mix.
- **For all homemade mixes:** Add a cup of balanced organic fertilizer to every 5 gallons (18.9 L) of soil. If using garden soil that usually needs lime, add about 1 tablespoon of agricultural lime to 1 gallon (3.8 L) of garden soil in the mix.

Fertilizing over the season: A generous supply of homemade or commercial compost in the soil mix provides slow-release nutrients, but the heavy watering schedule, which leaches out nutrients, and the smaller soil volume in a container means that plants will need supplementary fertilizer. Use fish fertilizer or other liquid fertilizers or make you own compost or manure extract (see Compost extract, p. 81). Depending on how many plants are in the pots and how they are growing, you may want to feed them with liquid fertilizer every two to four weeks.

Watering

Irrigation is a big challenge for container gardeners because plants use up the water so quickly in warm weather. The root zone is warmer in the summer than it would be for in-ground plants; therefore, the plants transpire more water. Containers often need water every day in the summer, and when it is hot, could easily need watering twice a day. Watering is critical for container plants: a day or two of neglect can kill them.

Think about the easiest way to get water to the containers so that it won't be neglected. Watering by hand is fine, of course, but someone has to be there to do the watering. Gardeners with a lot of containers often end up looking into automatic drip irrigation systems to ease the chore of frequent watering.

Watering spikes: The simplest "automatic" system is a perforated plastic spike that fits into the neck of a large plastic soft drink bottle. Fill the bottle with water, screw on the plant spike, and push the spike into the soil beside the plant. This releases a slow trickle of water to the roots. If you cut the bottom off the bottle so that it sits like a funnel beside the plant, it is really easy to refill. Plastic pop bottles or gallon jugs with the bottoms cut off can be used the same way, without the plant spikes, but use sticks to prop them upright or bury them deeper in the soil. Leave the lid on and unscrew it enough to allow a trickle of water. There are also ornamental versions of this kind of watering device that are nicer to look at.

Automatic drip systems: Installing a drip irrigation system that runs on a timer takes a lot of work out of watering. These give good results because the plants will be watered regularly, whether or not you are there to do it.

Inexpensive manual timers are available that you install between the tap and the hose of the watering system. Even a manual timer will reduce your watering work load considerably. More expensive fully automated systems are also available.

For small pots, a single dripper may be enough, but it is a good idea to put a flat stone under the dripper to help the water spread out. If the irrigation system will take the "shrubbler" type of fitting, these do a better job of watering evenly. These send out five gentle streams of water from the single fitting. It is easy to adjust the distance they sprinkle by turning the top of the fitting. You will need to experiment with how long to run a dripper/shrubbler watering system. It will usually take less than ten minutes and possibly as little as two to five minutes to deliver sufficient water to pots.

Self-watering containers: Large containers designed with a water reservoir in the bottom are available from garden suppliers, or you can build your own. They give excellent results because they provide an even supply of water to the roots, which reach the water through a mesh in the bottom of the soil compartment (some models use a wick to move water from the reservoir to the root zone). Since the filled reservoir can also last for several days in hot weather, you can get away for a few days without worrying about your plants.

7.6. A "shrubbler" fitting. An automatic watering system is very nice to have when there are a lot of pots to water.

Commercial models are expensive, but they do last a long time. They hold up to 12 gallons (45.4 L) of soil and 1.5 gallons (5.7 L) of water in the reservoir, making them also quite heavy when full.

If you are handy, you can make your own version of a self-watering container (there are lots of plans and videos on the web). Basically, all you need is a large outer container to hold the water (no holes in the bottom). Fit an inner pot inside, fixed so that the bottom of that pot sits 6 to 8 inches (15 to 20 cm) above the bottom of the outer container. Replace the bottom of the inner pot with wire mesh or else punch a lot of ¼-inch (0.5 cm) holes in the bottom so that roots can reach down for water. Make a hole in the side along the upper edge of the outer pot so that you can pour water through this to fill the reservoir with water. You can also buy plastic inserts with integrated water reservoirs that are designed to fit several sizes of pot.

Winter Vegetables in Containers

Many hardy greens can be grown in containers over the winter: corn salad, winter lettuce, leaf mustards, Swiss chard, kales, and spinach are some that I've had success with. If you have warm-season crops in pots, you can undersow them with lettuce or corn salad in late August. By the time your tomatoes or peppers finish producing, you will have a crop of greens started in the pots.

As well as using frost-proof containers, it is a good idea to move containers to a more protected place than the open garden. In a container, roots experience colder conditions than they would growing in the ground, and they don't tolerate as much cold as above-ground parts do. It is as if they were being grown two zones colder.

For winter, move containers closer to a wall, house foundation, or other shelter. For greater protection, you can group containers together and insulate between the pots with leaves, plastic, straw, or other materials. Wrapping a band of burlap or plastic around the outside of the whole group of containers gives the roots even more protection from freezing.

Fruit in Containers

Strawberries do well in containers, and it is possible to grow other berries or small trees in containers as well.

Strawberries: These have traditionally been grown in a strawberry jar, which is a very large pottery jar with openings for plants all around the sides. Roots reach into the soil in the center, and foliage sticks out the holes. You can make one from a large barrel by drilling 4-inch (10 cm) holes in the sides. I recommend planting everbearing or day-neutral varieties of strawberries because they produce berries all season.

When planting a jar or barrel planter, make sure the soil is well-firmed as you go; otherwise, the first time the whole thing is watered, the weight of the settling soil sucks the plants inside the barrel (trust me!). Fill the soil to the first line of holes, set a plant through each hole, with the roots spread out on the soil. Cover the roots with more soil and firm it well. Continue with each tier of plants until the container is filled, and then set the last couple of plants in the top opening.

Citrus: Dwarf Improved Meyer lemons and Bearss limes are now widely available in nurseries. These naturally small trees can grow for many years in pots. I have been pleasantly surprised at how productive these small trees are. Other citrus, such as smaller oranges, are sometimes available from nurseries as well.

Stone fruit: Dwarf fruit trees can be grown in large tubs, but eventually it becomes difficult to keep them in good condition. There are, however, genetic dwarf peach and nectarine trees that only grow 3 to 6 feet (1 to 2 m) high that can be grown indefinitely in a tub. They produce a pretty good little crop (two to three dozen peaches).

7.7. My Meyer lemon in a tub carries on, providing lemons year-round and spending the winter in the greenhouse.

Other fruit: Apple trees grafted onto super-dwarfing M27 rootstocks are better able to handle growing in containers than larger dwarf trees. Colonnade or "stick" apple varieties are very small trees that can also be grown in tubs. They fruit along the main trunk, rather than on branches, so they literally do look like a stick with leaves and apples all along the trunk. One tree doesn't produce much, though.

Figs can also be kept in tubs. Although figs will become very root-bound, with sufficient water and fertilizer, they continue to produce crops for about a decade. I have not grown persimmons or other small fruits such as blueberries in pots, but I've seen other people grow them successfully.

The challenge with blueberries is that soil pH tends to rise over time in pots; therefore, you may need to use sulphur (aluminum sulphate), available from a garden center, to acidify the soil.

7.8. A genetic dwarf peach isn't a big tree, but it is well-suited to life in a container.

CHAPTER 8

Year-Round Gardening Calendar

The crop schedule and harvest notes in this chapter are for the coastal regions of the Pacific Northwest, extending from Vancouver Island and the Lower Mainland on the south coast of British Columbia to Washington and northern Oregon, west of the Cascade Mountains. In the warmest microclimates and in years with early warm spring weather, spring planting can be a couple of weeks earlier than shown here (conversely, it can be weeks later if the weather is cold).

In more southerly parts of the region or if you have dawn-to-dusk sun on your garden all fall, dates for planting overwintered crops can be up to two weeks later. Don't plant later than suggested, though, if fall days in your garden are cut short by shading from nearby trees or buildings as the sun gets lower in the sky.

You will be making judgment calls every year, but over time you will fine-tune these planting schedules to suit your garden's microclimate(s). The coastal spring weather is so variable that you should be prepared to handle its rapid changes. Be ready to cover plants in a late cool spell and to mulch and shade them in an early heat wave.

Spring (February through May)

Once you establish a year-round garden, you won't need to battle unpredictable spring weather to get an early start for many crops. There will be plenty to harvest from March through May. Overwintered lettuce, kale, spinach, Swiss chard, and other greens grow new crops of leaves as the days warm and

185

TABLE 8.1. Year-round planting schedule for the south coast of British Columbia and Washington and Oregon west of the Cascades.

Dates	In the garden	Indoors or in a greenhouse
February	Sow broad beans.	Sow seeds of leeks, onions, celery, celeriac.
March	Plant strawberries, fruit bushes, and trees. If weather permits: sow peas, plant onion sets, and potatoes.	Sow indeterminate (tall) tomatoes, peppers, eggplants, summer broccoli, cauliflower, and cabbage.
April to early May	Sow peas, lettuce, carrots, beets, parsnips, summer turnips, radishes, scallions, Chinese cabbage and other leafy greens, Swiss chard, parsley. Plant potatoes. Set out summer broccoli, cauliflower, and cabbage seedlings and/or sow seeds. Transplant leek and onion seedlings.	Start melons, cucumbers, summer and winter squash, pumpkins, sweet basil, determinate (bush) tomatoes. Sow first planting of sweet corn in individual pots. Sprout beans in vermiculite.
Mid to late May	Transplant tomatoes and zucchini. If soil is warm, transplant peppers, eggplant, cucumbers, other squash, and pumpkin (or wait till early June). Sow Brussels sprouts and slow-maturing winter cabbage varieties in the garden or seedling flats. Plant sweet corn and bean seedlings.	Start more sweet corn, beans (or sow in the garden if soil is warm).
Early June	Transplant melons, sweet basil to garden. Sow more sweet corn, beans (or start indoors). Sow summer cauliflower.	
Mid to late June	Sow winter broccoli, winter cauliflower, quick-maturing winter cabbage varieties.	
Early July	Sow carrots, beets, rutabagas, endive and radicchio, Swiss chard/leaf beet, kohlrabi for winter harvest.	
Late July to early August	Sow last summer lettuce, radishes, summer cauliflower. Sow winter crops: arugula, fall and winter lettuce, leaf turnip/mizuna, collards, kale, daikon and winter radish, leaf mustards, komatsuna/mustard spinach, Chinese cabbage and other hardy greens, spinach, sweet onions and scallions, broccoli raab.	
Late August to mid-September	Sow corn salad, cilantro, arugula, winter lettuce.	
October	Plant garlic. Sow broad beans.	

lengthen. Leeks, carrots, beets, celeriac, and other roots left in the garden will be in good condition until April. Purple sprouting broccoli and winter cauliflower produce heads from late February through May. Indoors, you could still have potatoes, winter squash, onions, garlic, and apples if they have been stored well. In fact, I often have to make a point of using up the last of these in July.

So, go ahead and try planting early peas and potatoes in March if the weather permits, but don't worry about getting an early start for many other crops. If you wait until the soil warms up, it is a lot easier to get a good stand of seedlings. This also avoids the chance that biennials, such as onions, celery, and Swiss chard, will go to seed prematurely if there is a period of cool weather.

8.1. My spring planting is underway (under supervision).

If you are growing your own transplants, the main planting task for spring is starting seedlings (see Chapter 5). Otherwise, plan the garden, get your supply of seeds and soil amendments, and enjoy the harvest of overwintered crops.

Spring Planting Notes

For coastal gardeners, the best indicator of when to plant is the soil temperature. Pull back the mulch on beds where you plan to sow spring crops so the soil warms up and dries out. Wait until the soil is 50° to 60°F (10° to 15°C) to sow most seeds, and warmer for beans and corn (over 65°F/18°C).

To get a jump on the season, start peas, beans, and corn indoors three weeks ahead of planting dates. Peas and beans are easy to sprout indoors in vermiculite (see Chapter 5); doing so gets the seedlings safely past the danger of seedling pests and diseases before they go outdoors.

Set out squash, cucumbers, tomatoes, peppers, melons, and sweet basil after the weather seems to have stabilized into a warm summer pattern. Because the coastal spring is often long and cool, this might not be until late May

8.2. A bed of spring sown greens and sweetheart cabbage seedlings set out in April are ready to eat in May and June.

to early June in some years. If you set plants out earlier, be prepared to protect them from a late frost or cool spell, which would stop their growth.

To hasten sowing and transplanting dates, before planting, warm the soil by laying a sheet of clear plastic flat on the surface for a couple of weeks. After planting, cover beds with floating rows covers or plastic tunnels or cover the plants with cloches. Don't lay plastic directly on the soil as that would fry the seedlings.

Spring Harvest Notes

Carrots, beets, and parsnips: Roots still in the garden from last season start to grow again in the spring. When they do, they begin using up the stored sugars in their roots, so quality deteriorates the longer they stay in the garden. Keeping a thick mulch over the bed helps to keep roots cool and delay the start of growth in the spring. Root crops are usually fine up to early April, but can start growing in late March in warmer years. To preserve quality, dig up any remaining roots by April 1 and refrigerate them. They won't grow any bigger in the spring anyway, no matter how long you leave them in the ground, because they will direct their energy to flowering.

Leeks: Lift remaining leeks in April and refrigerate them, or just leave them in the garden. They will grow a seed stalk as the spring progresses. The stalk is tender and edible at first, so the whole leek can still be used. Once the stalk begins to toughen up, you can simply remove it (split the leek down the middle and lift it out) before using the rest of the leek.

Leafy greens: Overwintered leafy greens usually grow quickly in April. By the end of the month, there may be too much to keep up with, so remove surplus plants to make room for new crops.

8.3. After a particularly bad winter, leeks are still fine under their battered exteriors.

8.4. March harvest of overwintered leafy greens with Brussels sprouts underneath.

8.5. This Purple Cape cauliflower lost most of its leaves in January storms, but here it is in April, ready to pick a beautiful head.

You can leave spinach, kale, chard, and parsley in the garden even though they begin to develop seed stalks in the spring. The leaves that grow along the seed stalk are fine to eat.

Winter broccoli and cauliflower: No matter how battered these plants were by winter winds or heavy snow, as long as the stems weren't broken, they will recover. The plants grow new leaves and then form heads. The earliest purple sprouting broccoli varieties start heading in February. Later varieties start in April and continue producing useful shoots well into June.

What to Do Each Month

February

- Start seeds indoors if you can provide good growing conditions: leeks, onions from seed, celeriac, and celery.
- Sow broad beans outdoors if you didn't plant them last fall.
- Finish dormant pruning of fruit trees, bushes, and kiwi and grape vines (you can plan on pruning the grapes last, because they leaf out later than other plants).
- Gardeners in British Columbia: Attend your local Seedy Saturday to buy, sell, and swap seeds; hear speakers, and view displays. Most communities hold them on a Saturday sometime between late January and April.

March

- Start seeds indoors if you can provide good growing conditions: indeterminate (tall) tomatoes, peppers, and eggplants should be started now; also start summer cauliflower, cabbage, and broccoli for early planting.
- Peas: Sprout seeds in vermiculite for planting outdoors in two to three weeks, or sow directly in the garden if soil has warmed to 54°F (12°C).
- Onions: Plant onion sets outdoors at the end of the month if weather is warming. The best sets are smaller than a dime; larger ones may bolt to seed (use them as early scallions).
- Potatoes: Set a few seed potatoes on the windowsill to develop dark green sprouts. Plant them outdoors in late March for the earliest crop of potatoes. Protect early emerging sprouts from late frosts: hill up the soil over the sprouts or cover with mulch or plastic sheets.
- Set out strawberry plants and asparagus roots.
- Plant fruit trees, grapes, blueberries, raspberries, and other small fruit bushes, if you didn't do it in November.
- Finish pruning grapes.

April

- First week of April, dig any carrots, beets, parsnips, and celeriac roots still in the garden and refrigerate.
- If you can provide good growing conditions indoors, start seeds of summer and winter squash, pumpkins, cucumbers, melons, sweet basil, and determinate (bush) tomatoes.
- Sow lettuce, spinach, arugula, leaf mustard, and other salad greens in the garden if you don't have them as overwintered crops; sow parsnips.
- Plant more peas, potatoes, and onion sets; plant leek and onion seedlings later in the month.
- Plant fruit trees and bushes that have either been growing in containers or that have a good soil ball in burlap (avoid bare root stock, even if available, as it will be in poor condition by this time of year).
- By the end of April, start bean seeds in vermiculite indoors, also the first planting of sweet corn in individual small pots. In cool springs, delay the first sowing to early May.

May

- By the first week: plant onion and leek seedlings if not done in April.
- Sow summer beets, carrots, radishes, more lettuce, and other greens, Swiss chard, Chinese cabbage, and kale.
- Sow parsnips for fall and winter harvests.
- Sow more peas and plant main crop potatoes (for harvest in October).
- Set out cabbage, cauliflower, and broccoli transplants, or sow them directly in the garden.
- Plant out bean and sweet corn seedlings started indoors in April.
- Start another planting of sweet corn indoors, or sow outdoors in the garden if the soil is warm.
- Last week of May, in the garden or seed flats, sow Brussels sprouts and winter cabbages that take the longest to mature (110 to 120 days).
- Around the middle of the month, if weather is stable and warm, set out tomatoes and summer and winter squash plants.

Summer (June through August)

The delicacies available in the summer harvest make this the most wonderful time of year in the garden. Fresh peas and beans, tender summer squash, tomatoes, sweet corn, artichokes, strawberries, and early tree fruit add to the

8.6. Late June and everything is growing quickly in the long days.

bounty of salad greens, cauliflower, broccoli, carrots, beets, Swiss chard, sweet onions, and fresh herbs.

But it isn't all about harvesting: mid- to late summer is also the time to plant the vegetables you will feast upon next winter.

Mulch management: As the typical dry summer weather pattern along the coast starts to settle in, usually around mid-June, begin mulching the soil around the largest plants. Along the foggy, cool outer coast, wait until the end of June to allow soil to warm up before mulching. If dry conditions begin in May, start mulching then and be ready to put fine mulch around seedlings if there is an early heat wave.

8.7. Pinching out tomato suckers that sprout where the leaf joins the main stem keeps indeterminate (vining) tomatoes on track for an earlier harvest.

Summer pruning: Keeping order among the fruit and vegetables is an ongoing task over the summer. Pinch out shoots of grapes and kiwi, rub off watersprouts forming on fruit tree branches, snap off tomato suckers.

Summer Planting Notes

Succession planting: Sow vegetables that mature quickly (lettuce, radishes, salad greens, Chinese cabbage) at three- or four-week intervals over the summer months as spaces open up in the garden. Sowing bush beans, peas, and sweet corn two or three times, three weeks apart, spreads out the period of prime harvest.

Sow winter crops to fill your living refrigerator: Most vegetables harvested over the winter are started from seeds in the summer. Think of the winter garden as a living refrigerator: plants don't grow, but they keep in perfect condition for months because they are still alive. Since plants grow so little from November to February, what you are going to eat then has to have grown to full-size by the end of October.

Keep a planting schedule handy to remind you when to sow each crop. I also find it useful to keep all the seed packets for these later plantings together in one container. Here are the main summer planting windows for winter vegetables:

- July 1 to mid-July: carrots, beets, rutabaga, endive, radicchio, Swiss chard, and leaf beet, kohlrabi.
- Late July to mid-August: leafy greens, including kale, spinach, leaf mustard, and Chinese cabbage, fall lettuce; also winter radish/daikon, broccoli raab.
- Late August to early-September: winter lettuce, corn salad, arugula, cilantro.

Note that root crops, kale, and chard/leaf beet sown earlier in the garden will be fine for harvest through the winter. For these crops, the July planting date marks the *latest* date you can sow them and still get a mature crop by fall. In contrast, annual greens (spinach, leaf mustards, Chinese cabbage, arugula) for winter harvest shouldn't be sown before the end of July (early August in warm years), or the plants may go to seed before cold weather stops growth.

8.8. A bed of leafy greens for winter, sown August 1. Note how vigorous the komatsuna is (the tallest in the back row).

If you didn't start plants from seeds in time, you may be able to buy transplants of kale, Swiss chard, winter lettuce, and other greens, as well as overwintering varieties of broccoli, cauliflower, and cabbage. Just make sure the supplier is selling *winter* varieties of broccoli and cauliflower (it is common for suppliers to sell the wrong varieties of these crops at this time of year).

If you miss these dates and sow too late, seedlings will usually be too small by the time growth stops in the fall to provide much of a harvest. All is not lost, however, because surviving seedlings resume growing from late February onward and could still produce much earlier crops than you would get from a spring sowing.

Summer Harvest Notes

New potatoes: About ten to twelve weeks after planting, or when the potato plants flower, the first new potatoes are ready. (Note: not all potato plants flower.) Dig the whole plant or carefully rummage around the roots and pull off a few tubers, leaving the plant to continue growing.

Garlic and onions: Garlic planted the previous fall and onions grown from sets mature in July. Onions from seedlings take until late August or September to mature. It helps both kinds of bulbs to mature if you stop watering for one or two weeks before harvest, but it isn't mandatory. Onions and soft-neck garlic are ready to harvest when the tops have fallen over and the neck of the bulb is quite withered at the soil line. Hardneck (Rocambole) garlic is ready to harvest when the four or five lowest leaves have dried up and the outermost layers of the bulb are papery.

For details on curing and storage, see entries in A to Z Vegetables in Chapter 10.

8.9. The onion tops have fallen over, but wait another week or two for the bulbs to finish growing.

What to Do Each Month

June

- Sow succession plantings of sweet corn and bush beans up to the end of the month, indoors if it is cool, directly in the garden if the soil is warm.
- Plant more peas, lettuce, and other salad greens.
- By early June, set out celery and celeriac plants (set these out when the weather is settled to avoid risk of plants going to seed).
- By June 10, sow winter cabbage varieties that mature quickly (80 to 100 days to harvest).
- From mid- to late June, sow winter broccoli and winter cauliflower. If you have the space, seed them directly where they will grow or start them in flats or seedling beds and transplant them in July.
- By late June, harvest earliest varieties of garlic.
- Thin tree fruit around the end of the month (or in early July in cool years) after the June drop (see Chapter 6, p. 158).
- Continue pruning and training grapes and kiwi vines.

July

- First week of July: Mark the holiday by sowing a large bed of carrots for harvest all winter. Also sow beets, rutabagas, turnips.
- Sow radicchio, kohlrabi, and more Swiss chard and leaf beet.
- Plant out purple sprouting broccoli, winter cauliflower, and cabbage seedlings.
- Harvest garlic and onions that grew from sets.
- Last week of July through first week of August: Sow fall lettuce, kale, Chinese greens, spinach, sweet onions, hardy scallions, mustards, and other leafy greens to overwinter for early spring crops.
- Continue pruning and training grapes and kiwi vines; thin clusters of grapes to one per shoot.

August

- Early August: Finish sowing hardy leafy greens for winter and sweet onions for early spring harvests.
- Early August, summer prune fruit trees if required to slow growth of overly vigorous trees and keep trees compact.

- By the end of the month, sow corn salad, arugula, cilantro, and winter lettuce in beds or broadcast the seeds under vines of squash and other warm-season crops.
- Continue pruning and training grapes and kiwi vines (it never stops!).

Fall (September to November)

This is the time of year to finish harvesting the main warm-season vegetables and tree fruit and to prepare the hardy vegetables for winter in the garden. If you have a greenhouse or sturdy tunnel, fill it with hardy lettuce, spinach, Swiss chard, and other greens. You can transplant full-grown plants from other parts of the garden to make the most of this protected space.

To prepare the garden for winter, cover exposed soil with leaves, straw, or other mulch to insulate the roots of plants from cold, protect the soil from erosion by heavy rain, and control weeds. However, don't spread compost or manure on the garden at this time of year. The rain leaches the nutrients away (polluting water bodies with nitrogen and phosphorus), and it is too cold for nutrients to be available to plants or for the plants to use them.

8.10. The fall garden should be crammed full of food for winter harvest by October. The only empty space in this bed has just been planted to garlic.

Fall Planting Notes

Garlic: Garlic is much more productive when planted in the fall because it gives the roots time to develop over the winter. You might see small green shoots come up anytime from late fall onward; these are extremely hardy and won't be harmed by winter cold.

Prepare new ground: Prepare for next season's garden expansion by laying down thick layers of newspapers, cardboard, tarps, or mulches to kill grass and weeds. By spring, the sod will be dead and easy to dig in, leaving valuable organic matter in place.

Fall Harvest Notes

Winter squash: Harvest mature winter squash and pie pumpkins when the vines mature (leaves begin to die back, the skin of the squash feels hard, and the stem is shriveled and hardened). Winter squash and pumpkin fruit survive light fall frosts that kill the plants, but if a frost is expected, it is better to cover the plants or harvest the fruit and bring it indoors. Cure the squash for at least ten days in warm dry conditions to seal the skin.

Potatoes: Main crop potatoes are ready in September or when vines start to die back. Harvest on a dry day, and spread the tubers in the sun for a couple of hours to dry, or spread them on newspapers on the floor of a shed. Store the unblemished tubers in cool conditions in complete darkness.

Tomatoes for later: Before a killing frost damages the fruit, pick mature green tomatoes to ripen over the next couple of months. Store them in cool (not cold or refrigerated) conditions and bring a few at a time to room temperature to ripen.

8.11. This is truly backyard bounty! Fall fruit and vegetables are rolling in.

Pears and kiwi fruit: Most winter pears and kiwi fruit are ready to pick from late September to early October. For the best quality and storage ability, don't let the fruit ripen on the tree. Pears are ready to pick when the stem on the fruit snaps cleanly from the twig when the fruit is lifted upward. The skin of the fuzzy kiwi will be brown, without a green tinge; hardy kiwi (the one with small grape-like fruit) remains green, but usually one or two soften on the vine, showing that all the rest are ready to pick.

Preparing for Winter

Stockpile mulches: Collect as many fall leaves as you can. Use them for mulch around plants, and stockpile more in bins to decompose over the winter to make leaf mold. While you are at it, store a supply for next summer's mulch, but keep the leaves dry in plastic bags or in covered bins so they don't decompose. Where residents put out bagged leaves on the curb for pickup, cruise the neighborhood for bags to take home.

8.12. The garlic bed has disappeared under leaf mulch, and more leaves are being laid around the other plants to insulate the roots.

Bales of straw are usually cheaper in the fall than at other times of the year, so it is a good time to buy what you need for next summer's mulch. Leave the bale outside in the rain all winter to begin to break down and allow seeds to sprouts; turn it occasionally to smother seedlings.

Start mulching: For winter vegetables, mulching is not optional! Mulches keep the "shoulders" of root crops from freezing (and then rotting). Mulches also insulate the soil, which prevents wet soil from turning to ice, heaving up the top layers of soil, and tearing the fine roots of plants (called frost heave). Mulch also helps keep the soil warmer, so roots are still able to take up water in cold weather.

Fluffy mulches are best for winter protection: you can use whole leaves, straw, bracken fern, shredded corn stalks, or any other materials you can collect. Start mulching in November by working a 6-inch (15 cm) deep layer of mulch around the base of plants.

8.13. Cabbage family plants are top heavy and need support to prevent winter winds from breaking their necks.

Organize crop covers: For most of the winter on the coast, above-ground vegetables will be fine in the garden without covers. In the coldest gardens and when there is the occasional cold snap (below 23°F/–5°C), however, be prepared to cover leafy greens. They will survive with less damage if they are covered at least temporarily until the weather warms up. For a quick cover, you can use sheets of plastic or tarps weighted down with rocks or boards.

Brace for wind: Fall and winter windstorms on the coast are particularly damaging to cabbage family plants. These big top-heavy plants are easily blown down, especially in the soggy soil. In areas where heavy wet snow falls, the weight of the snow also pulls over leafy plants. Drive three or four garden stakes—such as bamboo, wood, or coated metal flower supports—around each stem to keep the plants from breaking during wind storms. Tomato cages also work if you are careful not to break the plant leaves while installing cages (you can wrap a tea towel around the leaves and gently pull them inward until you work the cage down around the plant).

What to Do Each Month

September

- The first week of September is the last date you can still sow corn salad and winter lettuce in the warmest areas. It is too late to sow anything else, but if you can find transplants to buy, and it is a warm fall, you might grow a small crop of hardy leafy greens. If they don't produce much, leave them in the garden, and they should give you have a head start on the spring season.
- Harvest winter squash (some may have been ready in August) and bring them indoors to cure.
- Dig potatoes when the tops begin to die down.
- Show off your produce at the local agricultural fair.

October

- In early October, pinch growing tips out of Brussels sprout plants to hasten development of sprouts.
- Sow broad beans.
- By early October, harvest winter pears and kiwi fruit.
- Dig mature plants of Swiss chard, leaf beet, kale, and other greens—retaining plenty of soil around the roots—and replant under tunnels or in unheated greenhouses.
- Plant garlic by the end of the month.
- If required to raise the pH, dig agricultural lime into empty beds where vegetables will be planted next spring. This gives the lime more time to start working, but can be done in the spring as well.
- Clear crop debris from the garden, and compost it or chop it up and use as mulch to protect the soil over the winter.
- Cover compost bins and manure piles so they shed rain over the winter.
- Move potted citrus and tender herbs to protected sites. Where more than

2 degrees of frost is likely in the winter, move these plants into an unheated greenhouse or cool sunporch. Where frosts are rare, plants can stay in a sheltered site outdoors, but be prepared to cover them or move them indoors temporarily if there is an unusual cold snap.

November

- Plant fruit trees, grapes, blueberries, and other fruit so roots will become established before spring.
- Cover the soil with a 6-inch (20 cm) layer of mulch around the stems of all overwintering plants.
- Mulch empty garden beds to control weeds and protect the soil from erosion.

Winter (December and January)

For the midwinter months, there is no weeding, watering, sowing, or planting to do, but there *is* the task of protecting crops from extreme weather. And, of course, harvesting continues for fresh salad greens, sweet and crisp carrots, cabbage, Brussels sprouts, and other crops.

8.14. The final layer of mulch over the carrots keeps frost off the shoulders of the root.

Protecting Crops

More mulch: In December (or late November if unusually early cold weather is predicted), add another layer of mulch, especially to beds of root crops. Make sure the roots are well covered up, and at this time, mulch right over top of the foliage. The leaves of celeriac are too tall to cover, so pile mulch well up over the tops of the roots; mulch kohlrabi to well above the bulb.

Temporary covers: The most damaging winter weather is the very rare extreme cold period with high winds and no snow. If temperatures are forecast to drop below 23°F (−5°C), lettuce, spinach, Swiss chard, and other leafy greens will suffer less damage if they are covered. Weight the covers down well with stones or boards because high winds usually accompany the Arctic outbreaks of polar air. Try to keep water or heavy snow from building up on the plastic for too long.

If it looks like it will dip below 14°F (−10°C), it is a good idea to cover winter broccoli and cauliflower and the less hardy varieties of leeks. The hardiest varieties of Brussels sprouts, leeks, as well as corn salad, parsley, and most kales are usually hardy to well below this.

8.15. Midwinter snows aren't daunting the leeks, Brussels sprouts, and root crops (under the snow in the foreground)

8.16. An Arctic outbreak lays low this bed of winter cauliflower and broccoli.

8.17. But wait! A couple of warmer weeks later, the plants have recovered. They produced a fine crop in the spring.

Effects of extreme cold: Occasionally, Arctic outbreaks bring extreme cold: below 5°F (–15°C). Such extreme cold is rare, but if there no snow on the ground, it kills the leaves of leafy greens and lettuce to the ground. This ends your midwinter picking, but don't discard the plants. Beneath the blackened leaves, the roots are usually still alive and likely to sprout a new crop of leaves in the spring.

Effect of snow: Cooler parts of the coastal regions receive occasional snow. Snow actually *protects* plants from low temperatures, but it is usually heavy and wet, so it can break plants, especially leeks and the stems of cabbage family plants. Use broken leeks immediately, before they start to rot at the break point. Leafy greens are flattened by heavy snow, but when the snow melts, they usually spring upright.

Effects of wind: In high winds, well-staked purple sprouting broccoli and winter cauliflower can lose quite a few leaves. They look very ragged, but as long as the main stems aren't broken, they will grow more leaves in the spring and produce a good crop.

Winter Harvest Notes

Above-ground vegetables: The main thing to remember about harvesting above-ground vegetables is not to pick while plants are frozen (unless they are going immediately into a cooked dish). Wait until they thaw out in a warm spell. This applies to leafy greens as well as leeks, Brussels sprouts, and other cabbage family plants. It may take cabbages up to a week to thaw completely inside. If you harvest while plants are frozen, they thaw into mush, but they will be fine if you allow the plants to thaw out in the garden and take up water again before harvesting.

To get the most from a bed of leafy greens, pick one or two outer leaves from every plant. This method of light overall harvesting allows each plant to retain the maximum leaf area to continue growth. Inner leaves are the hardiest, so continually using the outer leaves before they are damaged by frost ensures there is little waste over the season.

As leafy greens are harvested through the winter, the plants get smaller and smaller because there is hardly any replacement growth. Don't worry about

8.18. These greens are frozen right now, so wait until they thaw before picking them.

8.19. A January harvest of perfect roots.

nibbling them down to the smallest leaves, however, because growth begins to speed up in February with the first warm days.

Root vegetables: Even if you have to quarry through layers of snow to dig carrots, beets, celeriac, and other roots, they will be in perfect condition if they were well-mulched. Root vegetables keep well in the refrigerator, so choose a day with good weather and dig several weeks' supply at once (mark where to start digging next time).

What to Do Each Month

December

- Put a another thicker layer of mulch on beds, including right over the tops of root crops.
- Be ready to cover above-ground crops if an Arctic outbreak of extremely cold air is forecast.
- It is too late to start other vegetables, but it is never too late to start planning for next winter.

January

- Yahoo! Another garden year begins, and it is time to dream over seed catalogs (see Resources section for regional seed suppliers, p. 355). Ask other gardeners what grew well for them.
- Review your own garden notes from last year. Use them to plan the location of crops you want to rotate.
- If you will be starting your own seedlings, now is a good time to clean reusable pots and flats; buy or make your seedling soil mix.
- Starting in late January and continuing through February, prune fruit trees and bushes, grapes, and kiwi vines.
- US gardeners: On January 30, celebrate National Seed Swap Day. If you can't find a local event to participate in, organize one yourself!

CHAPTER 9

Managing Pests and Problems

Although you are probably concerned about pests in your garden, in my experience, more plant damage is caused by something wrong with the growing environment than by pests or diseases. Of course, that assumes your garden is well-protected from deer and rabbits!

The advantage of organic gardening, based as it is on building healthy soil, is that it produces healthy, resilient plants. By minimizing the use of insecticides and by planting to attract beneficial insects, organic gardeners can count on substantial help from the many insects that feed on pests. In fact, the more your food garden resembles a natural ecosystem—with mixed plantings and mulched soil—the easier gardening becomes.

Among the many possible insects and diseases that can occur, few regularly plague vegetables and fruit crops on the coast. In any one garden, you will likely see only a handful of these problems, and most can be prevented, once you know what you are dealing with.

Prevention

Prevention is the key. It is the first line of defense against insect pests, diseases, weeds, mammals, and other pests. Preventative methods are safe, mostly cheap, and they do a good job of avoiding damage altogether. Many provide solutions that last for the whole growing season. Here are some examples:

- Covering plants with insect netting or floating row covers to stop insects from laying eggs.
- Planting varieties that are resistant to diseases.
- Mulching the soil to prevent weeds from coming up.

Growing healthy plants is part of prevention because they are less susceptible to disease and more likely to survive pest attack and quickly replace damaged leaves.

Plants become stressed when they don't get enough sunlight, water, or nutrients. Sometimes there is no shortage of any of these in the environment, but conditions that the gardener can control, such as acid soil or poor drainage, prevent plants from getting what they need.

Another aspect of prevention working in favor of home gardeners is the fact that we grow so many different kinds of plants in a small area. Quite the opposite of a grower with a huge field of one vegetable, which gives the pests of that crop an unlimited supply of food. Insects and disease organisms stick to their particular host plants, so the mixed plantings in a small garden limit their ability to spread. For example, even if every one of your carrots were damaged by carrot rust fly, you could still have fine beets, onions, radishes, and other roots, because they are not acceptable food for that particular pest.

9.1. A typically mixed garden, from corn, apples, asparagus, leeks, and leafy greens to flowers and herbs, limits food for pests and attracts many beneficial insects.

Basics of Pest Management

Think pests are causing a problem in your garden? Here are some steps to follow that will help you decide whether or not there is a really a problem—and whether you need to (or can) do anything about it.

1. Make sure the problem is correctly identified. If you don't know what the problem is, there is no point in spraying or taking other action. You may *never* know what caused some kinds of the damage. However, because many things that go wrong with plants are caused by poor environmental conditions, you can always work on improving the growing conditions and see what happens.

Whether a problem is caused by insects, disease, or other pests, the cause must first be correctly identified before you can know what controls will work and how to prevent it in future. The use of the bacterial spray BTK (*Bacillus thuringiensis kurstaki*) is a good example: it only infects caterpillars, which are the immature stage of moths and butterflies. It doesn't affect other pests, including the sawfly larvae that look just like caterpillars. So, reaching for the BTK will do no good if your problem is sawflies.

The following individual entries describe the most common pests of food plants in this region, but not every problem that could possibly occur. To help identify problems, I have put an extensive database of photos on my website covering pests, diseases, disorders, and also beneficial insects. Other places to look for help (see Resources section for details):

- reference books and websites, especially ministries of agriculture (Canada) and university cooperative extension departments (US)
- local Master Gardeners
- gardener hotlines for phone queries and online forums
- experienced staff at local garden centers

You may be able to email photos to someone to help with identification (much better than a verbal description!). If you can't take a specimen to a Master Gardener clinic or a garden center for identification, bringing photos on your tablet or phone is the next best thing. Make sure photos are in focus and as close-up as possible.

2. Keep an eye on the problem. Regularly checking on a problem after you notice it can tell you whether it is getting worse or not and help in identification. People often notice leaf damage, for example, only after the critter that did the chewing has finished feeding and crawled away. By checking on the plants for several days, especially looking at the new growth, you can tell if fresh injury is occurring. If you don't see new damage, there is no point in spraying. You can, however, note the date when you first saw the problem. Next year, start looking a few weeks earlier than that for the first signs of damage so you can track down the culprits.

Get a magnifying glass to help you see, and keep notes and take photos so you have a record for next time.

3. Decide whether treatment is needed. It is important to distinguish between the kind of damage that reduces your crop or could kill plants and the kind of damage that doesn't really affect your harvest. A parsleyworm caterpillar chewing on carrot leaves isn't really doing much damage because it isn't attacking the part of the plant you want to eat. Anyway, you might be happy to allow the caterpillar to feed, knowing it will become a beautiful anise swallowtail butterfly. On the other hand, a codling moth caterpillar boring into the center of an apple is directly ruining the crop (though even in this worst case, the good parts of that apple can still be salvaged for applesauce).

What you consider "damage" can be a matter of personal taste and practicality. This is where the home gardener has a great advantage over the commercial grower. Because commercial produce is graded for perfection of appearance, growers control pests that merely do cosmetic damage. Home gardeners, on the other hand, don't need

9.2. Blasting with water works really well to control aphids—if you repeat it a couple of days later to catch the survivors of the first spray before they reproduce.

to waste food that has scars or marks, because they can simply trim off the blemished bit and use the rest. After all, how perfect does the skin of an apple need to be if the apple is fated to become apple pie?

The size of a pest population should also be considered in deciding whether you need to take action. Pests are naturally kept in check by weather conditions, natural enemies, and other factors. In certain years, some pests appear in high numbers; in other years, numbers are naturally low or nonexistent. It is by no means certain that a small infestation of insects will grow or that a disease you see on a few leaves will spread; the problem may die out. By regularly checking, you will be able to see whether the problem is getting worse.

4. Use least toxic and non-toxic controls. Many effective methods for managing pests do not involve using pesticides. Even the "safe" pesticides are best avoided if possible because they can also harm beneficial organisms. Your toolbox of non-toxic controls includes:

- **Physical controls:** These measures remove pests or kill them directly. For example, blasting aphids off plants with water sprays, pruning out diseased branches, picking off leaves that have insect eggs, or mulching to smother weeds are all physical ways to control problems.
- **Biological controls:** Most insect pests have natural enemies that can be relied on to keep numbers down to non-damaging levels. Birds are important predators of insects, especially in the spring when they are feeding chicks, but most insects are kept in check by other insects and spiders. You can increase the number of beneficial insects in your garden by planting flowers that attract them (see below).
- **Pesticides:** Most pesticides are chemicals (though a few contain microorganisms). Low-risk pesticides contain low-toxicity chemicals, such as soaps or compounds extracted from plants. These are only "safe" from the human point of view, of course, not for beneficial insects or other creatures. Most pesticides made from plants and other natural sources are permitted for use by certified organic growers, but with certain restrictions.

Some people make homemade mixtures on the assumption that these are safer than commercial pesticides. This is a mistake! Ingredients, such as soap, oil, salt, or mouthwash that don't harm people, can damage or kill the plants you spray them on. And remember that any mixture that actually works to control pests will also work to kill beneficial organisms, such as the insects that eat the pests or the "good" fungi that control disease-causing fungi.

The best thing you can do is avoid using pesticides of any kind. When some type of action is called for, try non-pesticidal methods first, and use pesticides as a last resort. You can minimize the harm from pesticides by choosing the least toxic product that will do the job. For example, if insecticidal soap will work, use that instead of pyrethrins (a nerve toxin extracted from pyrethrum daisies), which are more toxic and last longer on leaves. If you are spraying insecticides, spray only the plants, or parts of plants, that need treatment. Spraying where it isn't required isn't just a waste of time and money; it also needlessly harms other organisms and can leave an odor that repels beneficial insects from returning to the leaves.

The range of pesticides that home gardeners can use is now very restricted throughout British Columbia. A 2016 change to the provincial regulations limits what unlicensed people can buy to a specific list of least toxic products. Generally, these are considered safe for people without pesticide training to use, but that still doesn't mean the products are safe for non-target organisms. In the pest entries below, I have only included recommendations for pesticides that are acceptable for organic growers and for home gardeners living in British Columbia.

5. Follow up. Whether you take action or not, keep checking on the pest situation, and keep making notes. Your notes will tell you when problems appeared or disappeared, and how

Currantworm Control by the Calendar

Imported currantworm eggs look like white stitches along the veins on the underside of leaves. Because I wrote down when I first saw them on my red currant bush in previous years, I now know when to look for them. My records show eggs are laid on my bushes during the last two weeks of April. It only takes me a few minutes to pick off the leaves with eggs on them ensuring that the currantworms don't have a chance to do any damage.

Imported currantworm eggs on the underside of leaves. Pick them off now and the currantworms won't have a chance to do any damage.

well your approach worked. If you know when to expect a particular pest, you can prepare to deal with it while the infestation is still small or to prevent the problem altogether.

Attracting Beneficial Insects

There are thousands of species of native predatory and parasitic insects on the coast. You can benefit from these free pest control agents by attracting them to a garden that is safe (without insecticides) and hospitable (provides the adults with food).

9.3. Tiny bright orange aphid midge larvae are killing these aphids. The adult midges came into the garden looking for nectar flowers and stayed to lay eggs among the aphids.

The Lives of Insects

All insects start as an egg, which hatches into an immature insect called a *larva* (plural: larvae). When a larva grows to full size, it moults and becomes a *pupa*. Pupae are immobile and most look like oval brown cases, often protected by a cocoon of silk. Inside the pupa, the larva transforms into an adult insect, which eventually emerges and flies away. A familiar example is a caterpillar, which spins a chrysallis (a silken cover to protect the pupa) and changes into a butterfly inside. A complete life cycle can take a week (fruit flies) to several years (wireworms). Other terms are also used for larvae: caterpillars (larvae of butterflies and moths), maggots (flies), and grubs (beetles, wasps, bees).

A minority of insects, such as aphids, stink bugs, and earwigs, develop gradually without going through a pupa stage. Their larvae (also called *nymphs*), look more like an adult each time they moult. After the last moult, they are mature adults with reproductive organs and usually wings.

All insects have some development stage (often egg or pupa) adapted to survive winter.

9.4. This lady beetle is filling up on food from dill flowers.

For most beneficial insects, it is only the larvae (immature stage) that eat other insects. The adults sip nectar or feed on pollen. But when the adults have pollen and nectar to eat, they stick around, live longer, and the females lay more eggs. When these eggs hatch, the predatory larvae attack your pests. You can lure the parents of these hungry juveniles into your garden by growing flowers to attract them.

What to plant: The most attractive plants to beneficial insects are those that have a rich supply of nectar and pollen in tiny flowers—just the right

Companion Planting: Myth or Reality?

Much has been written about growing particular plants to repel pests, but I am afraid it is mostly wishful thinking. That's because plant-eating insects have an incredibly acute ability to "smell" their target plants, yet little ability to detect irrelevant scents. So an insect that eats cabbage can detect the mustard oil compounds in the leaves, but not necessarily the chemicals found in mint, dill, or other plants often recommended to repel pests.

But it isn't completely bunk: Some companion planting works very well, just not the way you might think. Many plants recommended as companions (those mint or dill plants, for example) are excellent for luring beneficial insects to the garden where they attack pests. While planting garlic is useless to repel aphids, research has shown that planting sweet alyssum works very well to attract aphid-eating insects. So forget the often contradictory companion planting lore and choose the best plants to attract beneficial insects (see Table 9.1).

Table 9.1. Herbs, flowers, and vegetables that have particularly attractive flowers for beneficial insects, including pollinators.

	Annuals and Biennials	Perennials
Herbs	Coriander/cilantro Dill Caraway Fennel Parsley Summer savory	Angelica Catnip Lavender Lemon balm Lovage mints Rosemary Sage Thyme and creeping thymes
Flowers	Calendula Candytuft Coreopsis Cosmos Feverfew Heliotrope Lobelia Mignonette Schizanthus Sweet alyssum	Alyssum Basket-of-gold (Aurinia) Coneflower Daisies Golden marguerite (Anthemis) Goldenrod Rudbeckia Verbena (especially *V. bonariensis*) Yarrow
Vegetables (when allowed to flower)	Chinese greens and mustards Kale Radishes Leeks and onions	

size for the tiny mouthparts. Plants in the carrot, aster, mint, and cabbage families are generally the most useful. Some, such as dill, cilantro, and parsley, are commonly grown in gardens anyway, so they just have to be allowed to flower (parsley will flower the year after planting). When you save seed from vegetables in these families, a great side benefit is that the flowers also feed beneficial insects. Some weeds, such as wild carrot, yarrow, chickweed, and wild mustard, are actually good insect plants too. But you don't have to encourage weeds, of course, as there are many other plants that attract beneficial insects (see Table 9.1).

Plant a few attractive plants among the vegetables or use them as edging plants or elsewhere in a flower border. I like to put a sweet alyssum plant or two in each long garden bed and also in my greenhouse (see p. 227 for photographs) to lure in aphid predators. It is important to try to have something in bloom from early spring to late summer by growing a variety of plants.

Controls for Common Insect Pests

Barriers for Insect Pests

Rather than repeating details on using barriers in individual pest entries in the A to Z Insect Pests and Problems section, I have put the relevant information all together, below.

Used correctly, barriers of all kinds are very effective at excluding pest insects from laying eggs on fruit and vegetables:

- Insect netting is used to cover entire fruit bushes and small trees to exclude apple maggot, currant fruit fly, cherry fruit flies, and spotted wing Drosophila.
- Insect netting or floating row covers are used over vegetable beds to protect carrots from carrot rust fly and cabbage family plants from cabbage root maggot.
- Bags of paper, organza, fine mesh, or sheer curtain materials are used to protect individual fruit or bunches of grapes from insects, birds, and other pests.

Give Your Beneficial Insects a Drink

One more thing you can do to attract beneficial insects is provide them with a safe water supply. They normally sip dew, but there is no dew in the driest part of the summer; with access to drinking water, studies show they live longer and lay more eggs. You can use any type of container as long as insects can't drown in it. A shallow bird bath with a rough surface, or a large clay plant saucer, is ideal. Put sand, gravel, or rocks in the water to provide safe islands for insects to perch on while drinking.

There are two essential rules for using all of these exclusion tools successfully:

- Put barriers in place before the pests show up.
- Ensure there are no gaps that could allow insects to get through the barrier.

Insect Netting

Insect netting products are sturdy, knitted, or woven high-density polyethylene mono-filament fabric designed to keep out insects while letting in over

90% of sunlight. They are sold in different widths and sizes of mesh for different pests. The netting is UV stabilized, and depending on the product, most are guaranteed to last seven to ten years. The fabrics let in rain and irrigation water so covers can stay in place until the attack period is over or the crop has been harvested. Although sheer curtain materials and mosquito netting look similar, they don't let in enough light for plant growth. Such materials could be used briefly, but for no more than two or three weeks.

For seedling beds and vegetables with soft foliage, such as carrots, insect netting should be supported above the plants. The fabric is strong enough to be held up on blunt sticks poked into the soil at the corners and along the center of the bed, or it can be laid over hoops or light frames. The netting is light and strong enough to simply drape over fruit bushes and trees and doesn't catch or tear on branches. Lengths of netting can be wrapped around individual branches

9.5. Insect netting protecting cherries from fruit flies, birds, and even rats.

(such as on a large cherry tree) or draped along rows of bushes to make a large tent. Secure the netting with clips, weight down the bottom edges to hold netting in close contact with the soil, or cinch it into a tree trunk with cord.

You can also use a regular sewing machine to sew insect netting into bags large enough to cover whole fruit trees or bushes. It can be sewn into small bags to cover single fruits or bunches of grapes (instructions on p. 279). Two insect netting products available in the region are:

- ProtekNet comes in a variety of weights, mesh sizes, and widths. Netting with 0.0335 inch (0.85 mm) mesh size or a 0.04 by 0.0236 inch (1.0 × 0.6 mm) mesh size will exclude spotted wing Drosophila. Heavier weight nettings (60 or 80 gr/m² weight) are the most durable. It is not necessary to buy the finest and most expensive mesh (0.0138 inch/0.35 mm).

- Agralan Enviromesh Standard is available online in the US; the mesh size is 0.05 inch (1.35 mm), which keeps out vegetable pests, but may not be fine enough to exclude 100% of spotted wing Drosophila.

Watch for other brands as they become available. Insect netting has been in use for years in Europe and Australia, and more products will find their way here. If you need large amounts, get together with other gardeners and order a roll from a wholesaler.

Floating Row Covers

These lightweight spun-bonded poly fabrics were invented to extend the growing season, but have been used for decades to prevent insects, such as cabbage root maggot and carrot rust fly, from laying eggs on vegetables. The fabric lets

9.6. Insect netting protects a bed of carrots from carrot rust fly attack.

in sunlight and water, so the covers can stay in place until harvest. It is light enough to float on foliage without requiring supports and lets in enough light that the covers can be left on for long periods. Floating row covers work well on vegetables beds but tear too easily to be useful on fruit trees and bushes. Thicker grades last longer, but exclude more light than the lightweight grades. For fruit, if you can't get the more durable insect netting, use floating row covers, but be careful to repair rips. Insects can find the smallest holes!

These fabrics were invented to hold in heat; therefore, they are not ideal for use in the hot weather. The lightest-weight fabrics trap less heat than heavier weights, but in a heat wave, it would be a good idea to lay shade cloth (see p. 114) on top of floating row covers to cool the plants.

Fruit Bags

Putting bags over apples and other large fruit makes a very effective barrier. Bags take time to install initially, but protect fruit from many insects at once, including fruit flies, codling moth, yellow-jackets, and stink bugs, as well as from birds and rodents. Bagged fruit is also very high quality. You can buy bags or sew them from insect netting or lightweight fabric (instructions on p. 279).

Organza gift bags: These are quick to install and work well on apples, figs, and bunches of grapes. They can be used for fruit with very short stems, such as peaches and some apple varieties. They are inexpensive from online wholesalers (but costly if bought retail). So far, mine have lasted for three seasons, though some have needed the ribbon drawstring replaced with more durable cord.

Paper bags: White or translucent bakery bags (for smaller fruit) or #2 size small brown lunch bags (for apples and pears) are cheap

9.7. Organza gift bags used to protect apples from codling moth and apple maggot.

and hold up well enough for a season, though they are quite fiddly to install. One method is to cut a 1- to 2-inch slit in the bottom of the bag, just large enough to fit over one fruit. Slip the slit over the fruit and straighten the bag so that the edges of the slit close against the twig. Staple or tape shut the edges of the open end of the bag to leave a pocket large enough for a mature fruit. Another method, for fruit with longer stems (such as pears): slip the open mouth of the bag over the fruit, pinch it together around the fruit stem, and staple it closed. If using opaque bags, removing them one to two weeks before harvest allows the color to develop on red varieties of apples. This is not necessary if you used translucent bags, or for green varieties of apples or other kinds of fruit.

Japanese fruit bags: Special fruit bags have been used for many years by Asian orchardists. The bags are made of a double layer of paper with an integral twist tie and are quick to install. Home gardeners in the US can buy Japanese fruit bags online.

Other bag materials: I tested plastic sandwich bags but found some of the apples had sunscald injury. Although some sources promote using nylon sockettes or "footies," studies show that codling moths and other insects can lay their eggs right through the thin stretchy fabric. Some recommend soaking the sockettes in kaolin clay (Surround®) before installing, but what a mess!

Exclusion Fences for Root Flies

Most adult cabbage maggot or carrot rust flies fly less than a yard above the ground, so a large proportion of them can be kept from reaching a crop by installing a mesh fence as a barrier. Although not as effective as covering beds with insect netting or floating row covers, exclusion fences can give adequate control for a home garden in areas where root fly populations are not high to start with. String a 40-inch-tall (1 m) fence of nylon window screen around the vegetable bed, with the bottom edge buried in the soil. Support the fence on stakes and allow the top 12 inches (30 cm) of the screening to fold and extend outward, away from the growing bed, to make a wide overhang. When the flies reach the fence and fly upwards, the overhang helps deflect them from flying over the top and into the bed. Exclusion fences do allow some flies to get into the crop (it is thought they crawl over the fence). Fewer carrot rust flies appear to be deflected by such fences than species that attack onions or cabbage.

Having tried exclusion fences, I have to say they are a real pain to construct and don't provide perfect control. Covering beds with insect netting is much easier and 100% effective if installed correctly, though there is a "laundry-on-the-garden" look to them that isn't great. Regardless of which method you use, be sure to rotate crops to make sure there are no root maggots in the soil from a previous crop.

Table 9.2. Least toxic pesticides acceptable for use in organic food gardens. Some products containing these active ingredients are certified for organic growing and some are not. Check product labels for OMRI certification if that is a requirement.

Active Ingredient	Pests	Mode of Action and Environmental Impact	Notes on Use
Insects			
Bacillus thuringiensis kurstaki (BTK)	Leaf-eating caterpillars.	Contains bacterial spores and protein crystals that infect and kill caterpillars. Non-toxic to other insects, animals, and people. Non-persistent; breaks down in a few days in sunlight.	Spray foliage while caterpillars are actively feeding. Caterpillars stop feeding immediately but may not die for 2–5 days.
Horticultural (Supreme) dormant oils	Overwintering eggs of aphids and some moth species; scale insects.	Contains highly refined petroleum oil or vegetable oils. Acts on contact, by suffocating, by toxicity, or by repelling insects. Sprays kill beneficial mites and insects; once residues dry, the sprayed area is safe for beneficial species.	If pests were present on trees in summer, spray deciduous trees and bushes when trees are dormant. Check label for list of plants that cannot tolerate oil sprays.
Horticultural (Supreme) summer oils	Soft brown scale, spider mites, whiteflies; also powdery mildew.	As above.	Use on shrubs and trees such as citrus, during the growing season, but not in hot weather. Check label for list of plants that cannot tolerate oil sprays.

Table 9.2. (cont'd.) Least toxic pesticides acceptable for use in organic food gardens.

Active Ingredient	Pests	Mode of Action and Environmental Impact	Notes on Use
Insecticidal soaps	Aphids and other sucking insects, caterpillars.	Contains biodegradable fatty acids. Acts on contact against insects and mites, including beneficial species. Once residues dry, the sprayed area is safe for beneficial insects. Residues of soap sprays can repel aphid predators from laying eggs among aphids on previously sprayed leaves.	Thorough spraying is required and repeat applications are usually necessary. Limit the number of times soap is applied to the same foliage, as it can damage leaves. Check label for plants injured by soap sprays.
Kaolin clay	Apple maggot, codling moth (1st generation), overwintering leafroller moths.	A mineral-based particle film. Sprays leave a barrier of fine white dust on fruit and leaves, which repels insects from laying eggs.	It is not toxic and can be used up to day of harvest, but is a white residue that has to be washed off fruit.
Pyrethrins	Flea beetles, other crawling and flying insects.	Active ingredients are extracted from pyrethrum daisies. Kills and repels beneficial insects. Toxins on sprayed leaves break down in a few days. Moderate human toxicity: avoid inhalation or contact with skin and eyes; can cause allergic reactions.	A last-resort pesticide due to toxicity to beneficial insects.
Spinosad	Leafrollers and other leaf-eating caterpillars.	Natural compound extracted from a rare soil microorganism. Fast-acting; remains active up to 4 weeks once sprayed on leaves. Highly toxic to bees and parasitic insects at time of spraying; low risk to beneficial insects once spray residues dry.	Do not apply to squash family plants. Limit the number of applications to any one plant to 3 times per year (fewer for some products according to labels). Avoid spray drift to water bodies.

Table 9.2. (cont'd.) Least toxic pesticides acceptable for use in organic food gardens.

Active Ingredient	Pests	Mode of Action and Environmental Impact	Notes on Use
Azadirachtin, Neem oil	Powdery mildew; aphids and other sucking insects, leaf-eating caterpillars.	Active ingredients derived from neem tree. Controls some plant disease fungi; repels chewing and sucking insects, also suffocates insects. Low toxicity, low environmental impact. Once dry, the sprayed area is safe for beneficial insects to contact.	Not persistent; reapply after a couple of days. More effective on immature insects than on adults. *Not registered for use in Canada at this time.*
Diseases			
Bacillus subtilis	Leaf diseases, powdery and downy mildews, *Botrytis*, also root rot fungi and club-root of cabbage. Not effective on leaf rusts.	Contains common soil bacteria that attack fungi on leaves. In the soil, the bacteria form a protective barrier around roots; US product is registered for control of some root rot fungi in soil, including clubroot of cabbage.	Apply at first sign of infection and at 7–10 day intervals. Used as a root dip or soil drench for root disease.
Sulfur	Many fungus diseases, including powdery mildew, rusts, apple scab; also controls spider mites.	Sulfur particles bind with fungus spores to prevent germination. Provides broad-spectrum control of fungi, also mites. Low toxicity to mammals, bees, birds, but toxic to beneficial mites. Once dry, the sprayed area is safe for beneficial insects.	Use only on plants tolerant to sulfur; can burn leaves of some plants (check label for list of plants).
Lime sulfur	Fungal diseases; also scales, mites, aphids on fruit trees.	Contains a calcium sulfur compound. Moderate toxicity to mammals, bees, birds; toxic to beneficial mites. Once dry, the sprayed area is safe for beneficial insects.	Use on deciduous fruit trees at 90% leaf drop in the fall, before buds swell in spring, or as midwinter dormant spray (can be mixed with dormant oil sprays). Will injure leaves of most plants. Use during growing season on plants as listed on label.

Table 9.2. (cont'd.) Least toxic pesticides acceptable for use in organic food gardens.

Active Ingredient	Pests	Mode of Action and Environmental Impact	Notes on Use
Bicarbonate, potassium or sodium	Powdery mildew.	Acts on contact to kill fungi. Low toxicity and low environmental impact.	Start applying at first sign of disease and every 1–2 weeks thereafter. *Not registered for use in Canada at this time.*
Fixed coppers: Tribasic copper sulfate, copper oxychloride sulfate. Not copper sulfate in British Columbia	Bacterial leaf spot, powdery mildew, and other plant diseases.	Moderate toxicity, but repeated use can build up toxic levels in soil. Remains active on the leaves 1–2 weeks after spraying. Highly toxic to fish and aquatic organisms. Fixed coppers are less toxic and persistent in the environment than copper sulfate.	Many plants are sensitive to copper (read labels), but fewer are affected by fixed copper than by copper sulfate. Avoid spray drift or runoff to water bodies. Copper sulfate (used in "Bordeaux mixture") is registered in Canada, but no longer allowed for use in BC by home gardeners due to high toxicity and long persistence.
Slugs			
Ferric (iron) phosphate bait; Ferric sodium EDTA bait	Slugs and snails.	Iron mixed in a granular bait attracts mollusks. Metal ions cause them to stop feeding, dry up, and die in 3–6 days. Non-toxic to people, pets, birds, insects, earthworms, and other wildlife. Remains active for a week.	Broadcast small amount of bait widely over the area. Do not surround plants with a ring of bait, as it attracts slugs to feed on the surrounded plant. Replace after prolonged heavy rain.

Note: There are too many products to name; therefore, I have only listed the active ingredient in the pesticide, which is listed in fine print on the label after "Guarantee." Always read and follow instructions on product labels.

A to Z Pests and Problems

Now, don't panic at the following list of possible disasters! Damage from most of them is preventable, and you may never see most of these. The worst threat to your harvest may actually come from the animals listed in the final section under Vertebrates (birds, deer, etc.).

Common Insects and Other Organisms
Aphids (many different species)
What to look for: Tiny pear-shaped insects, 0.1 to 0.2 inches (2 to 4 mm) long, clustered together in dense colonies on undersides of leaves or tips of young shoots. Colors range from light green to yellowish, pink, mahogany brown, or powdery gray.

Biology: Aphids suck plant sap, which distorts leaves, shoots, and flowers. They secrete "honeydew," which coats foliage with a sticky layer. Most species of aphids are adapted to feed on only certain host plants (e.g., rose aphids stick to roses, bean aphids to beans).

Management: Most aphids are naturally controlled by beneficial insects: lady beetles, aphid midges, hover flies, parasitic wasps, and many others. Planting flowers that attract aphid predators (see Table 9.1) can make a big difference in how quickly they control aphids in your garden. If natural enemies don't act fast enough, try spraying aphids with a strong stream of water.

9.8. Spring aphid control in greenhouse peppers: Sweet alyssum flowers attract syrphid flies, one of which is laying eggs (*top*); syrphid fly eggs among the aphids (*middle*); the same leaf a week later with two syrphid larvae and no aphids (*bottom*).

Credit: E. Cronin

9.9. Aphids of all ages.

This is quite effective if done twice, two to four days apart, to ensure that survivors of the first blast are knocked off before they can reproduce. Squashing aphids with your fingers or spraying them with soap, pyrethrins, or neem (azadirachtin) also kills aphids, but both methods also kill beneficial insects that are nearly always present, hidden under the aphids, by the time you spray. The insecticides also act as repellents to beneficial insects, which avoid laying their eggs on sprayed leaves even after aphids reappear, ultimately making aphid problems worse.

Apple Maggot (*Rhagoletes pomonella*)

What to look for: Dimples show in the skin of infested fruit. The maggots are usually discovered when fruit is cut open and their thin brown tunnels are visible in the flesh of the apple. Infested fruit quickly rots and becomes unusable.

Biology: Adult flies emerge from the soil in early summer. Females lay eggs singly beneath the skin of apples, crabapples, and hawthorn fruits (and sometimes plum and cherry) from July to early October. Eggs hatch in a week, and the maggots tunnel into the flesh of fruit. Mature larvae feed for two to four weeks, then leave the fruit to pupate in the soil, where they also overwinter. There is one generation per year.

Management: Always comply with local quarantines for this pest: it is illegal to carry backyard or non-commercial tree fruit into apple maggot-free areas of British Columbia, eastern and central Washington, and Oregon. Collect and destroy dropped apples every few days to prevent maggots in the apples from exiting to pupate in the soil. Place infested fruit in a sealed plastic bag and dispose of it or freeze the fruit to kill the maggots, then bury or compost it. Remove and destroy fruit from unmanaged or wild trees before August, including apple, crabapple, and hawthorn (better yet, remove unmanaged trees).

Bagging apples or covering entire dwarf trees with insect netting (See Barriers, p. 218) is a very effective way to prevent apple maggot damage. Remove and destroy any unprotected fruit outside the barriers. Sprays of kaolin clay (e.g., Surround at Home®) leave a barrier of fine white dust on fruit and leaves, which repels apple maggot adults from laying eggs. It is non-toxic, but there is a white residue that has to be washed off after harvest. Pyrethrins and spinosad sprays can be used by organic growers. To time pesticide applications correctly, use traps starting in June to monitor populations of apple maggot flies. Gardeners using traps for this purpose should learn where to place traps and how to identify apple maggot adults, because the traps catch other similar-looking insects.

Commercial or homemade apple maggot traps, consisting of red balls coated with sticky insect glue, can be used to catch adult flies. Some sources suggest hanging several traps in a small tree can reduce apple maggot numbers (it won't get them all), but others are not so optimistic (plus, sticky traps are also known to catch small birds). Commercial traps usually have a lure containing ammonia or fruit essences to improve attractiveness.

Beet and Spinach Leafminers (*Pegomya* spp.)

What to look for: Brown blotches on leaves of spinach, Swiss chard, beets, French sorrel, rhubarb, and related plants. These are caused by maggots (immature stage of the leafminer flies) feeding inside the leaves.

Biology: The flies lay tiny chalky-white cylindrical eggs in small parallel groups on the underside of leaves. When the eggs hatch, the small white maggots burrow between the upper and lower surface of the leaf, leaving behind blotchy "mines." They feed for two to three weeks, then exit the leaf and drop to the soil to pupate. There are two or three generations each season.

9.10. Leafminer eggs on the underside of a Swiss chard leaf.

9.11. Leafminer damage on a beet leaf looks like a brown blotch.

Credit: E. Cronin

Management: In light infestations, pick off the few blotchy areas on the leaves. When you see eggs laid on Swiss chard (they are not hard to see), you can harvest all of the large leaves at once and wash off the eggs. By the time the next crop of leaves grows again, that generation of flies is largely over. Don't do this on beets because removing the leaves stunts roots. Lady beetles and other predators eat leafminer eggs or pick apart the mines and pull out the maggots.

Where leafminer infestations are severe every year, cover beds with insect netting or floating row covers before the seeds come up to stop the flies from laying eggs on leaves. Sprays don't work because the insects feed within the leaves where sprays don't reach them.

Cabbage Maggot (*Delia radicum*)

What to look for: Plants in the cabbage family wilt in the midday sun despite being well-watered. The maggots are hard to see inside the roots, but distorted roots with tunnels in them are obvious in turnips and other cabbage family root crops. Low numbers of cabbage maggots may only stunt plants; higher numbers kill plants.

Biology: The first generation of flies emerges in early spring from pupae that overwintered in the soil. They lay eggs on the soil beside the stems of plants, starting in April. Larvae feed in the roots for about three weeks. The next generation of adults appears in early July. There are two or three generations per year. Generations later in the summer overlap, so egg-laying is continuous.

Management: In some years, crops planted after mid-June may escape severe damage because their roots are well-established by the time the summer generation of maggots appears. For plants that have been attacked but not killed, water well, and they may survive to produce a small crop.

There are no controls once the maggots reach the roots. The best approach is using barriers to prevent flies from laying eggs on plants. Cover beds of small plants, such as radishes or Chinese cabbage, with insect netting or floating row covers (see Barriers, p. 218) until harvest and to protect seedlings of larger plants until they are large enough for a barrier around the stem. Cover seedbeds at planting time, making sure the edges of the fabric are held tight to the soil, and leave the covers on until the crop is harvested or until late October, whichever comes first. Look under the cover occasionally to weed and thin seedlings (replace it the same day).

Protect individual plants, such as broccoli and cabbage, by placing barriers around the stem at transplant time or when you remove row covers to thin seedlings to the final spacing. Make these from 6-inch (15 cm) squares or circles of durable, flexible material (e.g., heavy waxed paper, heavy plastic bags, thin foam sheets, woven feed bags, several layers of newspaper). Cut a slit to the center of the square from one side; if the material is fairly stiff, cut a tiny X at the center to accommodate the stem. Slip the barrier around the stem of the transplant so the paper lies flat on the soil with the stem at the center X, fitting *snugly* at the base of the stem. Anchor the barrier with a stone to keep the slit closed and flat; leave barrier in place all season (apply mulch on top of the barrier).

9.12. Individual barriers around the stems prevent adult cabbage maggot flies from laying eggs.

9.13. Typical damage from carrot rust fly with a maggot visible near the root tip.

Carrot Rust Fly (*Psila rosae*)

What to look for: Carrot roots have tunnels filled with crumbly, rusty brown material. Tiny white maggots, up to ¼ inch (8 mm) long may be visible in the tunnels.

Biology: Adult flies emerge from mid-April to mid-May and lay eggs on the soil beside the stems of carrot family plants. When the eggs hatch, the maggots feed on roots for three to four weeks. The first generation of flies emerges throughout June. The second generation emerges from mid-July to mid-August and lays eggs into the fall. In the warmest areas and in years with a long warm fall, there can be a third generation in September–October. The maggots overwinter in the roots, and the pupae overwinter in the top layer of soil.

Management: This is a serious pest of carrots on the West Coast, especially where wild carrot (Queen Anne's lace) is common. In some areas, spring-planted carrots escape significant damage, but later plantings may be seriously injured. If rust flies are allowed to lay eggs on carrots sown in early July for winter harvest, the maggots will burrow in the roots all winter.

Delay sowing spring carrots until mid-May to avoid the overwintered generation. Carrots harvested before mid-July generally escape attack by maggots from second-generation flies. Covering beds with insect netting or floating row covers at seeding time provides the most reliable control (see Barriers, p. 218). The covers can be removed at the end of October, when flies are no longer laying eggs.

Codling Moth (*Cydia pomonella*)

What to look for: Apple and pears (sometimes walnuts, crab apples, or peaches) with a small hole in the fruit plugged with brown crumbly droppings. When the fruit is cut open, the dark track the caterpillar made boring into the core is obvious. Sometimes a pale pink or cream-colored caterpillar is visible inside.

Biology: Moths emerge about the time apples bloom. They lay eggs on the developing fruit or on leaves or twigs nearby. Caterpillars hatch in one to three weeks and immediately bore into the developing fruit, usually around the blossom end. They feed in the core for about a month, then crawl out of the fruit and down the tree trunk to spin a cocoon. Caterpillars pupate under loose bark or soil at the base of the tree, and most emerge in two weeks to lay eggs for the second generation in July and August. In the warmest areas and years, there may be a partial third generation in September.

Management: Where codling moth numbers are generally low to moderate, strict sanitation to destroy infested fruit as soon as it is seen may provide sufficient control, especially if combined with bagging fruit (see Barriers, p. 218). Starting when apples are the size of marbles, thin them to one fruit per cluster and 6 inches (15 cm) apart. Continue checking weekly, destroying every fruit with a tiny entrance hole filled with crumbly brown droppings (for best results, cut the fruit open and kill the caterpillar inside). Also, pick up dropped fruit immediately (same day) and destroy it. Soak fruit in soapy water for at least a

9.14. Codling moth exit holes and damage inside an apple.

week to kill larvae. Fruit bags provide good protection if installed before the moths lay eggs. This works best on early varieties; some moths may have already laid eggs before late apple varieties are large enough to bag. Install bags on apples and pears when the fruit is smaller than a nickel, usually at the same time fruit is thinned. Remove any unbagged fruit and destroy it. Tree bands can help reduce the number of caterpillars surviving to make a second generation. Starting in June, wrap bands of corrugated cardboard, 6 to 12 inches (15 to 30 cm) wide, around trunks and staple in place after scraping off as much loose bark as possible. Check every week and destroy cocoons and caterpillars found in or under the band; continue until September. If you are not vigilant in checking and destroying caterpillars, tree bands can actually increase the survival of later generations (which is why some experts don't recommend them for home gardeners). Kaolin clay (see Table 9.2) is a non-toxic spray that repels moths from laying eggs. It can give good results if combined with sanitation to destroy infested fruit. Spray kaolin when fruit is dime-sized, repeating every seven days as needed to maintain coverage as fruit and new leaves develop.

To control high populations (i.e., over 75% of fruit infested), spinosad insecticide sprays (see Table 9.2) are an option for organic growers. Timing is critical because insecticides are effective only for the short time after eggs hatch, before caterpillars burrow into fruit; once inside they are safe from insecticides. Starting a month after bloom, check fruit for tiny entrance holes, and spray immediately when one is found (also continue to remove and destroy infested fruit). Spray up to two more times, seven to ten days apart. Note that the number of spinosad sprays allowed per season is limited to three times for products currently registered in Canada (more for some US products). Spinosad must not be applied to fruit within seven days of harvest, and it is very toxic to bees. Sprays of soap, pyrethrins, or BTK (*Bacillus thuringiensis kurstaki*) do not work on codling moth.

Codling moth traps are available, but it is important to know that these sticky traps only lure male codling moth by mimicking the pheromones given off by female moths to attract mates. The traps do not directly control codling moth populations (since they don't catch female moths), but one trap in a home orchard can be used to time spraying of kaolin or spinosad. Check traps weekly, and start sprays when two moths have been caught in the trap for two weeks in a row.

Cutworms and Climbing Cutworms

What to look for: Overnight, young plants are chewed off at the soil line and small seedlings disappear. Climbing cutworms chew large ragged holes in leaves, sometimes well above the ground. To distinguish cutworm damage from slug damage, look for silvery slime trails (slugs) or pellets of dark excrement caught on the leaves (cutworms). The fat gray, tan, or greenish caterpillars curl into a characteristic C-shape when disturbed.

Biology: In early spring and sometimes late fall, cutworms feed at night on plants. A recent, but now widespread, invader is the large yellow underwing moth. This climbing cutworm is particularly damaging to winter vegetables because they are very cold hardy and feed during warm spells in winter through to spring. Cutworms hide in leaf litter or in the upper layers of soil during the day.

Management: Where plants show damage, look under them for the fat caterpillars in the leaf litter or just under the soil. They are easier to find just after dark; take a flashlight and search for climbing cutworms on plant leaves. Where other species of cutworms are chewing plants off at the soil line, protect transplants with a collar around the stem. Make them of light cardboard, 4 inches (10 cm) wide, or use small tin cans with lids and bottoms removed. Push the collar at least 1 inch (2 cm) deep into the soil. This collar does not stop *climbing* cutworms because they just climb right over it.

Credit: E. Cronin

9.15. An adult moth and a caterpillar with typical damage from the, unfortunately, now common, large yellow underwing moth.

9.16. Early spring damage from climbing cutworms. Suddenly, a lot of leaf area is chewed up overnight, but there is no sign of the culprit (it is hiding in the soil or under leaf litter).

9.17. Tuber flea beetle damage on potato leaves.

Flea Beetle, Tuber (*Epitrix tuberis*)

What to look for: Tiny round holes or pits punched in leaves of potato, tomato, and related plants early in the season. Tiny ¹⁄₁₆-inch-long (1 to 2 mm) shiny black beetles quickly jump from leaves (making them very hard to catch). Shallow dark brown pits and marks just under the skin of potato tubers (from feeding by larvae).

Biology: Adults emerge mid-May to early June and lay eggs in the soil for a month. Larvae feed on the plant roots for three weeks, then pupate. There are two or three generations per year. The last generation, which feeds from mid-August onward, is most damaging to potato tubers. On large plants, leaf damage from adult feeding is merely unsightly. The main damage is from larvae in the roots.

Management: Destroy all volunteer potato plants because they give overwintered flea beetles a head start on building damaging numbers in early spring. Plant early varieties of potatoes as early in the season as possible; they escape serious injury if harvested before the largest generation of flea beetles starts feeding on tubers in late August. Where flea beetles are a common problem, cover susceptible crops with insect netting to keep adults from feeding and laying eggs. On potatoes, do this before sprouts emerge from the soil; cover tomatoes at the time of transplanting. If there are large numbers of flea beetles attacking small plants, spray pyrethrins to control adults on leaves.

Flea Beetle, Cabbage/Crucifer (*Phyllotreta* spp.)

What to look for: Many tiny round "shot-holes" in leaves of cabbage family plants, also sometimes on spinach, beets, and lettuce, and occasionally other plants.

Biology: Adults overwinter in shrubby areas and leaf litter around gardens. They lay eggs around the roots of plants from May to early July. Larvae feed in roots for another six weeks or more. New adults emerge from late July onward and feed on leaves until fall, but they do not lay more eggs. Most flea beetle species that feed on cabbage family plants have a one-year life cycle, although there may be a second generation in warm areas and years.

Management: Large numbers of flea beetles attacking small seedlings or leafy greens can be very damaging. Damage to larger plants and those with waxy leaves, such as broccoli and cabbage, is usually not serious, but larvae tunneling in roots seriously damage radishes, turnips, and rutabagas. When the adults from the overwintering generation die off, there is a period when no leaf damage occurs while larvae are still feeding in roots. Sow root crops as late as possible to avoid overwintered beetles; roots sown in July for winter harvests generally escape damage because flea beetles are not laying eggs in late summer. Arugula, leaf mustards, or pac choi can be sown as a trap crop to lure flea beetles away from broccoli, cabbage, and other crops; start trap crops three weeks before sowing or transplanting crop plants. As a last resort, pyrethrins sprays are effective on adult flea beetles; spray at the first sign of shot-hole damage in early spring to stop adults before they lay eggs in roots.

Where cabbage family crops are grown continuously year-round, flea beetles number can become very high. To break the cycle, deprive flea beetles of host plants by removing all cabbage family plants from the garden before March or by covering them securely with insect netting before overwintering adults emerge to lay eggs. Control related weeds (mustard, winter cress,

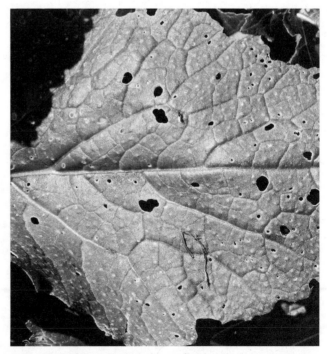

9.18. This leaf chewing by cabbage flea beetles is not serious, but the larvae could be damaging roots.

etc.) in and around the garden. Sow or transplant new cabbage family crops after June and cover these later-planted crops with insect netting at seeding time to continue depriving flea beetles of host plants (make sure no cabbage family plants were growing in the bed previously).

Imported Cabbageworm (*Pieris rapae*)

What to look for: Large ragged holes chewed in leaves of cabbage, broccoli, kale, and other cabbage family plants. Velvety green caterpillars in heads of broccoli and cauliflower. Caterpillars leave dark green pellets of excrement as they feed.

Biology: Adults are white cabbage butterflies. They emerge in early spring and lay tiny conical yellow eggs singly on the undersides of leaves of cabbage family plants. The caterpillars feed on leaves for about three weeks and grow to 1 inch (25 mm) long. They spin a chrysalis in debris around the plants and pupate for about two weeks. There are three or more overlapping generations per season, so they are present all summer.

Management: Although you may see many white butterflies and find eggs on leaves, little actual damage may result because birds and wasps eat lots of

Credit: E. Cronin

9.19. This cabbageworm escaped being hauled away by a yellowjacket wasp (so far).

cabbageworms. Feeding damage on outer leaves of mature cabbage looks bad, but the heads inside are usually fine. However, cabbageworms can destroy mid-summer seedlings, and they are a serious problem when they feed in heads of broccoli and cauliflower. Search daily to pick caterpillars off by hand or spray with BTK (*Bacillus thuringiensis kurstaki*), which is very effective. Products containing spinosad or neem (azadirachtin) also work, but also kill beneficial insects. Grow plants that attract these beneficial insects to your garden (such as dill, cilantro, or sweet alyssum) among the vegetables. Covering plants with insect netting to prevent butterflies from laying eggs can work if done in time to be certain no eggs have been laid on plants; it can fail spectacularly if eggs were already on plants because the netting then protects the caterpillars from their predators, such as wasps and birds.

Other Leaf-Eating Caterpillars

What to look for: The caterpillars (immature stage) of many species of moths and one or two butterflies feed on vegetables and fruit trees. Most caterpillars eat holes in leaves, starting with tiny holes and progressing to chewing larger ragged holes as they grow. Leafrollers are caterpillars that feed in the flower buds of fruit trees and other plants early in the spring, rolling up in the leaves at the tips of the branches.

Biology: Adult moths lay eggs only on food plants used by caterpillars of that species. Many species have only one generation during a season; therefore, the period of feeding damage is usually limited to a few weeks. After caterpillars reach full-size, they usually leave the plant to find a protected place to spin their cocoons. Adults emerge from cocoons a few weeks later, or more commonly, they overwinter in the cocoon and emerge the following season.

Management: Caterpillars have many natural enemies, including birds, parasitic wasps and flies, and yellowjacket wasps that usually keep numbers low enough to avoid damage. If you need to take action for a small infestation, it is usually easiest to pick them off by hand. Squash them or drop them in a bucket of soapy water to kill them.

For larger infestations, sprays of the bacterial disease, BTK (*Bacillus thuringiensis kurstaki*) are effective. Make sure leaves are well-covered with spray. Other pesticides that control leaf-eating caterpillars are soap, spinosad, and neem (which may be listed as azadirachtin on the product label) (see Table 9.2). All will harm the beneficial insects that eat caterpillars, and spinosad, in particular, is very toxic to bees; therefore, consider them *really* last-resort pesticides.

Imported Currantworm (Currant Sawfly) (*Nematus ribesii*)

What to look for: Large ragged holes in gooseberry or currant leaves, often with just the leaf veins left behind. The sawflies look like green caterpillars with black spots and dark heads; they grow to ¾ inch (2 cm) long. Eggs laid on the undersides of leaves look like white stitches along the leaf veins (see p. 214 for photograph).

Biology: Adults emerge from leaf litter under the host plants in spring, just as the leaves open. They lay eggs on leaves in the lower part of the bush. The larvae feed together in a group, chewing small holes in leaves on the interior part of the plant first, then dispersing to feed farther up. Left unchecked, they may defoliate bushes, causing loss of the crop. After feeding for about three weeks, they drop to the soil to spin cocoons. Most remain there until the following spring, but a few may emerge in July to make a small second generation.

9.20. These currantworms are what you are looking for if you didn't pick off the leaves with eggs before they hatched.

Management: Inspect bushes every two to three days from mid-April, looking on undersides of leaves for eggs; continue into June looking for larvae. Start by checking leaves in the lower center part of the bush first. Pick off leaves with eggs. Later, if you find larvae, either pick them off or spray them with insecticidal soap or pyrethrins. Note: BTK (*Bacillus thuringiensis kurstaki*) does not have any effect on these insects.

Pea Leaf Weevil (*Sitona lineata*)

What to look for: Tiny half-circle notches clipped out of the edges of leaves of peas and broad beans (also clover and other legumes). Adults are tiny grayish-brown weevils, about ⅛ inch (4 mm) long; they feed on plants at night.

Biology: There is one generation each year. Adult weevils overwinter in plant debris and become active in March. They feed on leaves and lay eggs in the soil around plants from March to May. The larvae survive best in cool wet spring weather, feeding on the nitrogen-fixing nodules in legume roots until June. They pupate for two to three weeks. New adults emerge in July and feed on leaves until August, but do not lay eggs at this time.

9.21. Small notches around the edges of pea leaves are characteristic of the pea leaf weevil.

Management: Feeding by high numbers of weevils can injure or even kill germinating seedlings in early spring. For planting in March and April, sprout peas on the windowsill for two to three weeks or until they are about 6 inches (15 cm) tall (see p. 125). When you plant them outdoors, make up for the loss of nitrogen nodules by fertilizing with a good supply of nitrogen as you would for any "heavy-feeding" vegetable. With seeds started indoors to avoid early attack, and nitrogen-rich soil, early peas can usually outgrow weevil attack and produce well. Peas sown from late May onward can usually be sown directly in the garden and without the extra nitrogen because egg-laying by the weevils has stopped by then. Ignore weevil notches appearing on leaves in late summer. Weevils emerging from the soil in July feed a little on leaves, but don't lay eggs.

Pillbugs and Sowbugs (*Armadillidium vulgare, Porcellio* spp.)

What to look for: Very tiny seedlings, especially carrots, beets, and lettuce, damaged or eaten entirely. Bean seedlings have the starchy "seed leaves" nibbled, and the first true leaves and often the growing point are destroyed completely, leaving just stems. Roots and stems of cucumber, squash, and melon

9.22. Typical damage to bean seedlings from pillbug feeding.

are gnawed at or below the soil line, and fruit has shallow scars. Pillbugs grow to ⅝ inch (1.5 cm) long and curl up into a tight ball when disturbed. Sowbugs are slightly smaller, a lighter gray, and are less damaging.

Biology: These land-living crustaceans feed on fungi and decaying and living plant material. They are common in compost piles and where there is rotting wood. Their numbers are highest in the spring, especially in cool wet years. They are very susceptible to drying out.

Credit: E. Cronin

9.23. Pillbugs roll up when disturbed.

Management: Remove rotting wood in the landscape and replace with stone, brick, or recycled plastic "wood." Start seeds, even carrots, in flats and transplant to beds once they are large enough to escape damage. Rake mulches away from seed beds, and keep the soil surface bare until plants are well-established. Irrigate in the morning, so the soil surface dries before evening. Wait until the soil is really warm before sowing beans, or better yet, start the seeds indoors for two to three weeks (see p. 123) because starchy seeds rotting in cool soil are very attractive to pillbugs. This attraction to fermenting material might explain the myth that spreading cornmeal kills them; it won't, but it might redirect their interest from your seedlings temporarily. Keep cucumber and melon fruit off of the soil. Combination baits are now on the market in the US, containing iron for slugs and spinosad to control pillbugs.

Slugs and Snails

What to look for: Large ragged holes chewed in leaves and shoots of emerging plants. You can usually see traces of their slime trails on damaged leaves. Slug eggs are perfectly round, translucent, and laid in masses in the soil.

Biology: Slugs and snails are essential decomposers of organic matter in our gardens, but they are also a West Coast scourge because they are most damaging in cool wet weather. Snails and some slugs climb up plants and shrubs to feed on leaves.

Management: Water in the morning to allow the soil surface to dry by evening. Use drip irrigation or soaker hoses to limit the surface area of moist soil. Pull mulches well away from seedling rows until plants are well-grown. Patrol the garden in the evening or early morning to kill slugs. Lay boards, slabs of damp newspaper, or grapefruit halves on the soil, and kill any slugs hiding underneath in the morning. Use strips of copper or zinc mesh around the edges of planters and on legs of greenhouse benches to repel slugs (this only works if you are sure there are no slugs or slug eggs already inside the area).

9.24. Slug eggs found under a plant.

Slug baits containing iron are very effective (several brands are approved for use by certified organic growers). Unlike the old toxic slug baits containing metaldehyde, these won't harm pets or wildlife. Sprinkle the granules sparingly, but widely, over a whole garden bed, and replace after heavy rain. Don't use it to encircle plants you are protecting because it is an attractant for slugs and acts slowly, leaving the slugs plenty of time to eat your plants before feeling the effects.

Spreading sharp materials, such as wood ashes, sharp sand, or diatomaceous earth (may be listed as silicon dioxide on the label), around plants is of little or no use, especially in wet conditions. Diatomaceous earth would also kill beneficial insects that walk across it. Drown slugs by attracting them to containers of fermenting liquids (slugs love yeast). The bait container should have holes cut in the sides to allow slugs access, as well as a lid to prevent ground beetles (important predators of slugs, see p. 22) from falling in. Set the container into the soil with the holes just above the soil surface. Fill it three-quarters full of beer, or use a mixture of water, baking yeast, and sugar.

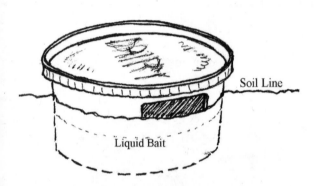

Soil Line

Liquid Bait

9.25. Homemade slug trap.

9.26. A maggot of the recently introduced fruit fly, spotted wing Drosophila, on a raspberry.

Spotted Wing Drosophila (SWD)
(*Drosophila suzukii*)

What to look for: Soft collapsed spots in ripe fruit and tiny white maggots inside the fruit or crawling on the outside of harvested fruit. Adults look like common "fruit flies" seen around compost bins and rotting fruit, with the exception that males have a single spot on each wing. They are especially attracted to raspberry, blueberry, cherry, strawberry, and blackberry, but are known to attack all stone fruit and berries, Asian pears, grapes, hardy kiwi, and many native plants. Damage is worst on later-ripening fruit when fly numbers are highest.

Biology: This new pest spreads rapidly and is now present throughout the PNW. Females saw tiny holes in the skin of ripening fruit and insert their eggs. Larvae hatch in a couple of days, feed under the fruit skin for three to thirteen days, then pupate in or around the damaged fruit. A complete life cycle takes one to two weeks at summer temperatures, and numbers rapidly build up in August. Adult flies overwinter in protected sites.

Make a Monitoring Trap for SWD

To make a simple trap that shows when and how many flies are present, punch or cut six to eight small holes (¼ in/0.5 cm) around the rim of a 16-ounce (0.5 L) plastic cottage cheese or deli container. Pour about 1 inch of apple cider vinegar into the container, snap on the lid, and set the trap in the garden (adding a little rice vinegar or merlot wine may improve catches, but are not required). Don't bother with recently recommended yeast baits: I found them smelly to deal with and no more effective than vinegar.

For monitoring, you only need one trap (in future, better baits may make it possible to control SWD with mass trapping). Start monitoring in early June, checking the trap at least weekly. Replace the vinegar every week or two. Male SWD floating in the vinegar are easy to identify by the single dark spot on each wing. When you see them, you can assume the fruit flies without spots are female SWD (hardly any "compost" fruit flies get caught in the vinegar trap). Record the date the first SWD are caught, and use that to install fruit covers before that date next year. If you are using pesticides, the first trap catch is a signal to start a spray program.

Management: The severe damage caused by this pest means a lot of research is going on. University of California researchers have found a promising natural fruit extract (butyl anthranilate) that repels SWD, and there may be other developments in future. Meanwhile, here are effective strategies for home gardeners: Plant early varieties of berries and cherries. If they ripen by early July, they may largely escape damage, unless a mild winter and early spring causes fly numbers to build up early. Prevent eggs from being laid on fruit by covering whole bushes or small trees with insect netting or by bagging individual fruit, starting about three weeks before the fruit ripens (see Barriers, p. 218). Netting should have a mesh size smaller than 0.04 inches (1 mm). Grow tall raspberries, blackberries, and other bramble berries in large cages covered with insect netting. Pick ripening fruit immediately or even a little early, and let it ripen indoors. Collect and destroy dropped fruit daily. Kill maggots in the infested fruit by burying it deeply, by freezing it, or by heating it in a sealed plastic bag in the sun for a week. Don't compost the material until you are sure maggots have been killed. Organic growers can use spinosad pesticides, starting as soon as monitoring traps show SWD are present. In the fall, to reduce the number of adults overwintering in the area, set out two or three monitoring traps (see above) to mop up as many adults as possible; keep refreshing the bait until early December.

9.27. A tent caterpillar egg mass on a finger-width branch of an apple tree. Look for these in the winter and scrape them off.

Tent Caterpillars (*Malacosoma* species)

What to look for: Groups of rusty-brown caterpillars feeding on leaves of fruit trees and other deciduous plants in April and May. They spin distinctive thick silken webs in the crotches of branches.

Biology: Moths lay egg masses in late summer on small branches of fruit trees and other deciduous trees. Eggs hatch in the April, and the tiny dark brown caterpillars stay together to feed, spinning successively larger web nests as they grow. In late May, tent caterpillars wander away from their webs in search of food and to spin cocoons in a protected spot. Populations go through seven-to-twelve-year cycles of extremely high numbers, followed by an abrupt drop as diseases and natural enemies kill off nearly all of the caterpillars. After several years, their numbers slowly begin to build, and the boom-and-bust cycle repeats.

Management: During high outbreak years, prevent fruit trees and bushes from being defoliated by removing egg masses in the winter and pruning out webs starting in April. Repeated sprays of BTK (*Bacillus thuringiensis kurstaki*) provide some control of caterpillars. If fruit trees and bushes lose all of their leaves, they grow more and usually don't suffer lasting harm, but won't produce a crop (pick off all fruit to reduce stress on the bush or tree).

Wireworms (*Agriotes* spp., *Limonius* spp., *Hypnoidus* spp.)
What to look for: Narrow tunnels or small round scars in potatoes, carrots, onions, and other roots. Larvae are golden to light brown, slender, leathery "wireworms," up to ¾ inch (2 cm) long, found in the soil, in tubers, and boring into large seeds and crowns of tender plants.

Biology: Adult beetles lay eggs in the soil, mostly in April and May, especially in the roots of grasses. Wireworms can be particularly damaging for the first few years after new sod is turned for a garden because there are usually many wireworms in the roots of the grasses. Larvae take three to six years to develop to adults. Damage is worst in spring and fall when wireworms feed closer to the soil surface. They burrow deeper in the soil in summer to avoid heat, and in winter to avoid cold. They can move a yard sideways through the soil as well, attracted to roots of plants.

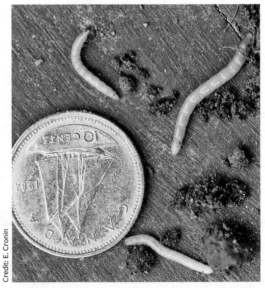

Credit: E. Cronin

9.28. Three wireworms with a dime for a size comparison.

Management: Planting as late as possible in the spring avoids some wireworms. Don't plant fall rye or other cover crops for overwintering because crops attract adult beetles to lay eggs on it in the spring (as do any weeds). Keep empty garden beds weed-free all winter with a thick layer of leaf mulch or other organic matter, and don't allow grass or weeds to grow in garden pathways. Sow extra seeds of peas, beans, and corn to allow for some losses. Lightly fork over the soil several times before planting and pick out the wireworms; their light color makes them easy to see. After several seasons of removing wireworms, numbers should drop considerably as long as you don't allow grasses or weeds to invade.

Here is a good wireworm control tip: First remove all crop debris and weeds from the garden bed. Then use chunks of potato and carrot as wireworm traps: Skewer each chunk on a short stick to act as a marker and bury the pieces an inch or two deep in the soil. Pull up the traps every day or two, and destroy any wireworms in the bait (the bait chunks can be reused for weeks). To clean up heavily infested soil, it might be worth trying trap crops. Starting with bare soil, about ten days before you want to plant the bed, sow rows of wheat or barley (about four seeds per inch/two per cm) about a yard (1 m) apart. The germinating seeds attract the wireworms if there are no other roots elsewhere in the soil. After ten days, dig up the grain seedlings, and destroy all wireworms found in the soil around the roots.

In 2016, a researcher for Agriculture Canada debuted a new trap for mass trapping wireworms in commercial potato fields. The Noronha Elaterid Light Trap (NELT) uses a solar-powered light to attract male and female beetles in large enough numbers to knock down the population. Research has shown effectiveness in potato fields; it isn't certain, yet, how well the traps will work for home gardens (it might lure more beetles to your garden than would have been there to begin with). Traps can be homemade, and the first commercial traps were marketed in 2017 (see Resources).

Note: Although nematode suppliers promote using insect parasitic nematodes for wireworm control, only some strains of nematodes have been shown to have a useful effect

9.29. Lure wireworms to buried chunks of potato to remove them from the soil.

on wireworms. So far, nematode species and strains sold to gardeners have had variable (even poor) results on wireworms; given the high cost, difficulty of timing application, and uncertain results, don't waste your money.

Common Diseases

Plant diseases are unfortunately a fact of life for coastal gardeners. The long wet springs and periods of cool humid weather even in the summer are especially favorable for the development of plant diseases. Once plants are infected, diseases are very difficult to control; therefore, the best way to deal with them is prevention.

Before a plant can become diseased, the three elements of the "disease triangle" must be present: a susceptible host plant, the disease agent (called a pathogen), and a favorable environment for the growth of the pathogen, usually, damp weather. Diseases cannot develop if any one of these elements is missing. Prevention and some control methods focus on removing one or more of these elements.

Choose disease-resistant plants. There are many resistant varieties of fruit and vegetables (see Table 2.1, p. 34).

Avoid pathogens.
- Be careful about bringing potentially diseased plants into your garden, and remove any obviously infected plant as soon as you see it.
- Buy only disease-free plants or grow your own from seed to avoid bringing a new disease into your garden. Always plant certified disease-free seed potatoes.
- Destroy infected plant material. Pick off diseased leaves, prune out branches with cankers (obviously sunken or injured areas), and pull out sick plants. Burn the infected material, bury it in soil, or dispose of it in the garbage. Some material, such as apples or apple leaves infected with apple scab, can be safely composted.
- Remove alternate host plants for diseases (example: remove junipers because they are also hosts for pear trellis rust that infects pears).
- Disinfect pruning tools between uses (mix 1 part hydrogen peroxide bleach to 9 parts water).

Environmental conditions. Although (obviously) there is nothing you can do about the weather, there are *some* things you *can* control:

- Promote rapid drying of leaves after rain. Prune, space, and train plants to ensure good air circulation around branches and through foliage.
- Keep leaves dry during infection periods. Grow susceptible plants under a roof overhang. Use soaker hoses or drip irrigation systems, which don't wet the leaves, or water early in the day so leaves dry quickly.
- Wait until the soil is warm enough for the type of plant before sowing (see Table 4.1, p. 91).
- Ventilate greenhouses and cold frames to circulate air and prevent condensation from wetting foliage.
- Observe three-to-five-year rotations for crops prone to soilborne pathogens, such as potatoes and the onion family.

9.30. Growing this peach tree under a roof overhang keeps the buds dry so it doesn't become infected with leaf curl.

Allium/Garlic Rust (*Puccinia allii*)

What to look for: Small patches or spots of rusty orange on leaves of garlic, leeks, and sometimes other onions and chives. Infections usually show first on new growth as small blister-like spots with a lighter yellowish ring around each spot. Later the spots turn dark brown.

Biology: Spores are spread very long distances by wind. There appear to be several strains of this rust present in the region. One strain mainly infects garlic, and sometimes onions or chives, while another strain infects garlic, leeks, elephant garlic, but not onions or chives. Cool wet spring weather provides ideal conditions for infection. This rust grows best on leaves that are wet for at least four hours (from fog, rain, or irrigation) and at moderate temperatures 50° to 75°F (10° to 24°C). It may overwinter as dormant spores in the soil and on infected overwintering leeks or perennial onions. It does not appear to be spread on mature garlic cloves, so you can plant cloves from infected garlic plants.

Note: There are many different rusts, and each stays on specific host plants, so allium rust won't spread to beans, blackberries, roses, etc.

Management: Early spring infections reduce the size of bulbs somewhat. Late infections (in June) seem to have little effect on garlic because the crop is almost done growing by the time the leaves become infected. On leeks, severely infected plants may be weak and stunted. Plants overfertilized with nitrogen or stressed by a lack of nutrients may be more susceptible.

Spacing plants for good air circulation allows leaves to dry quickly. Use drip irrigation or soaker hoses to water plants instead of overhead sprinklers. Where garlic is regularly infected, try growing early garlic varieties (e.g., Portuguese Red, which is ready about three weeks earlier than main crop garlic). If leeks are infected, harvest or destroy them before November to remove an overwintering host for the rust. Don't put infected leaves in the compost (bury, burn, or dispose). Sulfur sprays have little effect. Screening for resistant cultivars of garlic and leeks continues, but so far has not produced results.

Credit: E. Cronin

9.31. Allium rust on leeks. After starting out bright orange, the blisters later turn black.

Apple Scab (*Venturia inaequalis*) and Pear Scab (*Venturia pyrina*)

What to look for: Roughly circular corky scabs on the skin of apples and crab apples; on pears, scabs are often very small and cover most of the skin. Earliest symptoms are water-soaked spots on the undersides of early leaves that turn olive green, then black. In severe infections, fruit is misshapen, cracked, and covered with rough scabs.

9.32 Severe early apple scab infections ruined this fruit. (See Figure 6.2 [p. 146] for an apple with a moderate infection.)

9.33. Pear scab varies in appearance depending on the variety.

Biology: These diseases are caused by similar fungi that overwinter on old leaves beneath the trees (pear scab also overwinters on lesions on branches). In the spring, about the time flower petals fall, raindrops splash the spores back up onto the tree to start another year of infection. It takes as little as ten hours of continuously wet leaves at temperatures over 58°F (14°C) to infect tissue. Infections can continue to spread all season if wet weather continues.

Management: In light to moderate infections, a few scabs on the skin of fruit are merely unsightly. The fruit underneath is fine, although scarred fruit do not store well, and late infections in pears may show up later in storage. Given the likelihood of wet spring weather, coastal gardeners should choose immune or resistant varieties. Resistant apples include Akane, Bramley's Seedling, Elstar, Enterprise, Fiesta, Golden Russet, Jonafree, Liberty, Macoun, Mutsu, Prima, Priscilla, Red Free, Sunrise, Wagener, Wolf River, and Yellow Transparent. Note: McIntosh and Cox's Orange Pippin are among the *most* susceptible. Resistant pears include Orcas, Harrow Delight, Bosc, and Rescue, as well as Asian pears.

To minimize infections, prune trees to open up the centers for good air circulation so leaves dry quickly. Use drip irrigation or soaker hoses, rather than sprinklers or overhead watering systems. In the fall, rake up fallen leaves and remove any leaves remaining on branches. Compost them (in the center of a pile), bury them in the soil, or dispose of them.

On pears, apply dormant lime sulfur sprays as soon as leaves drop and again in late winter before buds swell. Growing-season sulfur sprays control apple scab if started early enough and reapplied repeatedly to ensure all new foliage is covered. For best results, start spraying as soon as buds swell, then spray every seven to ten days until mid to late June. Starting sprays later, immediately after the flower petals fall, can give adequate results—and means less spraying. Keep in mind that sulfur sprays kill beneficial mites that control pest mites, so only spray those trees with a history of serious scab infections. Far better to grow resistant varieties!

Black Knot (*Dibotryon morbosum*)

What to look for: Tar black or corky swellings grow on branches of cherries, plums, and sometimes peaches. The knots are elongated, spindle-shaped, and range from thumb-sized to much larger.

Biology: The fungus overwinters in the knots on the branches and grows quickly in late spring, shedding spores that are spread by wind, rain, and even birds. Spores infect new shoots in wet weather, and the knots grow over the summer, becoming hard and black by fall. The disease spreads slowly each year, eventually weakening or even stunting trees.

Management: Pruning out knots every year usually provides good control. Inspect trees in midwinter, and cut infected twigs and branches at least 4 inches (10 cm) below tumors; also remove knots in wild trees nearby. To avoid spreading spores, prune before buds begin to swell in the spring and disinfect tools between each cut. Burn or bury the infected wood. If there is a lot of black knot in wild trees in the neighborhood, avoid planting Stanley plums, which are very susceptible. The European variety, President, and Japanese varieties Shiro and Santa Rosa are reportedly more resistant to black knot than American plum varieties.

9.34. Well-developed black knot on a branch of plum.

Credit: E. Cronin

9.35. The progress of a Botrytis infection on strawberries, from left to right.

Botrytis/Gray Mold (*Botrytis cinerea*)

What to look for: Brown water-soaked spots on leaves, flowers, berries, or stems, later covered with soft, fuzzy gray spores. Often seen in the fall or after wet weather on overripe strawberries. Common on lettuce in cold frames in winter where there is little air circulation. Also occurs on stored fruit and vegetables.

Biology: The fungus is a weak colonizer, meaning that the main way it gets into plants is through bruised tissue and injuries caused by pests or other diseases. It also enters on spent blossoms and dying leaves. Once in the plant, the fungus spreads into healthy tissue. The gray fuzz that appears is a coating of zillions of spores.

Management: Botrytis thrives in damp, cool conditions, so the single most effective measure is to improve air circulation around plants. Give plants more space, prune and stake them; increase ventilation in cold frames, plastic tunnels, and greenhouses. Pick off old or damaged leaves to remove infection sites. Promptly pick off infected leaves and remove all parts of infected plants.

Brown Rot (*Monilinia fructicola*)

What to look for: Soft, rotting, grayish spots on plums, peaches, nectarines, apricots, or sweet cherries. Tufts of light tan or gray spores appear on the surface of infected fruit on the tree or in storage. Infections on twigs appear as oval brownish sunken patches of dead bark (cankers) or shiny patches on the bark; tips of twigs may wilt and die.

Biology: This common fungus attacks most kinds of stone fruit on the coast. The fungus overwinters in mummified fruit on the tree or on the ground as well as in infected twigs. In the spring, spores from these mummies are spread by wind, rain, and insects to fruit tree flowers. It takes as little as three hours of wetness at 70°F (21°C) to infect flowers, longer at lower temperatures. In warm wet weather, the disease can spread quickly to all fruit on the tree. It is particularly severe when heavy rains cause ripening fruit to split before harvest or when fruit is injured by insects, hail, or birds.

Management: Tart/sour cherries are less susceptible than sweet cherries; peaches are less susceptible than nectarines and apricots. Avoid overfertilizing trees with nitrogen. Prune trees to have open centers with good air circulation, which allows fruit and twigs to dry quickly after a rain. Thin developing fruit, so it is well-spaced.

Avoid irrigating with any type of equipment that wets leaves. Make sure trees receive adequate water while fruit is ripening, so fruit doesn't split if there is rain. Store only perfect fruit; handle it carefully to avoid bruising, and refrigerate immediately. Thoroughly clean storage containers between uses.

When infected trees are dormant, collect and destroy mummified fruit. Knock mummies from the branches (a long stick works for this), and burn, bury, or dispose of them in the garbage. Don't compost them. This sanitation step is extremely effective, but if it is skipped, sulfur sprays can limit the infection if timed correctly. Spray when blossoms first show a pink tinge and again before the petals fall. Spray again as fruit is ripening. Do not use sulfur on apricots because it is toxic to their leaves.

Cankers on Trunks and Branches

Two common types of cankers occur on fruit trees: European canker, a fungus disease of apples and pears, and bacterial canker, most common on sweet cherries, but also found on sour cherries, peaches, and other stone fruit.

What to look for: Foliage on affected branches begins to wilt or grow slower than others on the same tree. Look for a cracked or oozing lesion in the bark further down the branch or trunk. European canker is dry, roughly oval with concentric rings around the edges. The leaves above the canker wilt and die

9.36. Plums infected with brown rot and covered with tufts of spores.

9.37. European canker on apple where espaliered branch has rubbed on wire.

as the canker expands to encircle the branch. Bacterial canker causes rough lesions, usually oozing gummy, amber-colored sap, ranging from nickel-sized patches on small branches to large open wounds on trunks. Trees can hang on for years with either disease, but if cankers girdle the trunk, a tree can die.

Biology: Both are spread on pruning tools, and in wet weather by rain splashes and wind.

Management: Ensure that branches and trunks are not rubbing on posts or trellis wires (especially important for espaliered trees), and avoid injuring bark with mowers, string trimmers, etc. Prune out infected branches in dry weather, cutting at least 4 inches (10 cm) below the canker. When pruning infected trees, disinfect pruning tools between each cut, and only prune in dry weather, summer or winter.

Clubroot of Cabbage (*Plasmodiophora brassicae*)
What to look for: Cabbage family plants wilt in midday even though they are well-watered. Some die, others are stunted with yellowing leaves. When you

dig up a plant, it is obvious that roots are abnormal, with markedly thickened, whitish tumor-like swellings. After the plants die, the decaying galls turn brown and fibrous inside.

Biology: Clubroot is caused by a parasitic microorganism. It has tough resting spores that can survive for four to twenty years in the soil. When roots of a host plant grow nearby, the resting spores produce active spores in the spring; these swim in the soil water to the root hairs and enter the plant. They reproduce and spread through the roots, eventually forming large tumor-like masses in the root. The main group of host plants are in the mustard/cabbage (Brassicacea) family, but some unrelated plants also host clubroot without showing symptoms: strawberry, red clover, ryegrass, orchardgrass, corn poppy, dock (*Rumex* spp.), mignonette.

Management: This is a very serious disease because the spores remain in the soil for so long. The best defense is to never bring it into your garden: grow your own cabbage family plants from seed, or buy only plants grown in a soil-less mix (which is usually how commercial seedlings are grown). Don't accept plants from others' gardens unless you are certain they come from soil without clubroot. Clean and disinfect shared tools or rented cultivating equipment with 1 part chlorine or hydrogen peroxide bleach to 4 parts water before using them in your soil. If you know your soil is infected, you must clean and disinfect every tool you use in infected soil before using it elsewhere (or have a separate set of tools for infected soil), and never pass along plants from your garden to other people. Even if you stop growing cabbage family plants altogether, the soil remains infected for up two decades. You can continue to grow reasonable crops of cabbage family plants by heavily liming the soil. The clubroot organism thrives in acid soil, so raising the pH to

Credit: M. Hargrove

9.38. Clubroot symptoms on roots of kohlrabi.

7.0 or higher suppresses the disease. This takes a lot of lime, so test the soil pH regularly. If you can find them, grow clubroot-resistant varieties. More are listed by UK seed houses, but a few are available in North America, including a green cabbage (Tekila), Napa cabbages (Bilko, Jazz, Emiko), and rutabagas (Marian, Laurentian, Kingston, Invitation). There are different races of clubroot; therefore, resistance varies according to what race is present. A promising treatment is the use of *Bacillus subtilis* to treat roots at transplant time (see Table 9.2). This naturally occurring soil bacteria seems to work by protecting the roots and by producing compounds that help plants suppress infections from active clubroot spores; it doesn't remove clubroot from the soil. It has been most effective applied as a soil drench or seedling root dip at planting time and again as a soil drench two weeks later.

Damping Off

What to look for: Seedlings fall over and die, or seeds never come up. Close inspection of seedlings shows stems appear water-soaked and collapsed at the soil line.

Biology: Damping off can be caused by several fungi that infect germinating seeds and seedlings; it can also cause stem and root rots of older plants. Damping off can occur in the garden, but is most common in trays of seedlings. Cool wet soil favors damping off fungi. Damping off usually spreads through an entire seedling tray.

Management: Damping off fungi are common in soil, so focus on making conditions unfavorable for the disease:

- Start seeds at the correct temperatures (see Table 4.1, p. 91). Wait until the soil is warm before sowing outdoors.
- Avoid overwatering seedlings. Seed flats need only be kept damp, not wet.
- Make sure there is good ventilation around seedlings. Don't cover trays of germinating seeds.
- Use well-drained soil mixes with generous proportions of vermiculite, perlite, or other materials that aerate the soil.
- Disinfect pots and seedling trays before reusing them (soak in 1 part hydrogen peroxide bleach to 9 parts water).

- Unpasteurized seedling mixes that include finely screened, well-aged compost contain beneficial fungi that suppress damping-off fungi.
- Plant fresh (vigorous) seed at the correct depth.

Once damping off has started in a flat or row, it is usually too late to control it. Older plants sometimes survive, but their later growth may be stunted. Some gardeners recommend making a tea of horsetail (*Equisetum* spp.) or using compost teas to treat fungi in the soil; however, by wetting the soil, these remedies also risk making the problem worse. It is much better to prevent the problem in the first place!

Late Blight (*Phytophthora infestans*)
What to look for: Tomato plants rapidly collapse and rot. The earliest symptoms on tomatoes are dark blotches on stems and leaves, usually starting at the margins, but these are usually missed because the disease progresses very quickly. Infected fruit turns brown and leathery and quickly decays. In wet years, plants may die before any fruit ripens.

Biology: Late blight is caused by a fungus-like organism called a water mold. In cool damp summers, it is a widespread destructive disease of tomatoes and, sometimes, related plants. Spores spread on the wind and in splashes of water; they rapidly infect wet leaves. The late blight organism survives mild winters on plant debris in the soil and on volunteer potatoes left in the ground. Thick-walled dormant "spores" can also remain in the soil for years.

9.39. A well-ventilated plastic tunnel is one way to avoid late blight infections in tomatoes.

9.40. Late blight in tomatoes soon leads to rapid collapse of the whole plant.

Management: Plant resistant potatoes varieties; although none are immune, those that show resistance include Fundy, Kennebec, Sebago, Defender, Jacqueline Lee, Ozette. Plant only certified disease-free seed potatoes. Destroy volunteer potato plants because this is where late blight can overwinter and become the source of the next season's infection.

Grow tomatoes in the driest, sunniest place you have. Space plants out and prune and stake them to ensure good air circulation so leaves dry off quickly. Avoid splashing irrigation water on plants. Early-maturing varieties, such as cherry tomatoes, can usually produce a crop before infection strikes. The most reliable way to avoid late blight is to keep leaves entirely dry, which means growing plants in a greenhouse, under the overhang of a roof, or under some kind of well-ventilated cover to keep off rain. Make a simple roof for the tomato patch from a sheet of corrugated translucent plastic (e.g., Coroplast®) screwed to sturdy posts, or grow plants under tall plastic tunnels that have wide open sides and ends. It is essential to have excellent ventilation in greenhouses and tunnels to prevent condensation from dripping onto leaves and making them wet enough to allow infection. Although breeding for late blight-resistant tomato varieties continues, there are many different genotypes (strains) of late blight and tomatoes resistant to some strains are not resistant to others. To make matters worse, strains of late blight present in any region vary from year to year.

If late blight strikes, remove diseased plants and bury them deeply or seal them in a plastic bag and put them in the garbage. Do not compost diseased plants.

Peach Leaf Curl (*Taphrina deformans*)

What to look for: Twisted, puckered, and thickened leaves with reddish tinges on peaches or nectarines. Later in the season, affected leaves develop a grayish bloom and may drop. Infected fruit may be distorted or shriveled and often drops early in the season. Leaves that grow later in the season are not infected.

Biology: Peach leaf curl is caused by a fungus that infects buds of peach and nectarines. Spores overwinter in crevices in tree bark, on buds and twigs. *Taphrina* infects leaves in cool wet weather in early spring, just as the leaf buds begin to swell and show green tips. Spores develop on infected leaves (giving the grayish appearance) and are spread by wind and rain to trees. Prolonged wet spring weather allows spores to infect more leaf buds; infections stop in dry warm weather or when leaves have grown past the susceptible stage.

Management: Light to moderate infections do little harm, but in a severe infection (all too common on the coast), trees can be seriously weakened and lose most of the crop.

Grow resistant or tolerant varieties of peaches: Avalon Pride, Oregon Curl Free, Frost, Pacific Gold, or Renton. Redhaven peach shows some resistance,

9.41. Peach leaf curl distorts leaves.

but will still be infected to some extent. Train peaches and nectarines against a south-facing wall of buildings where the roof overhang will keep off rain. Devise a makeshift or permanent canopy to keep trees dry for the early spring period when leaf buds begin to swell. Lime-sulfur sprays reduce levels of infection by preventing spores from germinating. Spray in the fall when 90% of the leaves have fallen; if infection was severe the previous year, spray again in the very early spring (February) just before flower buds swell.

Pear Trellis Rust (*Gymnosporangium fuscum*)

What to look for: Bright orange irregular spots on pear leaves in early summer that continue to grow larger. In August, hard, irregular orange structures develop on the undersides of leaves where the spots are.

Biology: This fungus has two hosts: pears and juniper. The fungus stays dormant in juniper for most of the year, then produces masses of spores from April to early May on the branches. These are strange irregular, swollen growths covered with spongy bright orange masses of spores, which are carried on the wind to pear leaves. Spore-producing structures develop on the undersides of pear leaves, then they release spores capable of infecting juniper from late August until leaf fall. Pear leaves are usually newly infected each spring; the rust rarely remains in the trees over the winter.

9.42. Late stages of pear trellis rust on the undersides of pear leaves.

Management: This rust mainly occurs in the south coast areas of British Columbia and in coastal Washington. Only pears show damage; infected junipers look fine and continue to grow normally. Lightly infected pears suffer no harm either, but if the infection is severe, fruiting and growth may be reduced. Infections on pear trees vary from year to year, depending on rainfall and wind patterns, so a badly infected tree one year may not be seriously infected the next year.

The best (but usually impractical) way to protect pears is to remove all susceptible junipers within a 100-foot (30-meter) radius. Finding infected junipers is a challenge—and they are usually on someone else's property. If removing junipers can be organized as a neighborhood effort, remove the junipers before they form spores; before April 1, burn, bury, or dispose of them (do not chip or compost them). To prevent the disease from spreading from pears back to junipers, pick off infected pear leaves by mid-August (pear leaves can be composted because the rust dies when the leaf is picked). There is no point in spraying fungicides, especially dormant lime sulphur, since the fungus is not on the tree in the winter. If there are swollen growths on pear twigs, it shows that the infection has entered the tree; prune these out during the winter and dispose of the pruned wood.

Powdery Mildew (caused by several species of fungi: *Erysiphe*, *Sphaerotheca*, *Podosphaera*, *Oidium*, and others)

What to look for: White powdery patches on leaves, starting as small round, powdery white or gray spots, which quickly spread. Leaves eventually turn brown and dry up. Different species of powdery mildew fungi attack different host plants, including beans, peas, mustard family leafy greens, Swiss chard, tomatoes, grapes, strawberries, apples, and other fruit. In severe infections on fruit, the fruit becomes scarred and discolored with tan, russeted patches and scars.

Biology: Unlike other fungi, powdery mildews infect plants in dry weather. Spores germinate more quickly in humid conditions, but water on the leaves actually *stops* spores from germinating. Infections spread rapidly in the late summer and fall (before the fall rains start), when cool night temperatures and overnight dew raises the humidity around leaves. This is also when more old leaves are present, which are the first ones attacked by powdery mildew.

Management: Choose powdery mildew-resistant varieties of squash, cucumbers, peas, grapes, and apples (see Table 2.1, p. 34). Thoroughly rinse leaves (both sides) of susceptible squash and cucumbers with water at midday, several times a week. This prevents spores from germinating, but is only feasible if the plants are not at risk from other fungi that thrive on wet leaves (don't try this on apples, for example). Plant a second sowing of zucchini in mid-June to have young vigorous plants with less susceptible leaves present in late summer when powdery mildew infections are spreading. For late plantings of peas (May and June), shelling peas work well, because powdery mildew is only on the surface of the pods and the peas inside are fine.

The powdery mildew that infects apples overwinters in buds, giving them a whitish flattened appearance. To reduce the spread of the fungus, prune out infected buds when you are doing dormant pruning or before the buds swell in the spring. If there are many trees or too many infected buds on a tree to pick off, start a spray program with sulphur as soon as buds begin to swell.

Sprays of *Bacillus subtilis*, a biological control for many leaf-infecting fungi, also control powdery mildew. Spray according to directions on the label, as soon as the first sign of powdery mildew is seen.

Spraying leaves with a mixture of 9 parts water to 1 part milk, twice a week, has been shown to control mildew on cucumber and squash (but not on other plants).

Pesticides containing bicarbonate (baking soda) are registered for home gardeners in the US (not in British Columbia) to use on fruit and nut trees and

9.43. Powdery mildew on new apple leaves in the spring. (See Figure 2.9 [p. 33] for photograph of mildew on squash leaves.)

many vegetables. Sprays of sulfur or neem (azadirachtin) also control powdery mildew, but they must be used frequently to ensure new leaves are kept
covered with fungicide before the spores have a chance to spread to the new
tissue. Note: Frequent use of sulfur sprays can damage cucumbers and squash
leaves; it also kills beneficial mites on apple trees.

Root Rots of Garlic and Onions (*Sclerotinia, Fusarium, Botrytis, Penicillium, Embellisia* species)

Five main groups of fungi cause the most common bulb diseases in the onion
family. *Embellisia allii* only causes cosmetic blotches on the outer skins of garlic, but species of *Fusarium*, *Botrytis*, and *Penicillium* occasionally cause large
losses. By applying good sanitation and crop rotation practices, you can continue growing healthy onion family crops. White rot (*Sclerotium cepivorum*)
is an exception because it produces hardy dormant reproductive structures
(called *sclerotia*) that survive in soil for twenty to thirty years.

What to look for: Leaves turn yellow or start wilting, followed by obvious rotting in neck or bulb tissue. Single cloves or whole bulbs rot in the field or later
in storage. The color of spores and presence or absence of sclerotia helps to
distinguish between fungi, but it is not easy to identify specific diseases because symptoms look similar, especially in the later stages of deterioration.
Note that several root rots produce white or light gray mold growth and are
often mistaken for white rot. If you are concerned about disease in your crop,
send samples to your local plant health laboratory for an accurate diagnosis
(see Resources).

Biology: Fungi that cause root diseases mostly enter through injuries or around
the base of the bulbs. As the fungi grow in plant tissue, they eventually produce
spores or sclerotia, which remain in the soil. The number of infective spores
continues to build up in the soil if onion family plants are planted again in the
same place, but in the absence of onion family plants, the spores die out over
time.

Management: Prevention is the main approach to managing root rot diseases.
Common fungi that can cause root rots are present in most soils and are also

9.44. Despite the white mold growth, this is not the dreaded white rot disease. Crop rotation should prevent this root rot in future.

brought into the garden on infected bulbs. Prevention is the best defense: Maintain a three-to-five-year crop rotation (the longer, the better). Plant only healthy, perfectly intact garlic cloves and onion sets. If your garlic is healthy, use that for next year's crop rather than risk bringing in disease on purchased garlic. Grow onions from seed or buy them from a nursery that started seeds in a soilless mix; avoid field-grown onion seedlings sold in bundles in the spring. Plant garlic late in October to reduce risk of *Penicillium* spp. infections, which are more likely when soil is warm and relatively dry. Stop irrigating two weeks before harvest to allow outer skins to mature. Thoroughly cure bulbs in warm, dry conditions before storing. For long-term storage, choose the best bulbs and keep them very dry (outdoor sheds are much too damp). Control wireworms and onion maggots, which injure bulbs and allow fungi to enter. Ensure soil is well-drained over the winter for garlic crops. Feed the soil with compost to encourage growth of beneficial fungi and bacteria that suppress disease fungi and shield roots from attack.

Disorders

Disorders caused by nutrient deficiencies or something wrong with the growing environment injure plants. Irregular watering, heat stress, and calcium deficiencies, for example, are at the root of common disorders, from blossom end rot in tomatoes to bitter pit in apples. Many disorders look like insect or disease damage, so it may take some detective work to figure out what is wrong.

Bitter Pit (Apples)

What to look for: Small brown or gray corky lesions in the flesh of the apple, which may not be visible until the apple is cut open. In severe cases, dark depressed spots are visible on the skin and through-out the flesh, getting worse the longer fruit is stored.

What went wrong: Corky spots are due to the break-down of cells from a deficiency of calcium. Exces-sive nitrogen or potassium levels can cause calcium imbalances in tissues. Dry weather or lack of irriga-tion when fruit is developing makes it worse, as do practices that stimulate trees to produce rapidly ex-panding fruit (over-thinning or using nitrogen-rich fertilizer).

Remedy: Avoid varieties most prone to this problem: Braeburn, Jonagold, Transparent, Granny Smith, Jonathan, Golden Delicious, Gravenstein, Red Deli-cious, Cortland, Cox's Orange Pippin, Northern Spy. Manage trees to grow steadily but not quickly, main-tain soil pH and calcium levels, and avoid overfertil-

9.45. Bitter pit lesions on the skin and inside a Jonagold apple.

izing. Mulch trees and irrigate to keep soil evenly moist. To reduce vigor, prune susceptible trees in the summer only. Wait until the June drop is over to thin the crop, and don't thin fruit too much.

Blossom End Rot (Tomatoes and Peppers)

What to look for: Sunken tan or black areas at the blossom end of tomato or pepper fruits. On tomatoes, black spots may become quite large, taking up the bottom half of the fruit. On peppers and some paste tomatoes, the tissue may be tan and extend up the sides of the fruit near the blossom end.

What went wrong: Calcium deficiency in plant tissue. Your soil might have enough calcium, but it isn't available, or the plants can't take it up fast enough to keep up with rapidly expanding fruit. This is often because the movement of calcium inside the plant has been inhibited by drought stress, usually from irregular watering. It is often seen on tomatoes grown in containers that expe-rience alternating dry and wet soil. It can also be caused when plants grow too fast as a result of too much nitrogen fertilizer.

Remedy: Maintain even soil moisture with adequate irrigation and use of mulches. Use large planters for potted plants, and water often enough in hot weather to keep the soil evenly moist. Amend the soil with calcium (from lime, wood ash, or bone meal), and dig in more compost, which helps make calcium available to plants. Do not apply Espsom salts as this makes the problem worse by causing further nutrient imbalances.

Hollow Heart/Brown Core (Potatoes)

What to look for: Potato tubers have a cavity in the center, often star-shaped, and usually lined with a tan or brown layer. In extreme cases, the entire interior of the potato is affected, with dark bands in the flesh around the cavity. The dark areas are firm and not rotted.

What went wrong: Associated with calcium deficiency in the tubers from a sudden change in growth rate, often due to irregular watering, especially in hot weather, that allowed plants to become very dry, then very wet. Some varieties are more prone to this disorder than others: Atlantic, Russet Burbank, Norgold Russet, Yukon Gold.

9.46. Paste tomatoes (*upper left*) with blossom end rot. Both older and younger fruit are fine on this potted plant, so a temporary lack of water is likely to blame in this case.

Remedy: Potatoes with a small cavity can be salvaged for eating, although severely affected tubers are inedible. Revisit your irrigation system to ensure it provides a regular water supply, without overwatering. Even out soil moisture with the thick mulch of organic material (straw, leaves, etc.), plant in deep trenches, filling in the soil as shoots grow. Avoid overfertilizing with nitrogen, and ensure soil is well-supplied with calcium. Grow varieties noted for resistance to hollow heart: Sierra, Russet Norkotah, Sangre, Krantz.

9.47. This potato with a hollow heart can still be eaten.

Sunscald

What to look for: On leaves: Sunscald shows up as light tan, brown, black, or even purplish dead areas. Injury is worst on top leaves and parts of the plant most directly exposed to the sun. The injury shows up first on parts of the leaf farthest from veins, on leaf tips and margins.

9.48. Severely sunburned cucumbers struggling to survive.

On fruit: Sunscald appears as discolored spots that look "cooked." In tomatoes, damaged areas look like gray or white patches of papery or blistered skin on the side of the fruit toward the sun.

What went wrong: Direct heat injury occurs when temperatures become so high that cells in plant tissue die. Leaves and shoots suffer more damage if heat waves occur suddenly after cool weather or in early spring, because leaves that grow in cool, moist conditions have thinner layers of protective waxes. If hot weather continues, plants grow new leaves with thicker layers of waxes and other adaptations to heat.

If wet weather follows, rot organisms often infect the damaged tissue, making it look like the pathogens were the original cause of the damage.

Remedy: Be aware of weather forecasts so that you can water vulnerable plants well and shade them before hot weather hits. There is nothing to be done after the damage occurs, but if only leaves were burned, new leaves grow and the plants will recover. See Chapter 5 for how to harden off and protect transplants to avoid sunburn.

9.49. Sunscald on an apple. The rest of the apple is edible, but this one won't keep for long.

9.50. Green shoulders is a puzzling disorder—aren't tomatoes supposed to like heat and light?

Yellow/Green Shoulders (Tomatoes)

What to look for: Tomatoes have a hard green or yellowish area around the stem end of the fruit. Although the rest is completely ripe, the green area never ripens.

What went wrong: This can be caused when fruit is exposed to strong sunlight and intense heat, such as a period of unusually hot weather or in a glass greenhouse in the summer. A potassium deficiency in the soil may also play a role. Some varieties are more susceptible than others.

Remedy: Minimize leaf pruning to ensure there is enough foliage to shade fruit (fruit will taste better, too). Make sure there isn't a potassium deficiency in the soil. If this disorder has been a big problem in the past with your greenhouse crops, look for tomato varieties specifically listed for greenhouse growing.

Water Core (Apples)

What to look for: Glassy or water-soaked areas in the flesh of apples, particularly around the core. More severe water core shows as large translucent areas on the outside, often associated with sunscald. The glassy areas have a sweet taste and are edible.

What went wrong: A complicated disorder involving high temperatures and intense sunlight when fruit is ripening, possibly low calcium in the fruit, excessive nitrogen fertilization, and perhaps too much boron in the soil. It is most

9.51. External and internal glassy appearance of water core in a King apple.

severe when overmature apples are left on trees too long, when trees have a light crop, or the crop has been thinned too much, resulting in very large fruit.

Remedy: Avoid susceptible varieties: King, Transparent, Jonathan, Red Delicious, Granny Smith, Fuji, Honeycrisp. Pick as soon as apples are ready to be removed. Review tree care: ensure soil has enough calcium, irrigate fruiting trees in dry weather, avoid overfertilizing with nitrogen, and don't thin fruit too much.

Pollination Problems

Many things can interfere with pollination and fertilization of flowers. Unfortunately, you usually don't know there is a problem until there is no fruit. For summer squash or tomatoes, you might have time to remedy a problem as the season goes on. For tree fruit, however, once the flowers fall, there won't be more until next spring, so a pollination failure means a crop failure. And in corn, you won't know until you open the husks that some of the kernels weren't fertilized.

Tiny squashes form, but fall off. Even if a female flower is not pollinated, the little squash behind the flower can still continue to grow a bit after the spent flower drops off (see Figure 1.6, p. 15). The tiny squash soon turns yellow and drops. In wet weather, it may rot, making it look like disease stopped the squash from growing, but it was never fertilized to begin with. See entry for squash under A to Z Vegetables in Chapter 10 (p. 318) for information on hand pollinating squash.

Flowers appear, but no tomatoes. It might be too cold or too hot for fertilization. Most tomato pollen is damaged by temperatures below 55°F (12°C). The fruit may not form at all, or it might be partially pollinated, resulting in distorted or "cat-faced" fruit. Temperatures over 86°F (30°C) also sterilize tomato pollen. It rarely happens outdoors, but it is common for tomatoes in greenhouses or tunnels without enough ventilation. Flowers that were opening when the mercury went through the roof drop off, but later flowers developing in better conditions will be fine.

Fruit flowers appear, but no fruit. There are several possibilities:

- **Frost killed the flowers:** A late cold snap can kill blossoms of early fruit, such as peaches and nectarines.
- **Lack of pollinators:** Fruit trees, berries, and other plants need bees and other insects to transfer pollen. If the weather is cool and wet, bees won't come out. Native insects are better pollinators in cool weather than honeybees, but even these hardy natives cannot work in wet, cold conditions. Poor weather is only a problem for plants that were in bloom during the cool weather; varieties blooming in better weather fare better.
- **Lack of cross-pollination:** If fruit trees flower but don't set fruit year after year, they may be lacking a cross-pollinator. Nearly all apples and pears and many plum and cherry varieties need to receive pollen from a different variety to set fruit.
- **Birds ate the flowers:** House finches and sometimes other birds eat fruit blossoms to get the nectar inside. They can eat all of the flowers on a small tree. Cover trees with netting (the mesh has to be wide enough to allow pollinating insects to reach the flowers).

Lopsided or deformed fruit: Incomplete pollination is a common cause of oddly shaped fruit and berries. Insufficiently fertilized tree fruit falls off in the June drop, but partially fertilized fruit can mature completely despite being lopsided.

Corn with undeveloped kernels: Later-maturing kernels on the ear missed the boat when pollen was dropping, so they remain unfertilized and therefore undeveloped. This is common in home garden corn because the small number of plants shedding pollen at one time means that some silks can be missed (each silk is connected to a kernel, and each one must have a pollen grain to fertilize it).

9.52. They aren't pretty, but the developed kernels are perfectly edible.

Vertebrates

Deer, raccoons, rabbits, rats, and birds (not to mention the neighbor's cat or your own bouncing dog) can do more damage to a garden than all other pests put together. Deer are increasingly common in rural and suburban areas. As their numbers increase, more gardeners are finding it impossible to grow a food garden without fencing. This is an expensive investment, but if you live where deer pass through even occasionally, it will save a lot of grief if you put up a fence before you plant. A deer fence also keeps out pets, and you might as well design it to keep out rabbits while you are at it; they too are becoming a serious problem in more places.

A word of caution: Temporary measures, such as covering plants with floating row covers or plastic mesh keep out birds, but usually end in (your) tears when the deer show up. Deer are clever at pawing away, crawling under, or pulling down temporary fences or covers. Many a gardener, convinced they had a deer-proof fence, has discovered that once their aged dog passed on, the deer soon found a way past the fence. A fence backed up with a dog inside is an excellent deer deterrent, but try this only with dogs that don't dig holes or like to eat the crops. Repellents are also temporary measures that can be effective

9.53. I'm sure this little island black-tail is thinking about my garden...

enough for landscape plants that can take occasional damage, but don't rely on them to protect food crops, a.k.a. "deer candy." Some repellents are not for use on edible plants anyway, and deer have been known to ignore repellents, especially where they are short on food.

For orchards, an approach that may work for some people is to grow tall fruit trees (standard, not dwarf varieties), and prune them so crop-bearing branches are too far off the ground for deer to reach. Trees still need to be fenced to protect them from deer until they are tall enough.

Fences

I have seen a wide variety of deer fence designs, and I cannot swear that any are perfectly deer-proof. A motivated deer is a clever critter that will sooner or later get in; it will find a gap in the most improbable place, crawl under poorly secured fencing, or simply waltz through a gate left open. Where deer numbers are low, they are easier to keep out because they have other places to go. Where deer populations are high, there is a lot of pressure on your defenses, especially in the summer, when wild food supplies for deer are drying up.

When designing your fence, take into account the size of deer in your area. On Vancouver Island, where the deer are smaller island black-tails, fences 6- to 8-feet high are usually adequate. For the considerably larger white tails and mule deer on the mainland and Olympic Peninsula, however, plan on installing an 8- to 10-foot fence. Deer can jump vertical fences, but they are less inclined to try slanting fences or those with a projecting shelf at the top. These designs, however, take up more space than vertical fences and are harder to build.

Chain link: This is the ultimate defense—very expensive initially, of course, but it will outlast you and never need maintenance. Given the rigidity of chain link, deer cannot crawl under it. And, if there are no gaps between the ground and the bottom edge of the fencing, it is also effective against adult rabbits (baby rabbits may squeeze through it).

Deer and rabbit wire fencing: This is a woven wire fencing with the horizontal wires closer together at the bottom of the fence to make the openings smaller, though they are not actually small enough to keep out rabbits. It is available in several widths. Mounted on wood or metal posts, it is moderately priced, especially if you can do some installation yourself. Wooden posts will eventually need to be replaced, but the wire can be removed and restrung onto new posts after years of service. You can extend the useful height of this fencing by stringing a higher wire or two between the posts above the top edge of the fencing. Five-foot-high fencing can effectively be made 6 feet by stringing a wire 1 foot above the fence (tie plastic tapes to the wire so deer can see the wire).

Deer can crawl under woven wire if it is sagging or there are gaps along the bottom. One solution is to install a board or 2 × 2 crosspiece at ground level, spanning from post to post and screwed or nailed to the post at each end.

Staple the bottom edge of the fencing to this crosspiece. These crosspieces also make good supports for attaching sturdy wire mesh (such as ½-inch chicken wire or welded wire mesh) to keep out rabbits. The bottom edge of rabbit fencing must be in tight contact with the ground, either held down by stones or wire pins or by burying the bottom edge in soil, to ensure there are no gaps along the fence.

Plastic mesh fences: Plastic fencing ranges from large fairly sturdy mesh to finer "invisible fence" meant to be mounted on lightweight posts or metal fence stakes. Deer have been known to stand on their hind legs and pull these fences right off the posts, so don't trust plastic fences unless deer are only occasional visitors to the neighborhood. People have better results with this type of fence when it encompasses a larger area, so deer don't see the tasty

9.54. Deer and rabbit wire fence stapled to a bottom crosspiece, with a chicken wire strip to keep out rabbits. It still didn't stop deer from reaching their noses through the fence to graze on the plants inside.

garden plants. For temporary deer fencing, the sturdier plastic mesh, tightly stapled to wooden posts can be adequate.

Wooden fences: You can certainly build wooden fences of latticework or boards. They are more aesthetically pleasing than the more utilitarian fences just discussed; however, they block a good deal of light. Whether this is an important consideration will depend on where your garden beds are in relation to your fence (bear in mind the long shadow a fence will cast when the sun is low in the winter).

Other Barriers and Repellents

Motion-activated animal repellents: These devices have motion sensors that trigger a short but startling jet of water that works quite well to frighten animals. The ScareCrow® device has been on the market for many years (for products, see Resources). It is battery powered and connects to a hose; it only shoots a cup or two of water at a time, so the tap only has to be turned on to a trickle. The Spray Away® device has a solar-powered sensor and contains a water reservoir. For the greatest startle effect, point the startle device where the jet of water can hit leaves, as this amplifies the noise. This is effective for scaring away raccoons when fruit trees or grapes are ripening and deterring cats from using garden beds as litter boxes. Animals get used to them if they are always in the same place, though, so keep up the element of surprise by moving the device to different places every few days. Some dogs find it hilarious to run back and forth turning on the water, so you might want to turn it off during the day.

Netting: Many mesh or netting products are sold for covering vegetables and fruit. Plastic meshes are lightweight and most useful to keep out birds. But the lightest and cheapest mesh will make you weep with frustration as it tangles and snags on everything. Stiffer plastic mesh is easier to mount on stakes or lay over beds of strawberries without tangling, but it has to be pinned down or weighted along the edges to keep animals from getting under it.

Used fishing nets is another option. Because they are soft, flexible, and heavy, they drape easily over temporary supports and don't need weights along

9.55. Fish nets are easy to drape over beds to keep out small critters, such as rabbits and birds (but don't count on them to keep out deer).

the edges. They are bulky, however, and must be perfectly dry before you store them away.

Scare tapes: As a temporary measure, while fruit is ripening, you can string shiny tapes over the top of berry plants. These are usually made of Mylar or other reflective material and are designed to turn and twist in the wind and startle birds. They work pretty well if you string enough tape back and forth, and they are certainly easier to install than trying to cover a large berry patch with mesh. Variations include tying old CDs or strips of tinfoil to cords strung over the berry bushes, so they dance and flash in the breeze.

Fruit bags: Fastening bags over individual fruit or bunches of grapes sounds tedious, but it is easy—and about as pest-proof as you can get. Growers slip paper bags over Asian pears and sometimes other fruit to ensure perfection, but I use this idea in my garden for grapes. If you have ever struggled to cover a vigorously growing grape vine with mesh and tried to secure it so there are no gaps, you will appreciate how easy it is to slip a bag over each bunch, cinch

9.56. My homemade grape bags in operation. I love how easy this is! And now they also protect my grapes from fruit flies.

How to Make Fruit Bags

If you can use a sewing machine, you can easily make bags to protect bunches of grapes and other fruit. I sew them out of tough lightweight fabric with a tight weave, such as nylon curtains from the local thrift shop. I use a piece of fabric 8 inches wide by 24 inches long (20 cm by 60 cm) or two pieces 8 inches by 12 inches (20 cm by 30 cm). Sew them with a ½ inch (1 cm) seam allowance. Make a drawstring sleeve by turning under the top couple of inches (5 cm) of the (open) edge of each bag. Thread a shoelace or strong cord through the sleeve. Finished size of the bag is about 7 inches (18 cm) wide and about 10 inches (25 cm) long. If you sew five to ten bags each year as the harvest increases on a growing vine, by the time the vine reaches full production, you will have accumulated all the bags you need. At the end of the season, wash the bags and store them for next year.

9.57. Sheet metal barriers prevent mammals from climbing tree trunks.

up the drawstring and tie the string to the branch. Leave the bags in place until the grapes are ripe. The bags can be reused for years and provide protection from rats, birds, and wasps, even raccoons, if made of sturdy fabric. The bags don't interfere with summer pruning of the vines, and the grape leaves continue to receive full sun. They also work well for vines trained over arbors (which are impossible to adequately cover with netting), and they keep sun off the fruit, which is desirable for the best quality.

Metal tree collars: Critters that climb tree trunks—mainly raccoons, rats, and squirrels—can be kept out of fruit trees if you wrap wide metal flashing around the trunk during the period fruit is ripening. It should be at least two feet high to prevent their scrabbling claws from getting a grip on the trunk. For this to work, the tree has to be in the open where there is no other route into the tree from other trees, buildings, shrubs, fences, etc. The metal collars will only keep out squirrels if the tree is so far away from buildings or other trees that squirrels can't make the leap. Put flashing on all of the trees in a small orchard where branches overlap.

Where these vertebrate pests are a problem, when establishing the shape of a fruit tree, the lowest branches should start four or five feet above the ground, so there are no branches low enough for the animals to jump up and grab.

CHAPTER 10

A to Z Vegetables

This section includes what I think is key information for growing each vegetable successfully in a home garden. Unless mentioned otherwise, assume they all should be grown in fertile soil, with a pH 6.5 to 6.8, and that they all need irrigation in dry weather. The timing of planting and the overwintering information generally applies to the coastal regions of southern British Columbia and Washington and Oregon. Notes under Varieties provide examples updated for this new edition; it includes ones I have found most successful, but is far from being an exhaustive list of all that are currently available. For plants noted under Seed Saving as being at high risk of cross-pollination, make sure there are no related vegetables or weeds blooming at the same time. For information on cross-pollination and seed saving, see Chapter 5. For more information on the most common pest problems, see Chapter 9 and see Table 2.1 for disease-resistant varieties available at time of writing.

Arugula

Several different species of annual and perennial arugula have the same nutty, peppery flavor. Leaves of annual varieties are larger, but plants go to seed quickly in the summer, while the narrower leaves of perennial arugula can be harvested nearly year-round.

Culture: Sow annual arugula ½ inch (1 cm) deep at monthly intervals from April to early September for a continuous supply of young leaves. Perennial arugula grows readily from seed, eventually becoming large clumps; plant where it can remain for years. It is drought tolerant, and plants are hardy enough to survive most winters; mature plants also produce seeds, providing a supply of replacement seedlings.

Harvest: Use annual arugula from the thinning stage on up. Keep plants well-watered and fertilized for rapid growth; they become strong flavored in hot weather or when stressed by lack of water. For harvest all winter, plant perennial arugula in a protected site or move a couple of plants into an unheated greenhouse or cold frame.

Pests: Cabbage/crucifer flea beetles.

Species: Varieties of *Eruca vesicaria* are the traditional annual arugula or roquette; other annual arugulas are *Diplotaxis* species (Sylvetta, Red Dragon). *Diplotaxis tenuifolia* is the perennial or wild roquette.

Artichokes

These large ornamental perennials with feathery gray leaves and edible flower buds grow up to 5 feet (1.5 m) high. Some plants persist for many years, but most are not long-lived. They are not reliably hardy in the colder parts of the British Columbia coast or in poorly drained or heavy clay soils.

Culture: Plants grow readily from seed, but seedlings are quite variable. For a few plants, you might be better off buying plants from a nursery. Set plants 3 to 4 feet (1 m) apart in well-drained soil, rich in organic matter. Artichokes can manage with less irrigation than other vegetables. It is essential for winter survival that roots never sit in waterlogged soil and that crowns are protected from heavy rain and frost. In November, cut back stalks to 6 inches (15 cm) and mulch over the crowns with dry leaves or fluffy straw. Where winter temperatures dip well below freezing, cover each mulched crown with an overturned plastic pot (largest size) to keep the crown dry; mulch over the pot with another layer of leaves (push a stake through a drain hole in the pot to keep it in place). As soon as the weather begins to warm in February, remove the pot and pull back some of the mulch. Be ready to cover again if below-freezing temperatures are predicted.

Harvest and storage: Cut flower buds at any stage, from small tender buds until the tips of

10.1. This artichoke is at just the right stage for picking.

the bud scales begin to point slightly outward. The more mature the flower, the more fibrous and thistle-like the choke inside becomes.

Pests: Aphids, tended by ants, attack the flower stalks and feed between the bud scales.

Varieties: Green buds: Green Globe, Imperial Star. Purple buds: Violet Star, Violetta (purple varieties have been less hardy than Green Globe in my garden).

Asparagus

Growing your own is the only way to experience the sweetness of just-picked asparagus, but they do take up a lot of space for a few weeks of harvest. Expect to harvest five to nine shoots per crown, depending on variety, when the plants are mature.

Culture: Best in deep well-drained soil with a 7.0 pH; plants grow poorly in acid soil. Set one-year-old crowns (the usual size sold at nurseries) at the bottom of a trench 8 inches (20 cm) deep with crowns 1 foot (30 cm) apart in the row, rows 3 to 4 feet (1 m) apart. Lightly cover crowns with soil, gradually filling in the trench with soil as the shoots grow. Some people report better results growing asparagus in raised beds over 2 feet deep. Fertilize heavily with a thick layer of compost plus complete organic fertilizer, after growth starts in the spring; lime in the fall as required to raise pH. Wait until after two full growing seasons to begin harvest (waiting three years is better). Harvest for two weeks in the third spring; three to four weeks in the fourth year; and up to eight weeks thereafter, as long as shoots remain vigorous and a good size (finger width). You can grow plants from seed (note that they can take up to eight weeks to germinate), and they will be ready for harvest after four years. In the summer, stake up fronds, which can grow quite tall. Cut down fronds in late fall and mulch beds well.

Harvest and storage: Cut or snap off spears when they reach the desired length. If cutting, take care not to injure neighboring spears.

Pests: Slugs damage tips of emerging spears. Asparagus beetles (two species) usually don't cause significant damage to mature plants, but if necessary to protect new plantings, pyrethrin sprays are effective (never use soap sprays, which damage asparagus).

Varieties: Traditional open-pollinated varieties are the Washington series (Mary, Martha, Waltham). All-male hybrids are now widely planted because they produce more than female plants, which devote their energy to producing seeds. These include the Jersey series (Jersey Knight, Jersey Supreme) and a promising new hybrid, Guelph Millenium.

Beans

Good old beans: prolific, reliable, and popular! Snap beans are eaten fresh while pods are tender. Dry beans are shelled after they mature (young soybeans can be eaten fresh, as edamame). Bush beans produce a crop a week or two earlier than pole varieties, but stop growing when they reach full-size, whereas pole beans grow and produce all season.

Culture: Beans need less soil nitrogen than other vegetables because they produce their own. Wait until the soil is at least 60°F (15°C) before sowing. Plant seeds up to 1½ inches (3 to 4 cm) deep, spaced 2½ inches (6 cm) apart. For an earlier start and to avoid damage from pillbugs, sprout seeds indoors and set out plants when they have two true leaves (see Chapter 5). Sow bush varieties of snap beans monthly until late June to provide continuous harvests; spring plantings of pole beans continue all season, usually with a lull in late summer when a new flush of flowers produces a fall crop. Provide sturdy supports for pole beans, which grow quite tall.

Harvest and storage: Keep snap beans picked, even if you can't use them, because maturing beans stop plants from producing more flowers. For dry beans, leave pods on the plant until they are dry and yellow; finish drying indoors and then shell them.

Pests: Aphids; pillbugs. Leaf diseases, such as bacterial blight or bean rust, may occur in prolonged periods of wet weather. Use irrigation systems that keep leaves dry and avoid working among bean plants while leaves are wet.

Varieties: Snap beans: Both bush and pole varieties with green, yellow, and purple pods are available. Pole varieties are very productive in small areas. Romano pole beans (e.g., Musica, Hilda) have long flat pods and excellent flavor. Runner beans are a different species, also edible fresh. Dry beans: Many varieties, including soybeans, are available, and any snap beans can be left to mature for dry beans.

Saving seed: Easy. With the exception of scarlet runner beans, which are insect pollinated, bean flowers are self-fertile and won't cross. Allow pods to mature on the plant until the seeds inside are hard and the pods become papery. Finish drying indoors, then shell them.

Beets

Beets are two crops in one because the leaves are also delicious. Beets are very sensitive to acid soil, so if you have trouble growing beets, your soil pH may be too low.

Culture: Seed ½ to 1 inch (1 to 2 cm) deep. Each "seed" is a dried fruit containing several seeds, so plants must be thinned; space seedling 2½ to 3 inches (6 to 8 cm) apart. For a steady supply of baby beets, sow successive plantings monthly, starting when soil temperature is over 50°F (10°C), usually mid to late April. For winter harvests, sow beets in early July; soil must be very well-drained for good winter survival.

Harvest and storage: Roots and leaves are edible any size starting with thinnings. For most varieties, the best quality roots are up to 2½ to 3 inches (6 to 8 cm) in diameter. Leave beets in the garden over the winter, well-mulched, and dig them as needed.

Pests: Spinach leafminer. Varieties susceptible to Cercospora leaf spot show circular spots on leaves in wet weather, but the roots are not affected.

Varieties: Dark red, round beets: Detroit Dark Red, Detroit Supreme, and related open-pollinated varieties are the gold standard for quality (in my humble opinon!); Early Wonder, Red Ace F1 are also very reliable. Novelty yellow, orange, and white varieties are available. Cylindrical (elongated) beets (Cylindra, Taunus F1) are not the best choice for winter harvests because their high "shoulders" poke above the soil making them vulnerable to frost damage.

Saving seed: Easy. Overwintered beets flower in late spring, and seeds need most of the summer to ripen. High risk of cross-pollination because pollen is windborne. Beets can cross with Swiss chard.

Broad Beans or Faba/Fava Beans

Broad beans grow on upright plants with large fibrous pods sticking out from a main stem.

Note: Broad beans are toxic to some people, causing a kind of anemia called favism.

Culture: Sow 2 inches (4 to 5 cm) deep, thin to 6 inches (15 cm) apart in rows. They are more tolerant of acid soil than other legumes. Sow in March for summer harvest or in October for harvest early the following spring. They are very frost hardy, but plants are brittle and easily broken by heavy snow or wind.

Stake overwintering plants against wind, and in some areas wet snow, or grow them under a roof overhang or in a plastic tunnel.

Harvest and storage: Remove fresh beans from pods or allow seeds to mature and use as dry beans.

Pests: Bean aphids attack the flowers in late spring. Fall-planted beans avoid aphid damage because the beans are ready for harvest before aphids attack in the spring.

Varieties: Large-seeded: Broad Windsor, Aquadulce. Small-seeded: Sweet Lorane.

Saving seed: Easy. Flowers are self-fertile and won't cross. Allow pods to mature on the plant until beans inside are hard. Finish drying indoors and shell out seeds.

Broccoli/Broccolini

Broccoli is one of the most nutritious vegetables, and you can eat it fresh from the garden at least ten months of the year with the right choice of varieties. Broccolini is a broccoli crossed with Chinese kale, and broccoflowers may refer to broccoli crosses with cauliflower or just to the green-headed types of cauliflower; the same cultural methods apply to all. Summer varieties are harvested the same summer they are sown, while overwintering varieties produce heads in early spring the year after they are sown.

10.2. One of the purple sprouting broccoli plants that survived the freeze (see Figures 8.16 and 8.17) starts producing in late February.

Culture: Sow ½ inch (1 cm) deep, or start seedlings indoors in late March for planting out in early May. Space plants 1 to 2 feet (30 to 60 cm) apart: wider spacing is for sprouting broccoli. Keep plants well-watered because even short periods of drought severely reduce the crop. A spring planting of sprouting broccoli continues to produce side shoots until December. For a steady harvest from varieties with a large central head, plant a few new plants each month until early July. Start overwintering varieties by the end of June for plants to be harvested from next February to June; these plants may be kept going for several years if desired (they get quite large), producing a fresh flush of shoots every spring until a harsh winter brings them down.

Harvest and storage: Harvest heads and side shoots before individual florets begin to open or show yellow. Keep shoots cut, whether you use them or not, because plants stop producing if the flowers are allowed to bloom.

Pests: Cabbage root maggot; imported cabbageworm; cabbage aphids, clubroot of cabbage.

Varieties: Central head summer broccoli produces a large, dense central head followed by a modest yield of side shoots (Green Goliath, Waltham, and many hybrids). Green sprouting summer broccoli has a smaller central head followed by a larger continuous harvest of side shoots; plants grow well over 3½ feet (1 m) tall and often survive mild winters (Calabria, Italian Green Sprouting).

Purple sprouting winter broccoli is the main type of overwintering broccoli: Extra Early Rudolph is earliest (often February), but less productive than the excellent Red Spear (starts in March). There are also white sprouting winter varieties. Winter broccoli can live for several years, becoming huge, until killed by a particular severe winter. Recently introduced purple sprouting *summer* broccoli is causing confusion; these produce heads the first summer, not after wintering over: be sure you know which type you are buying.

Saving seed: Easy, but overwintering broccoli doesn't set seed until the second summer. High risk of cross-pollination with cauliflower, Brussels sprouts, and related plants. Allow the flowers to bloom and set seed pods. Harvest when pods are tan and dry.

Brussels Sprouts

A much-maligned vegetable, possibly because few people have tasted the sweet nutty flavor that develops after they have been frosted out in the garden.

Culture: Start seeds in late May to early June. Sow directly in the garden ½ inch (1 cm) deep or grow transplants in pots or in a nursery bed. Final spacing should be apart 1 to 2 feet (30 to 60 cm) because plants grow quite large. If started too early, the sprouts develop in late summer when aphids are more likely to damage them. If started too late, however, plants won't have time to produce sprouts before winter. To hasten sprout development, snip out the top cluster of leaves in late September or early October. Stake plants in the fall to prevent stems from breaking in wind and snow.

10.3. The top of this Brussels sprouts plant was pinched out in late September to hasten the growth of sprouts along the stem.

Harvest and storage: Leave plants in the garden all winter and snap individual sprouts off the stem as needed, leaving smaller sprouts to continue growing. If plants are frozen, wait until they thaw in warmer weather before harvesting. In the spring, overwintered plants grow tender shoots all along the stem where the sprouts were (and even if there weren't any sprouts)—this crop is well worth waiting for!

Pests: Cabbage root maggot; imported cabbageworm; aphids feeding inside sprouts ruin them; clubroot of cabbage. Root diseases are not common, but are best avoided by rotating mustard/cabbage family crops.

Varieties: Most are hardy to 14°F (−10°C), but Roodnerf is exceptionally hardy (to at least 0°F/−18°C that I know of). Hybrids often do better than open-pollinated varieties in variable or hot summer weather: Churchill F1 is particularly vigorous and cold hardy. Red varieties (e.g., Red Ball) are slower and less productive, but pretty.

Saving seeds: Leave plants in the garden all winter without harvesting the sprouts. Flower stalks come from each sprout in the spring. High risk of cross-pollination. Harvest when pods are tan and dry, and finish drying indoors.

Cabbage

There are so many types of cabbages suited to different seasons, it is hard to know where to start: green or red, ballhead (solid round heads), savoy (crinkly leaves), or pointed (conical) heads for summer, fall, winter, or spring crops. Time your planting dates based on the days to harvest for each variety, which can range from 60 to 210 days.

Culture: Be generous with irrigation to ensure heads grow rapidly. Seed directly in the garden, ½ inch (1 cm) deep or grow transplants. Early transplants should have stems smaller than a pencil when they are set out; larger plants may produce premature seed stalks or may never produce a head if there is a late cold spell. Final spacing should be 1 to 2 feet (30 to 60 cm). Some winter harvest varieties with large solid heads need 120 to 210 days to mature to full-size, while midseason cabbages take 70 to 85 days and early varieties as little as 60 days. For mid- to late summer harvest, sow early varieties from March to May. For fall and winter harvest, sow from mid-May to early June, depending on the variety; small varieties that take 50 to 60 days to harvest can be sown in early August. At the end of the summer, to stop mature heads from splitting in fall rains, tug or twist each head an eighth of a turn in the soil, just enough to break some fine roots and slow their growth.

Harvest and storage: Cabbages are ready to eat as soon as heads feel solid, but of course, heads will be bigger the longer they grow. Hardy varieties can stand in the garden all winter and stay in excellent condition. If the heads freeze in cold weather, wait until they have thawed completely in a warm spell before harvesting (it may take up to a week to thaw).

10.4. This Greyhound cabbage matures in just two months from sowing.

10.5. January King is an emperor of cabbages, with purple veins and blue-green leaves. Start seeds in late May for winter harvests because this one takes four to six months to mature.

Pests: Cabbage root maggot; imported cabbageworm; cabbage aphid, clubroot of cabbage. Other soilborne diseases, such as black rot, are best avoided by rotating mustard/cabbage family crops.

Varieties: For winter harvest, January King, Danish Ballhead, Langedijker Red are excellent (all take over 120 days to mature). Savoy cabbages grow quickly and are generally hardy. The large flat-headed Taiwan cabbages are very productive for summer and fall harvests. Small pointed-head cabbages (Greyhound, Early Jersey Wakefield, Caraflex F1) grow quickly and can be sown in early spring and again in August for a winter crop.

Seed saving: Not easy. Leave cabbages in the garden through the winter; they will send up flower stalks in the summer. In the spring cut an X, about one-inch deep, across the top of the cabbage to help the seed stalk to emerge from the center. High risk of cross-pollination.

10.6. Carrots and all the other hardy roots are a delight in midwinter.

Carrots

Baby carrots straight from the garden are a delight you can only experience if you grow them yourself. Carrots become sweeter in early fall as the cool nights cause sugars to concentrate in their roots.

Culture: The best soil is deep, loose, and without stones (stones cause forked roots). Sow thinly, ¼ to ½ inch (5 to 10 mm) deep; thin plants to 2 to 4 inches (5 to 10 cm) apart. Sow successive plantings to early July. In early July, seed a large bed of carrots for winter harvests. Carrot seeds don't tolerate deep planting, and the soil must be kept evenly moist for the germination period (seven to ten days in warm weather, longer in cool conditions). To achieve a good stand of seedlings in summer, shade the beds until seeds germinate. If necessary, you can transplant tiny carrots to fill gaps in a bed of winter carrots (worth doing because it is too late to plant more seeds).

Harvest and storage: Carrots are tasty from baby-size on up, and even the thinnings are good in salads. Spring-seeded carrots usually become woody (and huge) if left to grow until September. Dig overwintered carrots by early April to preserve their flavor because they use the sugar stored in roots to make a flower stalk when growth begins in the spring. Store carrots in the refrigerator, leaves removed, in loosely closed plastic bags or containers.

Pests: Carrot rust fly; tiny seedlings can be demolished by pillbugs and slugs (sow extra seeds to make up for losses).

Varieties: Stump-rooted or "half-long" varieties are best for shallow soil and planters. Scarlet Nantes and related varieties have excellent flavor. Chantenay types grow long carrots. There are also purple, dark red, and white novelty varieties (though I have found them disappointing compared to orange varieties).

Seed saving: Leave overwintered carrots in the garden to send up tall flower stalks in the spring. High risk of cross-pollination: if Queen Anne's Lace (wild carrot) grows in your area, don't try to save carrot seed.

Cauliflower

Tricky to grow, cauliflowers are sensitive to heat and to cold and are stressed by low fertility and uneven watering, any of which can cause distorted heads or small "button" heads. They are best when grown in cool conditions (60–65°F/15–18°C). Overwintering varieties produce the highest-quality heads (in my humble opinion) because they develop in the cool weather of March through April. Romanesco "broccoli" is a type of cauliflower.

Culture: Sow ½ inch (1 cm) deep, or start seedlings four to five weeks before planting out. Final spacing in the garden is 12 to 16 inches (30 to 40 cm) apart. If spring seedlings are too large (more than five true leaves or with stems larger than a pencil), a little cool weather or any other stress can cause

10.7. These cauliflowers were planted twelve days apart, but they were harvested the same day, after hot weather forced the later plant to produce a small head prematurely.

premature or "button" heads. Shade plants during heat waves; hot weather causes strong flavors and premature heads with separating florets. Sow overwintering varieties in mid to late June for harvest the following spring.

Harvest and storage: To produce white curds, break one or two inner leaves over the developing head to shade it; this isn't necessary for self-blanching varieties that have tightly wrapped inner leaves or varieties with colorful heads. Cut heads while the curd is fine-textured and compact, before florets begin to separate.

Pests: Cabbage root maggot; imported cabbageworm; cabbage aphid, clubroot of cabbage. Root diseases are not common, but are best avoided by rotating mustard/cabbage family crops.

Varieties: Of the summer/fall varieties, Snowball is an old favorite; Amazing is also an excellent open-pollinated variety; Snow Crown F1 is widely grown. There are also orange, purple, and lime green varieties, including broccoli-cauliflower hybrids. Romanesco is best grown as a fall crop as hot weather causes distorted or small heads.

Overwintering varieties: Galleon is a white variety, widely available; Purple Cape is extremely hardy, but getting harder to find.

Saving seed: Difficult! Start summer varieties for seed in the fall, and hold them over the winter in cold frames or very protected sites; winter cauliflower stands better over the winter under colder conditions. Both types eventually send up seeds stalks from the head, which take all summer to mature their seeds. High risk of cross-pollination.

Celeriac

Under the surface of this big ugly root (actually a swollen lower stem) is a creamy white, fine-textured vegetable, with a mild heart-of-celery flavor. It achieves greatness as the "cream" in cream of leek and celeriac soup.

Culture: Seeds are tiny, slow to germinate, and plants grow very slowly. Start indoors in February on bottom heat, or buy transplants in the spring. Set plants 8 to 12 inches (20 to 30 cm) apart each way in the garden. Seedlings with five true leaves or more may end up seed stalks if they are exposed to temperatures below 55°F (13°C) for a few days, so don't plant them outdoors until the soil is warm and a summer weather pattern has set in. Plants have short roots, so they need very rich soil and generous water (they are descended from marsh plants).

10.8. The shoulders of these celeriac will need to be well-covered with mulch before winter.

Harvest and storage: Mature plants are very cold hardy and can stay in the garden all winter. Mulch well to protect the shoulder of roots from freezing.
Pests: Trouble free.
Varieties: Limited selection.
Saving seed: Leave roots in the garden over the winter; plants send up large seed stalks in the spring. Seeds ripen over a long period, so collect them several times. Risk of cross-pollination (also crosses with celery).

Celery

Grow as for celeriac. Celery tolerates only few degrees of frost; therefore, it can only stay in the garden over the winter in the warmest, frost-free parts of the coast.
Culture, pests, seed saving: As for celeriac. Don't set celery out in the garden until the weather is reliably warm and stable.
Varieties: Limited selection; transplants are often available at garden centers. Most are self-blanching, meaning that the inner stalks remain pale and tender.

Cutting-leaf celery, grown for leaves to use as a flavoring, is easier to grow, but does not make wide stalks.

Chinese Cabbage, Leaf Mustard, Mustard Spinach, Leaf Turnip, Leaf Radish, and Related Greens

All of these greens are annuals and can be grown for summer harvest or for overwintering crops. Chinese cabbage varieties are the most sensitive to heat and poor growing conditions; the other greens are robust mainstays of a salad garden, and some are very frost hardy.

Culture: Sow ½ inch (1 cm) deep, thin to 4 inches (10 cm) apart in the row. Chinese cabbages are best sown after midsummer for fall and winter harvests because spring-sown crops may bolt to seed prematurely with the long days of June or in response to hot weather. For a (brief) spring crop, start indoors, and set plants out when conditions warm. Sow more seed of all of these greens mid- to late July for fall and winter harvests.

Harvest and storage: Use from the thinning stage on up. Cut full-grown heads of Chinese cabbage; for the other greens, pick leaves as needed and allow plants to continue growing. The pac choi types of Chinese cabbages are hardier than the wong bok types. The other greens listed are very hardy, and even small seedlings often survive the winter to produce excellent salad greens in the spring. After freezing weather, allow plants to thaw in a warm spell before picking leaves.

Pests: Cabbage root maggot; imported cabbageworm; cabbage/crucifer flea beetles; slugs, clubroot of cabbage. Root diseases are not common, but are best avoided by rotating mustard/cabbage family crops.

Varieties: There are many varieties among this large group of related plants. Chinese cabbage: pac choi/bok choy varieties have

10.9. Namenia leaf turnip greens are a mainstay of my salad bowl year-round.

loose heads of oval leaves on wide green or white ribs; wong bok/sui choi/napa cabbage varieties have tightly wrapped, upright, or barrel-shaped heads of pale green leaves. Leaf mustard: Osaka Purple, Green Wave. Mustard spinach: Komatsuna is extremely hardy and productive (but Red Komatsuna isn't). Leaf turnip: Namenia and Mizuna are similar, very hardy, with beautiful feathery leaves and mild flavor. Leaf radish has smooth mild leaves.

Saving seed: Easy. High risk of cross-pollination. Plants produce seed in the summer from a spring planting. Allow the flowers to set seed pods and harvest when pods are tan and dry.

10.10. Joi choi is a joy to grow as a late summer crop.

Corn

There is nothing like sweet corn harvested from the garden! Only a few open-pollinated varieties are early enough to mature in the cooler areas of the coast, but there many early hybrids that do well.

Culture: When the soil is warm enough for the type of corn you want to plant (see Table 10.1), sow two to three seeds in each spot or hill, 8 to 12 inches (20 to 30 cm) apart. Thin to one plant in each spot. Screen seedbeds to prevent birds from digging up the seeds. Early plantings are much more successful if seeds are started indoors in late April/early May in small individual pots; transplant to the garden, when seedlings are three weeks old and space them 8 to 12 inches (20 to 30 cm) apart. To avoid having all ears ripe at once, plant successive crops of early varieties three weeks apart until mid-June, or sow compatible early and midseason varieties at the same time. Don't remove the side shoots that sprout at the base of plants (the corn needs those leaves for maximum photosynthesis). Ensure plants are kept well-irrigated: ears of drought-stressed corn can be weirdly distorted.

Plants are wind-pollinated: the male "tassels" at the top of the plants shed pollen onto the silks that come out of the tip of the ears (the female part of the plant). For good pollination, grow corn in dense blocks rather than rows to ensure enough pollen falls onto silks.

Because kernels are seeds, their characteristics depend on the genes from both parents, so sweetness is affected by the pollen the flowers receive. There are several distinct types of sweet corn with different genetics for sweetness; cross-pollination between some types causes low-quality and mixed kernels within the ear (see Table 10.1). The easiest way to ensure good results is to grow just one variety of corn or only varieties of the same type of corn. If you do want to grow more than one, to avoid cross-pollination, different types

Table 10.1. Types of sweet corn for purposes of avoiding cross-pollination between types. Varieties may not be consistently identified by type in seed catalogues, and some newer varieties are hybrids between types; if in doubt, isolate varieties by timing plantings to ensure that pollination periods do not overlap.

Type of Corn	Minimum Germination Temperature	Characteristics	Examples of Varieties[1]
Sugary normal (SU)	60°F (15°C)	Most open-pollinated varieties and common hybrids. Kernels lose sweetness quickly after picking. Isolate from supersweet (SH2) types.	Golden Jubilee, Earlivee, Peaches & Cream, Silver Queen, Golden Bantam OP
Sugary enhanced (SE)	64°F (18°C)	Very tender kernels easily damaged. Contains more sugar than SU, but is better adapted to cold than SH2 varieties. Stays sweeter longer after harvest than SU. Isolate from SH2, but not SU.	Bodacious, Kandy King, Kandy Korn, Sugar Buns, Who Gets Kissed[2] OP
Supersweet (SH2) and improved super sweet hybrids	70°F (21°C)	Twice the sugar content of SU. Sugar does not convert to starch after harvest, so kernels stay sweet longest after harvest. Isolate from all other types.	Extra Early Super Sweet, Serendipity, Jubilee Super Sweet, Strong Start
Triplesweet & synergistic hybrids	70°F (21°C)	Isolate from SU and SH2 types.	Honey Select, Primus, Serendipity Triplesweet
Ornamental and Popcorn	60°F (15°C)	Isolate from all types of sweet corn.	Calico Popcorn OP, Pink Popcorn OP

[1] All are hybrids unless noted as OP.
[2] Who Gets Kissed can be sown in cooler soil than other varieties.

must be isolated from each other. Grow them at least about 75 yards (70 m) apart or separate them in time by sowing different types at least two to three weeks apart, so their pollen is not present at the same time.

Harvest and storage: Ears are ripe when the silks at the top of the ear have turned brown and dried up. Another way to check is to open a slit in the husk in the mid-section of the ear with a fingernail to check whether kernels are plumped up (mature) or still a bit flat and sunken (immature). Unlike traditional sweet corn, sugary enhanced and super sweet varieties can be refrigerated for several days without losing their sweetness (see Table 10.1).

Pests: Raccoons, squirrels, and rodents love corn on the cob; birds dig up seeds; wireworms attack seeds. The most destructive corn belt insects and diseases don't occur in the Pacific Northwest.

Varieties: See Table 10.1.

Saving seed: Very difficult. Very high risk of cross-pollination from any other corn growing within one-third of a mile (0.5 km), so if you want seed, it should be hand pollinated, and that's very complicated. See reference books listed in the Resources section for detailed instructions.

Corn Salad

Corn salad (mache, bird lettuce) is an excellent winter salad green. It is hardier and higher in vitamins than lettuce. Leaves have a crisp texture and a mild baby-corn flavor; they grow in a flat rosette of small leaves.

Culture: Will grow practically anywhere in any reasonable garden soil or in containers. Broadcast seeds over the surface of the soil from late August to mid-September, and lightly rake soil to cover. An ideal salad green to sow under squash vines, tomatoes, and other warm-season plants in late August. Don't grow as a summer crop: leaves are soft and soapy flavored.

Harvest and storage: The small rosettes are easy to handle if you cut individual plants off at the soil line, keeping the rosette of leaves together

10.11. Corn salad is the hardiest salad green you can grow.

for washing. When ready to use, cut off the base of the plant and drop the bite-sized leaves into the bowl. Leaf quality is best from fall through early spring. Plants produce dense roots, which are best left in the soil at harvest to add organic matter.

Pests: None. Even slugs don't bother it.

Varieties: Jade and Broad-Leaved Dutch produce larger leaves. Vit is smaller and darker green, with slightly cupped leaves.

Saving seed: Easy! Leave plants in the garden until the tiny white flowers turn into light tan seeds. Seeds shatter from the plants, so cut whole plants and dry on trays to avoid losses. Seeds are easy to shake from the dry plant material.

Cucumbers

These are not easy to get started in the coastal region because both seeds and seedlings die in cool, damp spring weather. Growing varieties with mostly female flowers (gynoecious varieties) greatly improves the yield per vine.

Culture: Start indoors three to four weeks before planting out. Plants need very warm conditions, so don't try to seed directly in the garden. Plant in rows with plants 8 inches (20 cm) apart, or in hills with three each, 3½ feet (1 m) apart. Allow vines to sprawl, or train them onto a trellis that supports the fruit. Train long English cucumbers up strings or onto a trellis and remove male flowers to prevent fertilization, which results in bulbous fruit with seeds.

Harvest and storage: Keep all cucumbers picked, even if you don't use them, or plants will stop producing flowers. Bitterness in cucumbers depends on variety and possibly temperature (fruit grown in cool conditions can be more bitter). Most of the bitterness compounds are concentrated in and just under the skin and in the stem end, so they can be removed by peeling.

Pests: Damping off and related root rots; powdery mildews (see Table 2.1 for resistant varieties).

Varieties: There are three main kinds. Pickling varieties are blocky, with short spines; pick them as gherkins (small) or medium-size for pickling. Slicing varieties are elongated, with smooth skin (Marketmore and Straight Eight are reliable old open-pollinated varieties; there are many hybrids). Lemon cucumber is a vigorous open-pollinated one, with a greater will to live than most; fruit is round with a light yellow skin, but tastes like other cukes. Long English cucumbers (usually grown in a greenhouse) are long and seedless, with very tender smooth skin.

Saving seed: Difficult. High risk of cross-pollination, so flowers must be isolated in bags or taped shut so that you can hand pollinate them. See Chapter 5 for detailed instructions on seed saving.

Eggplant

Mini and long Asian varieties are generally early and are most likely to ripen on the coast. Large-fruited varieties need hotter weather than is usual for this region and are best grown in a greenhouse or tunnel.

Culture: Seed indoors mid-April, eight to ten weeks before setting out (mid to late June); space 12 inches (30 cm) apart. Plants to be grown in greenhouses can be started and set out a few weeks earlier. Grow in the warmest possible conditions. All varieties do well as container plants.

Harvest and storage: Pick fruit before it is completely mature, while the skin is glossy. Skins can get quite tough if the fruit is left on the plant until the skin is dull or turns brownish.

Pests: Tuber flea beetles; aphids.

Varieties: Most are deep purple or purple streaked; there are also white varieties. Mini types are the smallest; Asian eggplants have long slender fruit (e.g., Ichiban). For best results growing large-fruited eggplants, choose the earliest varieties currently available.

Saving seed: Self-fertile, but there is a risk of cross-pollination by bees, so only grow one variety at a time for seed, or cover seed plants with screening. The greatest problem is having enough time for the fruit to remain on plants to ripen; in this region, a warm greenhouse is really a requirement.

Endive, Chicory, and Radicchio

This is a confusing group of related plants. Chicories are perennials, and most are winter hardy (e.g., radicchio, sugarloaf). Endives are less hardy annuals or biennials that form loose heads (e.g., escarole, frisée). Oddly enough, forced or Belgian endive (also known as witloof) is a really a chicory.

Culture: All are easy to grow from seed, but are sensitive to crowding. Space seedlings a foot apart, and keep plants evenly watered. Sow endives from early spring though July for a succession of salads. Endives may bolt in response to cold spring weather or very hot summer weather. For milder flavor, blanch centers for two to three weeks by tying outer leaves closed in dry weather (centers rot in wet conditions) or by covering plants with a large pot. Sow chicories and radicchio when the soil is warm, from late June to early July. Not every radicchio plant produces a head, but their leaves are still useful in winter salads. Sow Belgian endive in June for roots to be dug in October for forcing (leaves are too bitter to eat).

Harvest and storage: Chicories and radicchio are hardy enough to overwinter outdoors. Pick individual leaves or cut whole heads above the root (new leaves often sprout from the stumps in the spring). Escarole and frisée are least hardy; harvest before heavy frost in the fall or cover with a cold frame. To force Belgian endive, dig roots in late October, cut off leaves ½ inch (1 cm) above the top of the root. Stand roots upright close together in a container tall enough to hold the full length of roots (trim tips of longest roots if necessary); fill around the roots with soil or sand and water well. Turn a bucket or pot upside down over the planted roots, ensuring it blocks all light. Keep roots cool outdoors for a month, then move to warmer conditions (e.g., basement, garage, unheated greenhouse) for forcing. Creamy yellow buds sprout in two to three months. Cut just above the top of the root and allow new leaves to sprout: large roots can yield four to six cuttings by spring.

Pests: Trouble-free.

Varieties: Chicories: Radicchios have round or oblong heads with red or mottled leaves; sugarloaf endive has tall narrow heads with tightly wrapped leaves. Forced Belgian endive/witloof produces pale yellow blanched buds. Endives: Escarole has crimped creamy yellow, self-blanching center leaves; frisée has deeply cut fringed leaves, pale and frilly in the center.

Saving seed: Easy for the hardy chicories (endives should be moved into greenhouses or cold frames

10.12. Forcing endive is worth the effort for these crisp, mild-flavored heads in January.

to overwinter). Flowers are not generally self-fertile; therefore, allow insects to move pollen between plants or hand pollinate. High risk of crossing between all endives, chicories, and wild chicory.

Garlic

Wonderfully strong and flavorful varieties are available to gardeners: Hard-neck (Rocambole) varieties have the most intense flavor and are easy to peel. Soft-neck garlic, what is usually seen in grocery stores, keep longest.

Culture: Plant garlic in the fall, so it has time to grow a large root system before the increasing day lengths of May and June stimulate it to make bulbs. Separate cloves from the bulb (leave the skins on); plant them pointed end up, with the tip just covered, 8 inches (20 cm) apart each way. Mulch beds for the winter. The following June, hard-neck garlic sends up a curving central seed stalk (scape); snap these off as they appear, and eat them (in stir-fries, pesto, etc.). If possible, stop irrigating about two weeks before harvest, which is about mid-July for most varieties.

Harvest and storage: Hard-neck garlic is ready to harvest when four or five lower leaves have turned brown and dry and the outermost layers of the bulb become thin and papery. Soft-neck garlic is ready after necks wither, causing the tops to fall over. Lift the bulbs and hang whole plants in bunches or braids, or spread them in trays one layer deep. Keep in a warm, dry airy place for three weeks to cure; don't leave bulbs in direct sun. When bulbs and leaves are thoroughly dry, rub off loose skins and dry soil; cut the stalks of hard-neck garlic just above the bulb or leave a long enough stem to tie them in bunches. Store garlic in cool, dry, well-ventilated conditions (i.e., not in closed containers or outdoors in a garden shed).

Pests: Allium rust; garlic root rots are common. If your garlic crop is healthy, save your own bulbs for planting to avoid the risk of bringing in root diseases.

10.13. Just harvested hard-neck garlic (*left*) and soft-neck garlic (*right*).

Varieties: Buy your first garlic from seed suppliers (not the grocery store) to ensure bulbs are disease-free. There are many varieties of white skinned and reddish/purplish skinned garlic with differences in flavor and harvest dates. Portuguese Red is a very early variety that matures mid to late June; Music is an excellent main crop hard-neck garlic.

Saving seed: After harvested bulbs are cured and cleaned, select the best ones and reserve them to plant for the next crop.

Jerusalem Artichokes, Sunchokes

A root crop with fans and detractors, Jerusalem artichokes have nothing to do with artichokes. They are tall perennial sunflowers with small yellow flowers that produce a large crop of egg-sized, somewhat elongated, knobby tubers in the fall. If not kept in check, the plants develop dense, invasive stands and once established are nearly impossible to eradicate later if you change your mind (you have been warned!).

Culture: Plants grow in any soil and tolerate drought, but the best tubers are grown in fertile soil with some irrigation in the dry season. Plants are hardy perennials that grow over 6 to 10 feet (2 to 3 m) tall. Every fragment of root left in the soil grows, so don't plant them in annual vegetable beds. Suggestions for limiting their spread include growing them in large pots or in beds surrounded by root barriers sunk 2 feet (60 cm) deep in the soil. Don't discard uncooked tubers in compost piles or with garden waste; they could survive to generate another stand of invasive plants.

Harvest and storage: Roots are ready for harvest after flowers die in the fall; flavor is reputed to improve after frost. They don't store for long once dug, but can remain in the soil all winter to be dug up as needed.

Pests: None.

Varieties: There are no named varieties, but there are differences in tuber color and flavor between strains. Before planting tubers, try eating a few to check the flavor.

Saving seed: Propagated from tubers, pieces of tubers, tiny fragments of tubers.

Kales and Collards

The reliable productive kales are champions in the winter garden, when their leaves are so tender they can be used as salad greens. Kalettes are kale-Brussels sprout crosses that grow rosettes of leaves all along tall stems, and collards are a different plant with a distinctly different flavor; grow them both like kale.

Culture: Seed ½ inch (1 cm) deep; thin to a final spacing of 6 to 12 inches (15 to 30 cm) between plants. Plants sown earlier for summer harvests can remain in the garden through the winter, or they can be sown in early August for winter harvest. Both tolerate low temperatures of 14°F (−10°C), but cover plants if temperatures threaten to drop lower in an extreme cold snap. Established plants can sometimes continue for several years if left in place (they become quite tall).

Harvest and storage: Frost improves flavor; winter crop leaves are tender, sweet, and mild. Wait to harvest frozen leaves until the plants have thawed out in a warm spell.

Pests: Cabbage root maggot; imported cabbageworm; cabbage aphid, clubroot of cabbage. Root diseases are not common, but are best avoided by rotating mustard/cabbage family crops.

Varieties: Few varieties of collards are available. There are many kale varieties: Winterbor has dark green frilly leaves; Siberian has flatter tender leaves. Red Russian, Winter Red, and Redbor add color to salads. Tuscan/Lacinato or "dinosaur" kales have dark green plume-shaped leaves on large plants. Ornamental kales are also edible.

Saving seed: Easy. High risk of cross-pollination. Allow overwintered plants to flower in spring; harvest seed pods when they are tan and dry, usually by late July.

Leeks

Leeks grow beautifully in the coastal climate, and the hardy varieties are outstanding vegetables for winter harvests.

Culture: Start seeds indoors February to March (or buy seedlings later). Plant seedlings outdoors in late April to early May, spaced 8 inches (20 cm) each way. Sowing seeds at that time will produce baby leeks for fall harvest, but not full-sized plants. Leeks need rich soil because their roots are short. Don't bother planting in trenches; this is a widespread garden myth. Seedlings planted at a normal depth grow long straight (and clean!) white stalks. If seedlings are too large when set out (more than the width of a pencil), they may go to seed later if there is a late spring cold spell. In late fall, mulch around the plants as

10.14. No need to plant leeks in trenches—and these Unique leeks have the ribbon to prove it!

far up the stalks as possible. Although some varieties are unscathed at lower temperatures, if the forecast is for below 14°F (–10°C), cover them with a tarp.
Harvest and storage: Leeks can be harvested at any size, as desired. If over-wintering leeks freeze solid, wait until plants thaw out in a warm spell before harvesting.

By spring, leeks still in the garden have a ragged outer layer of leaves, but the stalks are fine underneath. Overwintered leeks develop seed stalks in the spring, but remain edible to May or later (cut leeks lengthwise and strip out the center stalk).

Pests: Trouble-free. Rotate crops to avoid root rots that attack onion family.
Varieties: Summer/fall varieties (Lancelot, Elephant, Autumn Giant) are not as hardy as winter varieties, such as Unique (outstanding quality and cold toler-ance), Durabel, Siegfried Frost, Bandit, and Saint Victor (a beautiful purplish color).
Saving seeds: Easy. Allow overwintered leeks to flower; it takes the whole sum-mer to mature seeds. High risk of cross-pollination, including with onions. When seeds turn hard and black inside the florets, cut the heads and finish drying indoors. It is difficult to separate seeds from chaff.

Lettuce

This favorite salad green comes in an amazing variety of leaf textures and colors. With the right choice of varieties, it thrives in coastal gardens all year-round.

Culture: Sow ¼ inch (5 mm) deep, or in early spring, broadcast seed on the soil surface (cover with screen if birds are a problem). Thin plants to 3 to 4 inches (8 to 10 cm) apart. Sow small amounts at two to four week intervals from early spring to late July. Plants produce harvestable leaves in three to four weeks, and grow to full-size heads in six to eight weeks. After that, they go to seed and leaves become increasingly bitter. Sow frost-hardy varieties in August for winter and early spring harvest. Lettuce survives winter in better condition when it is protected from heavy rain under a plastic tunnel, cold frame, or building overhang. Overwintered plants apparently crushed by winter often sprout beautiful heads in the spring, so don't be in a hurry to pull damaged plants.

Harvest and storage: Useable from thinning stage on up. Pick individual leaves or harvest whole plants at any size.

Pests: Slugs; Botrytis occurs in cool, poorly ventilated conditions, such as in closed cold frames.

Varieties: There are thousands of varieties among butterhead, romaine/cos, loose leaf, oakleaf, and iceberg types. Nearly all can be grown as spring lettuce. For summer, choose heat-tolerant varieties: Red Sails, Jericho, Anuenue, and Batavian (crisphead) varieties. Choose frost-hardy varieties for overwintering: Winter Density, Rouge d'Hiver, Arctic King. A few varieties do well in summer and winter: Continuity (a.k.a. Merveille des Quatre Saisons), All the Year Round.

Saving seed: Easy annuals. Allow the best plants to go to seed. Little risk of cross-pollination, but best to save only one variety at a time. Seeds ripen unevenly, so collect them over a month. Every couple of days, shake flower heads vigorously over a bucket to knock loose ripe seeds.

Melons

A challenge for even experienced gardeners, melons are delicate, need a lot of heat, and are often disappointing in coastal gardens. But when they work out, they are wonderful!

Culture: Start seeds indoors five to six weeks before planting out. Plant in rows or in hills, three plants each, 3½ feet (1 m) apart. Set plants outdoors only after the soil is very warm and the weather is stable, which may take to mid-June. Most varieties need warmer weather than the coastal climate provides; they are usually best grown in a greenhouse or plastic tunnels unless the garden is particularly warm and sheltered. Hand pollinate flowers of plants growing under covers or where bees are scarce.

Harvest and storage: Melons don't continue to ripen off the vine, so wait to pick them until the fruit slips easily from the stem.

Pests: Pillbugs; powdery mildew.

Varieties: The smaller-fruited earliest varieties have the best chance of maturing outdoors in most areas. Large-fruited later varieties may only ripen in the warmest inland sites or in greenhouses or tunnels.

Saving seed: As for cucumbers.

Mesclun

This is a term for a mixture of leafy greens, meant to be cut for baby salad greens. They liven up a salad with a variety of colors, leaf textures, and flavors, from tangy, hot, or bitter to mild and sweet.

Culture: Grow as for lettuce and other small leafy greens. Sow ¼ inch (5 mm) deep, or broadcast seed on the soil surface. Don't thin plants unless they are exceptionally crowded. Sow small amounts at two- to four-week intervals from early spring to early September.

Harvest and storage: Harvest at the baby leaf stage three to five weeks from sowing. Use scissors to shear leaves from all of the plants in a section of bed. Cut plants will sprout new leaves, which can be sheared repeatedly. Leaves can also be harvested individually as plants get larger.

Pests: Slugs.

Varieties: Typical ingredients include kales, red and green lettuce, corn salad, leaf mustards, arugula, endive, joi choi, and other leafy greens. You can make your own mix, according to taste, or buy mesclun blends from seed suppliers.

Onions and Shallots

If you are only familiar with grocery store onions, you might be amazed at the variety you can grow: from small shallots to huge Kelsae Giants, in colors of magenta, dark red, yellow, and white, and flavors from sweet and mild to extremely pungent.

Culture: Onions and shallots have short roots, so they need steady moisture; they grow best in soils with a neutral pH (7.0). Start seeds indoors six to twelve weeks before planting out in mid-April to early May, or buy seedlings or sets (tiny bulbs that grow into full size onions). Space plants 6 to 10 inches (15 to 25 cm) each way. Seedlings larger than half the width of a pencil or sets larger than a dime may go to seed in response to a late cold spell in the spring.

Onions are sensitive to increasing day length. Most varieties suitable to the Pacific Northwest need thirteen- to sixteen-hour day lengths to start forming bulbs. Plant by late April/early May, so they have time to grow roots before the long days of June stimulate bulb formation. Sow bunching onions from April through August; some are quite hardy and stand all winter. Sweet onions can also be sown in late July to produce very early mild onions the following June; however, heavy snow and cold snaps take their toll, and sometimes few survive over winter. Plant perennial onions any time from seed, sets, or bulbils (tiny bulbs that form on the top of stalk), and harvest as needed.

10.15. Thoroughly curing storage onions ensures they keep for months.

How to grow onion sets: To avoid importing root diseases on commercial sets, you can easily grow your own. Choose good storage varieties, sow mid- to late May in average garden soil (do not add compost or fertilizer before planting), two to three seeds per square inch. Dense planting keeps bulbs small (ideally dime-sized). When necks wither, harvest and cure as for table onions; store in cool, dry conditions until planting in early spring.

Harvest and storage: Pull onions of any size for immediate use. Onions from sets mature in July; those grown from seedlings mature in August or September. Harvest mature onions after the neck withers and the tops fall over, but don't be in a hurry: bulbs continue to put on weight after the tops start to wither.

To help cure onions, stop watering a week or two before you expect to harvest. Don't bend tops down artificially, because damaged tissue may become diseased. Pull mature bulbs and spread them in trays or hang them in bunches in warm, dry conditions (out of the sun) for three to four weeks. When bulbs are thoroughly dry, rub off dry leaves, soil, and loose skins, and store them in cool, dry conditions. The ideal temperature is just above freezing, but under 46°F (8°C) will do. Well-cured storage varieties keep for six to twelve months. Sweet onions keep two to four months.

Pests: Onion maggot (biology and control similar to cabbage root maggot); Allium rust (occasionally); rotate crops to avoid garlic and onion root rots.

Varieties: Storage onions: Red Wing F1 is an outstanding red; while yellow

Onion Seedlings: To Trim or Not to Trim?

Leaves of onion seedlings started indoors can be floppy and tangled, so clipping them back to 4 inches (10 cm) is often recommended to make sturdier plants. However, removing leaf area can also slow their growth and reduces the size of the later bulbs. Some gardeners never trim the tops, others always do, and everyone seems happy with their results. Whether or not you trim seedlings (I never bother), at planting time, if the tops are flopping over, cut them back to 6 inches (15 cm) to reduce the leaf area while roots recover. Don't bother if the seedlings are shorter than this at planting time.

storage onion sets are usually unnamed, seeds of many excellent storage varieties are available: Sturon is outstanding for storage and sets; also Copra F1. Sweet onions: Walla Walla (large, white, mild), Tropeana Lunga (Italian red torpedo onions). Shallots: Grow from sets or seeds (Ed's Red, Ambition F1 both produce large bulbs). Bunching onions/scallions: Kincho Japanese Bunching (also winter hardy). Perennials: Egyptian walking onion, perennial bunching onions (a.k.a. Welsh onions).

Saving seed: Hold the best bulbs until spring and replant in the garden. They will grow tall stalks with a large ball of florets at the top. High risk of cross-pollination, so ensure no other onions or leeks are flowering at the same time. Cut seed heads after the seeds have turned black and hard; spread in trays to dry because ripe seeds drop easily.

Parsnips

I don't like parsnips, so reader alert: the following information lacks the benefit of personal experience, though it has been vetted by people who do grow them.

Culture: In early spring, seed ½ inch (1 cm) deep; seeds are slow to germinate. Thin to 3 inches (8 cm) apart as soon as possible to avoid overcrowding. Get fresh seed every year because seed is only viable one to two years. Some people sow in April or May for their winter crop; others sow in June, but the soil may be too warm by then for good germination (shade seedbed). Protect roots with a thick layer of mulch for the winter.

Harvest and storage: Leave them in the garden for the winter, and dig as needed. Roots are sweeter in the fall, and aficionados claim the flavor is best after several weeks of freezing weather.

Pests: Carrot rust fly.

Varieties: Limited choice: Hollow Crow and Harris Model are standard varieties; a few hybrids are also available.

Saving seed: As for carrots.

Peas

It is an enormous pleasure to eat raw peas straight from the vine (in the interest of researching the optimum time to pick, of course). Peas can be grown in coastal gardens from spring through fall in most years unless the summer is exceptionally hot.

10.16. Pea enation virus shows up when aphids arrive on peas in midsummer, so grow resistant varieties.

Culture: Sow 1 inch (2 cm) deep, space plants 2½ to 3 inches (6 to 8 cm) apart. Very early plantings (in March) often have high losses to pests (cutworms, slugs, birds) with little gain in earliness of harvest.

Peas can germinate in soils at 39°F (4°C), but it is slow (optimum is actually 75°F/24°C). For heavy wet soils that usually can't be worked until late spring, prepare the seedbed the fall before, and mulch to control weeds over winter. In the spring, pull back the mulch for a couple of weeks to warm the soil, then poke the seeds into the soil without cultivating. For an early start and to avoid pests, sprout seeds indoors, and set out when plants are thee to four weeks old. Pea roots produce their own nitrogen, so there is usually no need to provide nitrogen amendments before planting unless peas are attacked by pea leaf weevil (see entry on p. 241). Tall varieties need tall trellises because some grow 2 yards (2 m) or more; short varieties can be allowed to sprawl, but are easier to pick if trellised. Sow two to four crops in succession from early spring to late June for fresh peas through October. For summer crops sown May through June, choose varieties resistant to pea enation mosaic virus and powdery mildew.

Harvest and storage: Pick shelling peas when the pods have filled out. Snap peas can be eaten pod and all at any size, but are at their maximum crunchy sweetness when pods are plump rather than flat. Snow peas (also called sugar peas) are meant to be harvested while the pods are flat; if they become overgrown, pods become tough and stringy, but you can still shell out the peas.

Pests: Pea leaf weevil; powdery mildew and pea enation mosaic virus are best managed by planting resistant varieties. Birds and rodents dig up seeds, so you may have to screen seedbeds until plants are several inches high.

Varieties: See Table 2.1 for disease-resistant varieties. Shelling peas: Green Arrow, Sabre, Aladdin. Snap peas: Cascadia, Sugar Ann, Sugar Snap. Snow peas (e.g., Oregon Giant) are generally more tolerant of hot weather than shelling or snap peas.

Saving seed: Easy. Flowers are self-fertile. Leave pods on the vine until they have become dry and leathery. Pick and dry further indoors, then shell out seeds.

Peppers

It takes a longer, warmer season to ripen large sweet bell peppers and some hot peppers than coastal gardens usually experience, but there are early varieties of all types that do ripen fully. Colors range from green (unripe sweet peppers) to red, orange, yellow, purple, and dark brown; flavors range from crisp and sweet to spicy hot to blistering.

Culture: Seed indoors in late March to early April. Plant out in late May to mid-June after the soil is very warm, spacing plants 1 foot (30 cm) apart. Plants need as much warmth as possible, so benefit from being kept under cloches or row covers at the beginning of the season. Poor fruit production outdoors is usually due to low temperatures, whereas in greenhouses, it is usually due to high temperatures. All peppers ripen earlier and produce larger crops in greenhouses or tunnels; they also do well as container plants, and because they are perennials, will continue over the winter if moved indoors to a warm greenhouse or sunroom. Stake plants or support with tomato cages. Pinching the tips of branches makes plants bushier and produces more flowers, but delays ripening of fruit.

A common, but puzzling, complaint is hot peppers that don't develop the expected intensity of heat. This may be due to picking fruit before it is fully mature or to natural variations between plants or to adverse growing conditions (don't let plants become drought stressed).

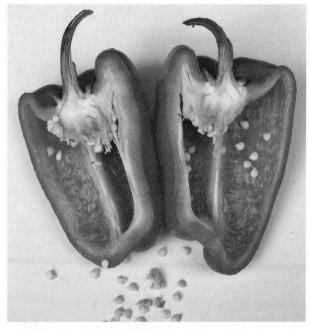

10.17. Saving pepper seed is easy as long as you prevent bees from moving the pollen around.

Harvest and storage: Sweet peppers are edible from green through all stages of ripening; they are quite sweet when fully ripe. Sweet peppers freeze well without blanching, while hot peppers are traditionally dried for long-term storage. Pull whole plants and hang up in a dry place to ripen the last fruit, or harvest ripe peppers and spread them on trays or thread them onto a string and hang up to dry.

Pests: Aphids are common on seedlings, but are usually controlled by beneficial insects when plants are set outdoors.

Varieties: Unless plants will be grown in a greenhouse, choose earlier varieties (i.e., sixty to eighty days to harvest). Hot peppers: Most have small to medium-sized, slender red, green, or yellow elongated fruit with varying intensities of heat (Habanero is many times hotter than Jalapeño). Sweet peppers: Ace F1 (early), California Wonder (blocky, bell type); Italian Ramshorn or Bull's Horn peppers have sweet elongated fruit; Pimento peppers are also available.

Saving seed: Flowers are self-fertile, but there is a high risk of cross-pollination. Grow only one variety, or screen plants to prevent visits by insects. Leave fruit to mature on the plant to the point of overripeness. Cut open fruit, and spread seeds on a plate to dry. Wear rubber gloves when handling hot peppers!

Potatoes

Potatoes grow well in the coastal climate and are very productive in a small space, even producing good crops when grown in bags of soil. A yard-square (1 m²) bed can yield 20 to 40 pounds per square yard (10 to 20 kg per m²).

Culture: Potatoes grow best at pH 6.5, but will tolerate more acidic soil, though with slightly lower yields. Plant seed potatoes (small potatoes that are planted whole, not cut up) from March through May. Set them 2 to 4 inches (5 to 10 cm) deep (up to twice as deep in sandy soil), 8 inches (20 cm) apart in rows or hills 12 to 18 inches (30 to 45 cm) apart each way. Plant only certified seed potatoes (organic seed potatoes are available); there is a high risk of importing soilborne diseases on uncertified stock, which can also spread to tomatoes and related plants. Though often stated that spuds must be grown in acid soils, that is only to prevent infection by scab (see Figure 3.8, p. 79), caused by bacteria that don't tolerate acid soil. Scab is usually not a problem in home gardens unless infected potatoes were planted (such as table potatoes); there are many varieties with moderate to high resistance to scab. Apply a thick mulch to keep soil cool and moist, or keep the soil well hilled up around plants to prevent tubers from being exposed to light and turning green (green areas are toxic). Tuber growth is determined by day length; they grow faster as days get shorter at the end of the summer.

To grow potatoes in large bags or containers (5 to 10 gallons [18.9 L–37.8 L]), fill each container with a fertile, loose soil mix and plant with two to four seed potatoes. For the largest crop, use the largest container and choose late season (indeterminate) varieties; start with the container one-half to two-thirds full of soil mix; keep adding soil around the stem as the shoots grow to increase the formation of tubers along the stem. Earlier (determinate) varieties (e.g., Red Pontiac, Colomba) largely stop producing new growth once the first tubers form; they also grow well in containers, but it won't increase the yield to bury the shoots as they grow.

10.18. Potatoes can be grown in large bags or containers to save space.

Harvest and storage: New potatoes are ready about eight to ten weeks after planting or when the flowers bloom (some plants don't flower). To harvest new potatoes, dig the whole plant or gently feel down around the roots to remove a few tubers, leaving the plant to grow. Harvest main crop potatoes September to October or a couple of weeks after the vines die down, for maximum maturity and storage ability. On a dry day, leave the potatoes in the sun for a couple of hours to dry and harden the skin, or spread them to dry on newspapers on the floor of the garage. When dry, brush off the soil, and store them in opaque containers (burlap bags, cardboard boxes) in cool (50°F/10°C is ideal) completely dark conditions. If stored in a refrigerator or left in the garden for the winter, potatoes develop a sweet taste and the texture changes. Potatoes have a natural dormancy, so they won't

10.19. Sprouting seed potatoes on a windowsill, called chitting, gives them an early start.

sprout for several months, even in less than perfect storage conditions. Don't leave potatoes in the garden through the winter: in addition to producing an odd flavor, this also potentially allows late blight to overwinter in the garden.

Pests: Tuber flea beetles, aphids; late blight. To manage common scab, plant resistant varieties (see Table 2.1) and rotate crops. Disorder: hollow heart.

Varieties: Early to midseason varieties: Red Pontiac, Chieftain, Colomba, Goldrush, Norland, Seiglinde, Warba, Yukon Gold. Late varieties for storage: Russet Burbank, Bintje, German Butterball, Kennebec, Orchestra. There are many varieties, including white, yellow, red, and blue potatoes; different varieties are suited for different uses (baking, chips, as new potatoes). A few late blight-tolerant varieties are available, including Defender, Jacqueline Lee, Ozette, Satina.

Radishes

Summer radishes are the fastest vegetable to mature (and the fastest to become overmature!). For a steady supply of prime summer radishes, sow small amounts every week or two, and don't hesitate to discard overgrown ones. Winter radishes, such as the many varieties of daikon, grow much larger and keep well in the garden for harvesting in the winter.

Culture: Sow ½ inch (1 cm) deep, thin to 1 inch (2 cm) apart, any time from March through August. Interplant them with slower-growing vegetables, or sow a few seeds in the rows with carrots and parsnips; radishes break the crust on clay soils and will be half-grown by the time the other plants germinate. The key to mild radishes for summer harvests is growing them fast by keeping them well-fertilized and watered; they become strong flavored in hot weather or when stressed by lack of water. Sow winter radishes in late July to early August for large, overwintering roots; these remain mild with a sweeter flavor as they mature in cool weather.

Harvest and storage: Harvest summer radishes starting when they are the size of a nickel. They keep well in the refrigerator. Leave winter radishes in the garden, well-mulched, for winter harvests. Green pods that form on flower stalks of plants allowed to go to seed are also edible.

Pests: Cabbage flea beetle; cabbage root maggot can be very destructive, especially to overwintering varieties. Root diseases are not common, but are best avoided by rotating mustard/cabbage family crops.

Varieties: Summer radishes: Many varieties of round red, long red, or white radishes; White Icicle; French Breakfast (elongated heirloom variety). Winter radishes: Many varieties of daikon (long, carrot-shaped roots), watermelon radishes (red inside, such as China Rose, Starburst, Red Meat), Black Spanish (round, with tough black skin, but tender white interior). Wasabi radish is a type of daikon as hot as the real thing.

Saving seed: Easy. Leave roots in the garden to send up seed stalks later in the season (winter radishes go to seed in the spring). Allow seed pods to dry, and harvest. High risk of cross-pollination with turnips, Chinese cabbage, leaf mustard, and wild mustards.

Spinach

If you have been frustrated by how quickly spinach bolts to seed, try sowing it in August. You can pick leaves all fall and some in the winter, depending on the weather. Overwintered plants grow a whole new crop of leaves starting in March and on through May. New Zealand spinach is a vigorous, unrelated tender perennial that produces fairly spinach-like leaves all summer (sow outdoors in June after soil has warmed).

Culture: Spinach is sensitive to acid soil. Sow seeds ½ inch (1 cm) deep; thin plants up to 1½ inches (2 to 3 cm) apart each way. Seeds germinate best in cool soil; in warm soil, sow extra seeds to compensate for lower germination rates. Rapidly increasing day lengths in spring cause spinach to go to seed, as does heat stress, so late spring- and summer-sown plants don't produce much. Sow in early to mid-August for the overwintering crop. Shade the seedbed during the germination period. Seedlings of most varieties stand up to late summer heat well, with only a few going to seed prematurely. Spinach does better in winter when it is protected from low temperatures and heavy rain under a plastic tunnel or cold frame or in a bed under the overhang of a roof.

10.20. Planted last August, growth is really taking off in March. By June, I have had enough spinach and am happy to see it going to seed!

Harvest and storage: Pick leaves from August-sown plants over the fall and winter. No matter how battered the plants look by February, from March through the end of May, they will produce a large crop of new leaves before going to seed.

Pests: Spinach leafminer; downy mildew (see Table 2.1 for resistant varieties).

Varieties: Long Standing Bloomsdale and related varieties (e.g., Bloomsdale Dark Green, Bloomsdale Savoy) are reliable, winter hardy; Giant Winter or Viroflex is well-suited to overwintering. Many disease-resistant hybrids are also available.

Saving seed: High risk of cross-pollination. Pollen can travel a long way on the wind. If there is no other spinach flowering in the area, allow your plants to set seed, and leave them until seeds ripen. Save seed from the last plants to bolt, not the first.

Squash and Pumpkins

Summer squash are very large productive plants, so don't plant too many! Many winter squash and pumpkins need quite a lot of space because they have sprawling vines, but they can be directed to run over non-garden areas and pathways if growing space is at a premium.

Culture: Start seeds indoors five to six weeks before planting out. Theoretically, summer squash can be sown directly in the garden in early to mid-June if the soil temperature is over 60°F (over 77°F is better) (16°C, over 25°C is better), but the crop will be late. Plant in rows or hills with three plants per hill, 3½ feet (1 m) apart for bush varieties, somewhat wider for vine types. Dig in a generous supply of compost and amendments high in nitrogen before planting.

Open-pollinated varieties usually produce male flowers for several weeks before female flowers appear. In poor soil, they may never produce female flowers. Some hybrids produce only female flowers for the first few weeks; for such plants, pick off the early female flowers because premature fruit set stunts the plant. Be prepared to hand pollinate flowers (see text box for instructions), at least in early summer, before bees are numerous. Pollen must be transferred to flowers within the same *Cucurbita* species group (see Table 10.2). Large-fruited winter squash (e.g., Hubbards, large pumpkins) take all

10.21. Keep summer squash, like this zucchini, picked to ensure plants continue to flower; if you planted too many, remove a few plants.

Hand Pollinating Squash

We can't rely on bees to pollinate flowers, both because their numbers are lower than they used to be and because they don't fly in the spells of cool weather that are common on the coast. The most important plants to routinely hand pollinate are the squash family. To make sure of a crop, hand pollinate your squash, pumpkins, melons, and gourds. Here's how:

Male squash flower (*top*) and female flower (*bottom*). Note the small squash below the female flower.

Transferring the pollen to the female flower.

1. First, find an open female flower: they have a miniature squash attached below the flower.
2. Then find an open male flower: they have a straight stem with no miniature fruit below the flower, and you can also see pollen, like bright yellow dust, on the center structure of the flower.
3. Pick the male flower, peel back the petals, and dab some of the pollen onto the center structure of all the open female flowers. You can dust several female flowers with the pollen from one male flower.

Squash flowers only last for a day in the summer, so pollinate in the morning, before the blossoms wilt later in the day.

There is, however, one complication to keep in mind: Three different species of squash are grown in this region, and pollen from one species won't pollinate flowers of a different species (for commonly grown varieties in each group, see Table 10.2). As long as you stay within the species group, you can use pollen from one variety to fertilize the flowers of another variety. The species is usually listed on the seed packet or in the variety description, but if you don't know which group your squash or pumpkins belong to, just stick to transferring pollen from male flowers to female flowers within plants from the same variety.

summer to mature; keep the first two fruit that set on each vine, and pinch off any squash that sets after August 1 because they won't have time to mature. Small-fruited winter squash (e.g., Acorn, Delicata, Festival) can usually mature four to six fruit per plant.

Harvest and storage: Summer squash: Usable at any size, but best when small (6 inches/15 cm long for zucchini). Squash flowers or the flowers along with the tiny fruit still attached are also edible. Winter squash: Harvest when the vines mature (leaves begin to die back) and the squash stem is shriveled and dry (you won't be able to dent it with a fingernail). Winter squash and pumpkins can survive light fall frosts, but if a frost is expected, cover the plants or harvest the fruit and bring it indoors. To harden and seal the skin against rot organisms, cure fruit for at least ten days in a warm (80–86°F/27–30°C) dry location with good air circulation. When fully cured, the stem is dry and gray (and as hard as wood). Gently brush soil off cured squash, and store them

Table 10.2. Common squash within each species group. When hand pollinating flowers, stay within the species group.

Cucurbita pepo (Most summer squash)	Zucchini, Romanesco Yellow crooknecks Acorns Vegetable spaghetti Delicata, Festival, Sweet Dumpling Stripetti Scallopini/Pattypan Sugar pumpkin, most pie pumpkins* Vegetable marrow
Cucurbita maxima (Most winter squash)	Buttercups Bananas Hubbards Kuri, Kabocha Turbans Rouge Vif d'Etampes pumpkin Most mammoths Sweet Meat, Sweet Mama
Cucurbita moschata	Butternuts Tromboncino

*There are some "pumpkin" varieties within each species group.

10.22. This squash is dark orange and looks ready to pick, but the stem is still soft—so give it more time.

10.23. Butternuts are the one type of squash you might be able to save seeds from without a high risk of crossing, because there are so few other varieties in the same species group.

in cool (60°F/15°C) dry conditions. Most keep at least three months and some for nine months or more. Some people wipe the skins with bleach solution (1 part hydrogen peroxide bleach to 9 parts water) before storing them, but I haven't found this necessary. Banana and acorn squash do not need to be cured; they only keep two to three months in cool dry conditions. Check stored squash at least monthly for signs of rot.

Pumpkins: For jack-o'-lanterns or Thanksgiving pies, the fruit is fine even if frost has killed the vines. To store sweet pumpkins over the winter, harvest them before frost, and cure and store as for winter squash.

Pests: Powdery mildew (see Table 2.1 for resistant varieties).

Varieties: Summer squash: Zucchini comes in many varieties including dark green, light green, yellow, even round (Eight Ball); Romanesco is striped light green, very vigorous; Partenon F1, Cavili F1 are parthenocarpic varieties for earliest fruit without pollination. Other summer squash: Vegetable marrows, yellow crooknecks, pattypans (like little flying saucers), vegetable spaghetti, Italian Tromboncino (a type of butternut with long narrow necks).

Winter squash: Many colors and shapes, most are vining; a few are bushes better suited to small areas. Varieties with large fruit (Hubbard, large buttercups, Banana) take longest to mature. Small-fruited varieties ripen more reliably in cooler regions:

Gold Nugget, Delicata, Sweet Dumpling, Acorn, Festival F1 (an Acorn–Delicata hybrid that is an exceptionally long keeper).

Saving seed: Difficult. For advanced seed savers only. Flowers must be isolated for hand pollination: bag them before they open, or tape them shut. Don't save seed from squash if flowers weren't isolated because the resulting fruit is usually poor quality. When hand pollinating for seeds, transfer pollen only between flowers within the same variety.

Sweet Potatoes (Yams)

What grocery stores label as "yams" are actually sweet potatoes. There are many orange-fleshed varieties, including early sweet potatoes for northern gardens, as well as purple- and white-fleshed sweet potatoes.

Culture: Plants grow well in moderately fertile soil, and they tolerate acid soil, but grow best where they can feel subtropical heat in the root zone. In very warm gardens with full sun all day, they can be grown in raised beds. Wait until soil is at least 55°F (13°C) to set plants outdoors; space 12 to 18 inches (40 to 60 cm) apart. It helps to use clear plastic to warm the soil for two to three weeks before planting and a clear or black plastic mulch during the growing season. In cooler years and cooler gardens, plants will produce much more when grown in large black pots (1 plant per 5-gallon [18.9 L] pot), set out along a wall where the full sun shines directly on the pots.

Harvest and storage: Harvest in the fall when temperatures begin to drop consistently below 50°F (10°C), usually mid- to late September. Stop watering two weeks before harvest. Cure tubers for a week at 77°F (25°C). They keep in cool (60°F/15°C), dry conditions for six to eight months. Use up small, finger-width roots immediately: they don't keep for long, but are delicious.

10.24. Propagating sweet potato slips from a tuber takes time, so get started in January.

Pests: Spider mites, aphids.

Varieties: Georgia Jet is very early with light orange flesh; Beauregard, Superior are dark orange; white and purple varieties are also available (look for tubers of the latter in Asian food markets). Watch for new early varieties being selected in Canada for northern growers.

Propagating: Start plants from cuttings or slips sprouted from tubers. Cuttings: At harvest, take 6- to 10-inch (15 to 25 cm) cuttings from the tips of vines. Remove lower leaves, and stand cuttings in a glass of water. Roots sprout within days, and cuttings can be potted within a month. Grow in warm, bright conditions indoors until spring. For slips: In early January, prop a small tuber upright in a jar filled halfway with water, or lay it on its side in coir or a planting mix with half the tuber buried. Keep it in a very warm place or on bottom heat until leaves sprout. Move the tuber to a warm, sunny windowsill, and let shoots grow until roots appear at the base of the shoots. When shoots have their own well-developed root systems, carefully sever the tiny plantlets from the mother tuber, keeping the roots intact, pot them up, and grow in a sunny window until spring.

Swiss Chard, Leaf Beet

These vigorous leafy greens with large upright leaves yield an outstanding amount in a small space, for a full year, from one planting in May.

Culture: Chard grows best at a high soil pH of 6.5 to 7.5. Seed ½ to 1 inch (1 to 2 cm) deep; thin seedlings to 2½ to 3 inches (6 to 8 cm) apart. Each "seed" is a seed ball containing several seeds, so seedlings must be thinned. Spring-sown plants carry through the following winter and spring. Sow more plants by late July for winter harvest, especially leaf beet varieties, which are hardiest.

Harvest and storage: Chard survives better under some type of cover, even just a plastic sheet, in the coldest weather. Allow frozen leaves to thaw out in a warm spell before harvesting. In a severe cold snap, leaves of broad-ribbed chard can freeze to the ground, but don't hurry to discard plants because roots usually sprout new leaves in spring.

Pests: Spinach leafminer; powdery mildew. Some varieties (e.g., Rhubarb chard) are susceptible to Cercospora leaf spot (many tiny round leaf spots) in wet weather.

Varieties: Swiss chards: Bright Lights (red, yellow, purple, and white stems); Fordhook (heavily savoyed dark green leaves, wide white stems). The cold-hardiest chards are Lucullus (broad stems, light green leaves) and Leaf Beet (also called Perpetual Spinach or Bietina) (narrow stems and smoother leaves).

Saving seed: Easy. Overwintered plants send up a seed stalk in late May; flowers appear in June, and seeds mature in July. Strip the seeds from the stalks, and dry the seeds thoroughly. High risk of cross-pollination because pollen is windborne; can cross with beets.

Tomatoes

Probably the food crop grown by more people than any other. Tomato varieties are generally determinate or indeterminate (some are in-between). Determinate, or bush varieties, are shorter plants that stop producing new shoots and flowers after reaching full-size. The fruit ripens early, over a relatively short period. Indeterminate, or vine tomatoes, continue to grow new shoots and flowers until they are cut down by their gardener or killed by cold; vines can grow over 8 feet (2 m) long in a greenhouse. Tomatillos and ground cherries, or husk tomatoes, are related plants.

Culture: Start bush tomatoes indoors in early April, six to eight weeks before setting out (usually mid-May to early June, after the soil is warm). Start vine varieties up to twelve weeks before setting out. Or buy transplants, which are widely available. Space bush varieties 1 foot (30 cm) apart; vine varieties may need up to 2 foot (50 to 60 cm) spacing, depending on the staking system. Bush tomatoes can be allowed to sprawl on the ground (but mulch the soil first to keep the fruit clean), or staked up to save space and reduce disease risk. Vine tomatoes should always be staked or supported. Plants grow best at 79° to 86°F (26° to 30°C); higher temperatures can kill flowers, delay ripening, and produce bland flavors. Large-fruited and long-season varieties (e.g., Brandywine) don't ripen many fruit in cool summers or cooler microclimates unless grown in a greenhouse or tunnel.

To speed ripening and prevent vine tomatoes from becoming a dense jungle, pinch out shoots (suckers) that form between a leaf stem and a main stem. After late August for outdoor plants or early October for greenhouse plants, force ripening of existing fruit by pruning off new shoots and flowers and cutting back on irrigation. To improve air circulation in the center of plant, remove oldest lower leaves below the ripening fruit. For best flavor, however, keep as many upper leaves as possible, consistent with training the vines and ensuring good air circulation.

Because of the high risk of late blight infection, it is essential to keep leaves of tomatoes dry. Bush tomatoes grow well in containers, and small-fruited varieties can be grown in hanging baskets. Bring container plants indoors to a sunporch or greenhouse to extend the season. Because tomatoes are perennials, it is possible to cut back small container plants and overwinter them indoors to produce a crop next year.

Tomatillos and ground cherry: Grow as for indeterminate tomatoes, space 2 feet apart and support in tomato cages.

Harvest and storage: Before killing frost damages the fruit, pick mature green tomatoes (full-size and light green). Spread them out one layer deep in shallow boxes or trays. Stored at 50° to 60°F (10° to 15°C), they will hold for several months. To finish ripening, bring tomatoes to room temperature; exposure to light increases their color, but is not required for ripening. You can also pull whole vines and hang them in a shed and allow fruit to ripen (spread newspapers below!). Check stored tomatoes often to remove ripening or rotting fruit.

Harvest tomatillos when the paper husk begins to loosen and the fruit inside becomes lighter green to pale yellow. For sweetest flavor, harvest ground cherries when the paper husk is completely dry and fruit is starting to fall off the plant.

Pests: Tuber flea beetles; late blight. Disorders: blossom end rot; green shoulders. Pollination problems: Most varieties can't set fruit at temperatures below 50°F (10°C) or above 86°F (30°C) (heat sterilizes pollen). While flowers present during a heat wave may die, flowers developing in cooler weather will be fine.

Credit: J. Standen

10.25. Brandywine tomatoes need lots of heat and a long growing season (this one was grown in a greenhouse).

Varieties: Too numerous to mention! Zillions of red varieties, also green, yellow, orange, brown, black, and striped. Grow at least a few early varieties to ensure ripe fruit in cool summers; parthenocarpic varieties (e.g., Oregon Spring, Siletz) can set fruit without fertilization in cool weather (45°F/7°C). Siberian tomatoes (e.g., Sasha's Altai) produce a respectable crop in cool weather. Paste tomatoes contain less juice and make excellent sauces. Large-fruited and paste tomatoes are more prone to disorders than small-fruited varieties.

Saving seed: Easy. Plants are self-pollinating, and there is low risk of crossing for most varieties; exceptions are older "heritage" varieties, such as Brandywine, with more open flowers (separate these from other tomatoes by 15 yards [13.7 m]). Leave fruit on the plant until it is slightly overripe; squeeze pulp and seeds into a glass of water. Allow to ferment for two days to break down the gel coating on the seeds, then pour off the water and rinse seeds well in a sieve. Spread the clean seed on a plate to dry (not on paper because they stick). Some people skip the fermenting stage and just dry the seeds.

10.26. Fermenting tomato seeds for a few days removes the coating.

Turnips and Rutabagas

Turnips grow quickly, and both the root and leaves are edible. Rutabagas (also called swedes) are larger yellow roots, with a distinctively different flavor, usually grown for winter harvests.

Culture: Sow ½ inch (1 cm) deep, thin to 2 inches (5 cm) apart (up to 6 inches/ 15 cm for rutabagas). Sow small amounts of turnips at two to three week intervals from March to mid-July. Sow enough for fall and winter harvest by end of July. Sow rutabagas for winter harvest by July 10. The best roots grow in deep soil without stones.

Harvest and storage: For best flavor, harvest summer turnips when they are 2 inches (5 cm) in diameter. Overgrown turnips become woody. Rutabagas grow much larger; leave them in the garden for the winter, well-mulched, and dig as needed.

Pests: Cabbage root maggots are particularly destructive; imported cabbage-worm. cabbage/crucifer flea beetles; slugs; clubroot of cabbage. Other root diseases are not common, but are best avoided by rotating mustard/cabbage family crops.

Varieties: Turnips: Purple Top, White Globe, Tokyo Cross. Rutabagas: Laurentian, Marian (resistant to clubroot).

Saving seed: Easy. Overwintered roots send up flower stalks in the spring. Harvest when seed pods are tan and dry. High risk of cross-pollination; will cross with radishes, Chinese cabbage, leaf mustard, and wild mustards.

CHAPTER 11

A to Z Fruit

All fruit trees and bushes described below grow best in full sun and well-drained fertile soil. Unless stated otherwise (blueberries are the main exception), grow them in slightly acid soil (pH 6.5 to 6.8). To produce the best crop, fruit should be irrigated during summer dry periods. If possible, avoid using overhead sprinklers, which prolongs the length of time leaves are wet and thus susceptible to fungal diseases. Details on planting and pruning tree fruit, table grapes, figs, and kiwi are given in Chapter 6. Pest and disease problems are covered in greater detail in Chapter 9. For berries and cherries in particular, the biggest change since the first edition of this book has been the invasion by a new fruit pest in the region (spotted wing Drosophila). The need to protect fruit from this tiny fly may affect what you choose to grow and how you prune to make it possible to cover plants with insect netting.

Apples

There are many apples varieties (thousands?), from favorite heritage varieties to recent selections. Named varieties of apple trees come from cuttings (called scions) grafted onto rootstock because apples are natural hybrids. They don't come true from seeds, which means fruit of seedling trees differs from the parent tree. Many varieties are available on dwarfing rootstocks; these grow to 8 to 10 feet (2.5 to 3 m) high and about as wide, though with pruning can be kept smaller. Trees grafted onto an even more dwarfing rootstock, called M27, stay under 5 to 8 feet (2.5 m), which is ideal for small gardens. Semi-dwarf trees grow to about 12 to 15 feet (3.5 to 4.5 meters). Multi-graft trees have three or

11.1. Spartan apples on a multi-graft dwarf tree. Reliable and scab-resistant, these lovely crisp apples keep for up to eight months in good conditions.

more varieties grafted onto one trunk and are almost always on dwarfing rootstock. Columnar apple varieties bear fruit along the trunk; the crop is small, but several can be planted close together for a small garden.

Culture: Plant dwarf trees 10 to 12 feet (3 to 3.5 m) apart and that distance away from hedges and other landscape plants. Apples grafted on M27 rootstock can be planted just 3 to 6 feet (1 to 1.5 m) apart. Allow 15 feet (4.5 m) around semi-dwarf trees. Install at least two permanent support posts (three is better) for each dwarf tree, or espalier them against a wall or fence, making sure the bark doesn't rub on the wires. When branches are heavy with fruit, they may also need temporary props to prevent breaking.

Pruning: If you see shoots coming from the base of the tree, they are probably coming from below the graft. Cut them off, and pull away enough soil to make sure the graft union stays above ground. After the June drop, thin to one to two apples per cluster. In years

Table 11.1. Approximate harvest period for common varieties of apples growing on southern Vancouver Island. Ripening will be earlier in warmer microclimates and warmer summers.

Harvest Period	Cultivars
Late July–early August	Yellow Transparent,* Pristine, Lodi
Mid to late August	Lodi, Sunrise, Summerred
Early to mid-September	Redfree,* Ginger Gold, Akane,* Gravenstein (ripens over a month), Sunrise,* Golden Delicious, Chehalis
Mid-September–early October	Ambrosia, Elstar,* Gala, Fiesta,* Jonafree,* Honeycrisp, Macoun,* Liberty,* Priscilla,* Spartan,* Prima,* Cox's Orange Pippin
Mid to late October	Empire, Melrose, Criterion, Golden Russet, Enterprise,* King,* Mutsu,* Jonagold, Bramley's Seedling,* Belle de Boskoop,* Cortland
Early November	Braeburn, Fuji, Granny Smith, (all need a long growing season; not for cooler coastal gardens); Pink Lady, GoldRush, Northern Spy
* Resistant or immune to apple scab	

with poor set, this won't be necessary, but when there is a heavy crop, thinning is important to ensure a crop next year.

Pollination: Nearly all apples must to be cross-pollinated by another variety (Yellow Transparent is partially self-fertile). If you don't have much space, plant two dwarf trees on M27 rootstock or grow one dwarf multi-graft tree. Varieties on multi-graft trees will have been chosen to be compatible for pollination and blooming time. Gravenstein, Mutsu, Jonagold, and Winesap varieties won't pollinate each other or other apples, but still need a cross-pollinator.

Harvest and storage: When a few apples drop from the tree, it shows the crop is maturing. Ripe apples part easily from the twig with a gentle tug; not all fruit is ripe at once. Good storage varieties keep until May or longer in ideal conditions: 35° to 41°F (2° to 5°C) with high relative humidity. Store apples in loosely closed plastic bags or containers to keep humidity high, but allow a little air exchange. Don't store apples with other fruit or potatoes because apples give off ethylene gas, which speeds up ripening (or sprouting) of other produce. Check regularly for signs of rot in stored apples.

Varieties: By choosing well, you can extend the harvest of fresh apples from late July to November if desired (see Table 11.1 for approximate harvest dates). Harvest dates vary by a couple of weeks either way from year to year, and it can take two to four weeks (e.g., Gravenstein) for all apples to ripen on a tree. Early apples don't keep for long; however, varieties that ripen in late fall generally store well. Some very late varieties (e.g., Braeburn, Fuji, Granny Smith) don't always ripen fully in cool years or in cooler microclimates on the coast. Cox's Orange Pippin, MacIntosh, Pink Lady, and Gala are so susceptible to apple scab they make poor choices for coastal growers.

Pests: Apple maggot; codling moth; leafrollers; apple scab; powdery mildew; European canker.

Blueberries

Blueberries thrive on the coast. Highbush blueberries and half-high hybrids (highbush crossed with eastern native lowbush blueberries) are most commonly grown. The bushes have beautiful red or yellow leaves in the fall. Grow huckleberries (available at native plant nurseries) and low-bush blueberries as for blueberries.

Culture: Blueberries grow best in cool, moist, well-drained acid soil (pH 4.5 to 5.5 is ideal). Don't lime the soil or use bonemeal, wood ashes, or other amendments that raise the pH. If your soil is not acid enough, amend with sulphur (aluminum sulphate is available at garden centers for this purpose) and lots of leaf mold (composted leaves), or grow bushes in containers with an acid soil mix. Mulch with a thick layer of leaves, pine needles, or shredded bark mulch to keep roots cool, control weeds, and help acidify the soil. When setting out plants, take into account how you plan to protect plants from spotted wing Drosophila: a few plants can be covered individually with insect netting; larger plantings can be set out in double rows to make it easier to cover with long tents of insect netting.

Pruning: Prune while bushes are dormant, up to late February. Remove crossed, broken, and weak branches. Shape the bush to be narrower at the base with a wider top. Thin out crowded branches to make an open center. Plants begin to decline after eight to ten years, so starting when the bush is seven years old, cut back one or two of the oldest branches at ground level each year, and allow new ones to take their place.

Pollination: Plant at least two varieties to improve pollination.

Harvest and storage: Blueberries look ripe long before they are; wait until they turn deep blue-black under the bluish bloom. With their waxy skins, blueberries keep in the refrigerator longer than other berries. They freeze well and are excellent dehydrated (too excellent, in fact: you won't be able to keep them long).

Pests: Spotted wing Drosophila; birds, raccoons.

Varieties: Plant early varieties to avoid the main population of spotted wing Drosophila. If you protect the bushes from fruit flies (with insect netting or sprays), growing a mix of early to late varieties provides a longer harvest (July to early September). Most varieties are partially self-fertile, but fruit set is improved by cross-pollination. Early: Earliblue, Duke, Spartan, Reka, Patriot (adapted to heavy, wet soils). Midseason: Bluecrop, Northland, Hardyblue, Blueray. Late: Brigitta (a tall productive hybrid). Half-high hybrids: Northland (early), Northsky (midseason), Northblue (late).

Blackberries and Blackberry Hybrids

When Himalayan blackberries already grow widely on the coast, you might wonder why anyone would plant more. But there are domestic blackberries (including thornless) as well as blackberry crosses with raspberries and other brambleberries that have unique flavors well worth growing. Besides, with the recent spread of spotted wing Drosophila, wild berries are often too infested to enjoy; when you grow your own, you can protect the berries from attack.

Culture: All blackberries thrive in deep soil as long as it is well-drained in winter. These are large vigorous plants that produce large crops when grown in good soil with summer irrigation. Spread a layer of finished compost (not manure) around the base of plants each year, and mulch well to control weeds. Keep on top of the task of removing weak canes and any shoots that come up in pathways and away from the main crowns because blackberries can quickly get out of hand.

Pruning: Each cane is biennial: it grows the first year and fruits the second year. After that it should be pruned out entirely. One system to keep trailing types (most varieties) well-organized is to grow them supported on a trellis with four to six parallel wires or rails. The first year, allow new canes to grow unchecked, but train half of them to grow to the left, tied to the lower wires, and the other half tied to the lower wires on the right. Next year these become fruiting canes. In the spring, untie them, shorten them to six to eight feet long, and fan them out and tie to the upper part of the trellis. Allow this year's new canes to grow in either direction along the lower part of the trellis. At the end of the second season, cut off at the ground any canes that have just finished fruiting. Every year, thin the canes to leave a total of twelve to fifteen per plant (half would be first-year and half would be second-year fruiting canes). Keeping such tight control over trellising also makes it easier to cover plants with insect netting against fruit flies.

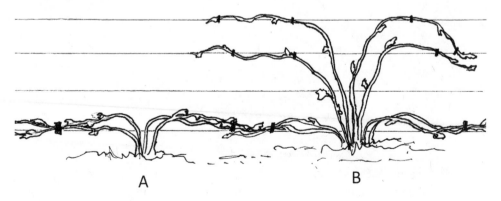

A   B

11.2. Brambles trellising system.

Harvest and storage: Good frozen and as jam, jelly, or juice.

Pests: Spotted wing Drosophila; powdery mildew and leaf rusts sometimes occur, but usually don't have much effect the yields.

Varieties: Thornless blackberries and marionberries are domesticated blackberries. Loganberries, tayberries, and boysenberries are hybrids with a blackberry parent, each with a different flavor.

Cherry

A standard sweet cherry can grow 30 feet (9 m) high, but on Gisela dwarfing rootstock, it is possible to keep them to 10 feet (3 m), much more practical for pruning, picking, and pest management!

Culture: Give dwarf trees a 6- to 10-foot (2 to 3 m) diameter growing space around the tree.

Pruning: At planting time, know how you intend to protect the fruit from birds and fruit flies when it reaches full-size, so that you can begin pruning the tree accordingly. Key to harvesting a crop is pruning to keep the tree small enough that you can cover it with insect or bird netting or grow it inside a

11.3. A perfect crop under the insect netting that is protecting the cherries from fruit flies, birds, and other pests.

netting-covered frame. For trees that are too large to cover, plan to cover individual branches with netting.

Harvest and storage: Some varieties are almost black when ripe, others are lighter red, making a taste test the best way to determine when to pick the red varieties. Cherries don't keep very long: eat them fresh or freeze or preserve them immediately.

Pollination: Sour cherries (pie cherries) are self-fertile. Varieties that need cross-pollinators include Angela, Bing, Early Burlat, Rainer, and Van. Self-fertile varieties include Craig's Crimson, Lapins, Stella, Sweetheart, and Vandalay. Varieties on multi-graft trees have been chosen for pollinator compatibility.

Pests: Spotted wing Drosophila and cherry fruit flies; brown rot, bacterial canker, black knot. Birds and raccoons can be very damaging.

Varieties: Early varieties such as Early Burlat, Lapins, and White Gold (yellow with red blush) are more likely to ripen before spotted wing Drosophila numbers reach damaging levels. Sour cherries are easiest to maintain as small trees.

Citrus, Lemons, and Limes

Sour citrus trees can tolerate a degree or more of frost when hardened off for winter. Limes and dwarf Meyer lemons do well in containers and ripen good-quality fruit in the coastal climate. Some gardeners grow oranges and other citrus; these are generally larger trees and need a longer warm period to ripen than lemons and limes. Experimenting with them is for gardeners who can provide especially warm growing conditions and winter shelter, usually in a greenhouse.

Culture: Soil pH 6.0 is ideal; too much lime in the soil causes iron and zinc deficiency. Leaves turn yellow with green along the leaf veins and take a long time to turn green. Because citrus nutrition is very tricky, I recommend supplementing additions of compost with a complete citrus fertilizer available from nurseries. Avoid overwatering citrus. For winter, move containers to a very protected site where temperatures won't dip lower than 30°F (–1°C) over the winter (e.g., unheated greenhouse or glassed-in porch). Trees survive 25° to 28°F (–4° to –2°C), though the fruit on the tree at the time may drop. Citrus are much better off in cool or even cold, humid, bright conditions than they are inside a house; they often drop leaves when brought indoors where it is too dry and light levels are low.

Both lemons and limes can be planted outdoors, but will need supplementary heat to survive the lowest winter temperatures. Here is a tried-and-true method, from Bob Duncan of Fruit Trees and More (Sidney, BC): thread a string of incandescent Christmas lights through the tree and cover the tree with floating row cover. [I live in a colder microclimate so I wrap a sheet of clear plastic around the sides of my outdoor lemon and just use floating row cover over the top of the tree for ventilation.] Turn on the lights when temperatures drop to 32°F (0°C), and leave them on until temperatures rise above freezing. This protects trees from surprisingly low temperatures: my lit-up lemon has so far survived several periods of 16°F (−9°C).

Pruning: Little to do except for thinning crowded branches or pinching back tips to keep plants compact. The trees regularly set too many fruit for the size of the tree; thin developing fruit to 6 inches (15 cm) apart on the branches.

Harvest and storage: Fruit color isn't a reliable indicator because ripe limes can be yellowish and ripe lemons light green. Citrus are ripe when the seeds turn brown; however, some have few or no seeds. Ripe fruit can stay on the tree for long periods without deteriorating, so picking timing is not critical.

11.4. Soft brown scale is a very common pest on citrus, but at least it can be safely controlled with horticultural oil sprays.

Pests: Soft brown scale is common: These are sucking insects that look like tiny brown bumps along stems and on undersides of leaves. The most noticeable symptom is sticky patches of honeydew on leaves, and often sooty mold grows on the sweet liquid (just wash it off; it isn't attacking the leaf). In the fall, spray trees with horticultural oil mixed according to package directions for a "growing season" spray. Make sure to thoroughly cover the undersides of *all* leaves. (Note: Soap and other sprays are largely ineffective for scale.)

Varieties: Two widely available sour citrus are Improved Dwarf Meyer lemon and Bearss lime. Yuzu (*Yuzu ichandrin*) is a hardy sour citrus (fragrant lemon-lime flavor) that can survive winter outdoors on much of the coast; reports of hardiness vary: mine was badly damaged, but not killed, by lows of 16°F (–9°C). Other sweet and sour citrus are available from specialty nurseries.

Currants and Gooseberries

Depending on your passion for these, you may only need one bush to meet your needs for red currant jelly or gooseberry pie, but you will require several black currant bushes to make a useful quantity of juice.

Culture: Avoid wet, poorly drained soils and also hot, dry sites. Space plants about 3 to 4 feet (1 m) apart (farther apart for black currants, which are larger). Mulch to keep soil cool and moist. Most varieties have self-fertile flowers and do fine as a single bush, but they produce larger fruit if cross-pollinated by another variety.

Pruning Tips: For gooseberries, red, and white/pink currants: Prune to keep an open center, and remove branches low to the ground. Fruit is produced on young branches one to three years old; those four years and older produce very little. In years two and three, leave three to four new stems and keep six to eight of the older ones. To make it even simpler: after four years, start removing the oldest, most ragged canes every year and keep about the same number of new shoots.

11.5. The small marks on each of these developing currants show that a currant fruit fly egg has been laid inside.

Black currants and jostaberries: Plants produce the best fruit on the last year's canes; therefore, once plants start fruiting, annual pruning consists of cutting out old canes. If growth was good, remove most of the old wood that fruited (old stems are darker, with loose or peeling bark; new stems are light brown, with smoother bark). If there aren't many new canes, cut out about a third of the old branches at a time.

Harvest and storage: Strip ripe currants from bushes by hand or clip off trusses of berries. To pick thorny varieties of gooseberries, wear gloves and long sleeves to protect yourself.

Pests: Imported currantworm. Currant fruit fly lays eggs on developing fruit between early May and mid-June: larvae are white maggots that feed on seeds inside each berry, then exit the fruit leaving a black mess behind; attacked currants ripen and drop first. To prevent flies from laying eggs, cover plants with insect netting tied firmly into the trunk; leave it on for the four- to five-week egg-laying period and remove in mid-June.

Varieties: Only a few varieties are widely available, and you may not have much choice. If you have 5-needle pines in your landscape, choose white pine blister rust-resistant varieties (currants are an alternate host). Red currants: Red Lake is a very old favorite; Viking is also very good and resistant to white pine blister rust. Black currant hybrids immune to white pine blister rust include Ben Sarek, Crusader (not self-fertile), Titania. White and pink currants are also available. Gooseberries come in both green- and pink-fruited varieties, including some without thorns (Pax). Jostaberries are black currant and gooseberry hybrids (tart fruit, disease-resistant, vigorous).

Figs

Figs are beautiful tropical-looking trees with smooth gray bark. The key to being able to enjoy a crop in the Pacific Northwest is planting the right variety. Most varieties have two crops over a long growing season, but only the figs from the first crop will ripen reliably in this region. Choose a variety with a good first crop and prune to make the most of the first crop.

Culture: Figs grow fine in any well-drained soil, but prefer a higher pH (6.0–7.8). Plant them in the warmest, sunniest site you can, such as against a building or rock wall where reflected heat helps ripen fruit. Avoid fertilizers high in nitrogen, which cause trees to produce more leaves than fruit. Mulch to protect roots for winter. Unpruned trees grow up to 30 feet (9 m) tall, but they can be pruned to much smaller dimensions and still produce a good crop. They can be grown in large containers, such as half barrels, and kept to under 10 feet (3 m) in height. Figs are always the last trees to leaf out in the spring (so don't panic when they are late).

Pruning: Don't follow pruning methods from warmer climates, which are aimed at maximizing the second crop at the expense of the first crop (second crop figs almost never ripen in the Pacific Northwest). First crop figs are produced on the new growth from last summer; therefore, don't cut back the ends of branches when trees are dormant as that removes the only fruit that will ripen fully (details on fig pruning are in Chapter 6, p. 159). Winter temperatures, below 16°F (–9°C), can kill some first crop fruit embryos and tips of some branches, but most of the tree will be fine.

Pollination: Common figs available in the PNW are parthenocarpic, meaning fruit actually sets without pollination. You may have heard that fig wasps are required, but they are not present in the region; some warm climate figs grown in California, such as Calimyrna, do require pollination by fig wasps.

Harvest and storage: Figs don't ripen further once they are picked, so leave them on the tree until they are perfectly

11.6. Small second crop figs remaining on the tree in the fall will be killed over the winter.

11.7. The neck on the upper fig has collapsed, showing the fruit is ready to pick. The lower fig is not yet ripe.

ripe. A fig is ripe when the neck is so soft that it collapses and the fruit droops over. Figs don't keep long at all, but are delightful fresh, frozen, or dried.

Pests: Birds, raccoons, and other vertebrates; yellowjacket wasps feed on juice from cracks in ripening fruit.

Varieties: Desert King is reliable in the PNW (fruit has a golden green skin and pink inside); Peter's Honey (a Lattarula or Italian Honey fig with a good first crop of honey sweet, straw-colored figs); Brown Turkey (dark purplish brown fruit). More good varieties are becoming available, but before buying, be sure your choice is notable for producing a large first crop.

Grapes, Table

American grapes (*Vitis labrusca*) and American grape hybrids need less heat to ripen than European table grapes, and the early varieties ripen pretty reliably on the coast. They are also hardy to at least 0°F (–18°C), so can be grown in northern coastal areas where there are Arctic outbreaks in winter. Note: Wine grapes are mostly European grapes (*Vitis vinifera*), which need a long warm season to ripen.

Culture: Grapes do best in deep soil, but garden vines manage in shallower soils as long as it is fertile and well-drained. Grow grapes in the warmest part of the garden where they can be supported on a trellis, along a fence, or over an arbor. Space plants 8 feet (2.5 m) apart.

Pruning: See Chapter 6.

Harvest and storage: Leave grapes on the vines until fully ripe for maximum sweetness. A mature table grape produces twenty-five to forty large bunches of grapes depending on how large the vine is allowed to grow. A couple of vines can produce surplus to freeze, dry for raisins, or make into juice.

Pests: Birds, raccoons, and other animals usually do the most damage. Powdery mildew infects European varieties, but American and American hybrid varieties are resistant. Blister mites cause puckered spots on grape leaves, but even large numbers have no effect on the harvest. Spotted wing Drosophila are known to attack grapes; bagging bunches of grapes (see p. 165) or covering vines with insect netting to protect fruit from fruit flies also protects it from wildlife.

Varieties: Seedless American hybrid table grapes: Himrod (very early white); Interlaken (very early green); Price (very early blue); Canadice (early light red);

Coronation (early blue-purple); and Vanessa (early red). *Very* early varieties produce a reliable crop in most places; however, early varieties and, especially, midseason varieties may not ripen fully in cool years or cooler microclimates; late varieties may only ripen in the warmest inland sites.

Haskap or Honeyberry

Your experience of these blue-fruited relatives of honeysuckle may or may not be in line with what you hear from promoters. I wasn't impressed with the ones I grew and have heard the same from others; but then, coastal gardeners can grow superb blueberries, and that's a hard act to follow. Honeyberries certainly have their enthusiasts, however, and breeding for improved flavor continues, so you might like them (I suggest you taste some before you invest). The following notes are from other sources: I did not keep my plants.

Culture: Plants grow in any moderately fertile, well-drained soil, with pH between 5.0 to 7.0. Space plants about a yard (1 m) apart in rows to make a hedge or a somewhat wider spacing to maintain them as individual bushes. Amend the soil with compost as for other fruiting plants.

Pruning: For the first few years, little is required except removing broken and crossed branches. As the plants get older, it will be necessary to thin out dense interior branches, but no more than 25% of the branches in any one year.

Harvest: Berries ripen in June and are mostly hidden under leaves. They turn blue before they are completely ripe; therefore check that they have turned purple all the way through, which shows they are fully ripe.

Pollination: Two varieties are necessary for pollination, but not just any two varieties: they have to be genetically compatible, and they must bloom at the same time. Tundra, Borealis, Blue Belle, and varieties in the Indigo series won't pollinate each other, but Honeybee, Berry Blue, Aurora, and Cinderella can pollinate those as well as each other (none are self-fertile).

Varieties: Breeding programs in Japan and Russia generated two groups of haskaps with differences in flavor and other qualities. Canadian and US plant breeders have been hybridizing the original types and selecting for improved flavor and productivity. All varieties are extremely hardy, but the Russian varieties had a tendency to come out of dormancy too early in warm spells that are common in a coastal winter; therefore, look for varieties that are specifically described as suitable for growing on the coast.

Pests: Powdery mildew (on some varieties); birds eat the berries so cover with bird netting. Fruit ripens so early that it isn't likely to be damaged by insects, including spotted wing Drosophila.

Kiwi

The fuzzy (grocery store) kiwi fruit is hard to manage in a small yard as they are large and extremely vigorous. Some hardy kiwis are a bit less rambunctious and easier to manage, but also produce small fruit and a smaller crop.

Culture: Grow vines in moderately fertile soil and avoid overfertilizing with nitrogen. Vines do best in full sun, in the warmest part of the garden (as for grapes). It can take five to seven years for female kiwi plants to flower, but once vines begin fruiting, they usually come into heavy production rapidly.

Harvest and storage: A mature fuzzy kiwi vine can produce hundreds of pounds of fruit. Pick them before they ripen, in late September to early October. The skin of the fuzzy kiwi will be brown, without a green tinge. The skin of the smaller hardy kiwi is smooth and remains green. Store for three to four months in ideal conditions (35° to 41°F, 2° to 5°C). As needed, remove fruit from cold storage and hold at room temperature to ripen. As the storage period lengthens, the time it takes to ripen when brought to room temperature decreases.

Pruning: Kiwi vines grow 10 to 20 feet (3 to 6 m) or even more in a season, but can be kept much smaller with regular pruning. Prune vines in both winter and summer; they produce many strong shoots, which should be kept pruned back over the season.

Pollination: Kiwi plants have either female flowers or male flowers, which means you need to plant one of each for pollination. The hardy kiwi, Issai, can set fruit without pollination.

11.8. The fruit of hardy kiwi is small, but tasty, and vines produce large crops.

Pests: None. Animals are not usually a problem because the fruit is picked before it is completely ripe.

Varieties: The fuzzy-skinned kiwi (*Actinidia deliciosa* or *A. chinensis*) have egg-sized fruit with rough skin. Females: Saanichton, Hayward; Male: Chico.

Hardy kiwi (*A. arguta*) have small fruit (up to 1 inch/2.5 cm long) with a smooth skin that doesn't have to be removed before eating. Varieties: Issai (self-fertile) and Ananasnaja (needs a male pollinator). Other kiwis (e.g., *A. kolomikta*), some with variegated leaves, also produce small tasty fruit.

Peaches, Nectarines

Peaches on the coast are a hit-or-miss crop because they flower early, when cold rainy weather may keep pollinators away and late frosts can ruin the flowers. Fruit quality often doesn't measure up against peaches and nectarines grown in hotter climates, but they are a treat nonetheless.

Culture: Grow peaches and nectarines in the warmest part of the garden. If possible, plant the tree against a south- or southwest-facing side of a building that has enough of a roof overhang to keep winter rain off the tree. This prevents peach leaf curl disease and provides a warmer microclimate to ripen fruit. Nearly all varieties are self-fertile.

Pruning: Trees can be trained into an open center structure or trained against a wall or trellis. Fruit is produced on one-year-old branches (the previous season's growth); therefore, trees should be pruned heavily each year. As a general rule, remove about ⅔ of the branches during the winter or head back the shoots by ⅓ to avoid having fruit develop at the ends of long branches. To control excessively vigorous growth, prune

11.9. Peach trees often grow rampantly and benefit from summer pruning to reduce vigor.

in summer, removing watersprouts and heading back long branches in early August.

Harvest and storage: Fruit is ready to harvest when they part from the branch with a gentle tug. Where raccoons and other animals make it difficult to achieve tree-ripened fruit, pick fruit before it is perfectly ripe and ripen indoors.

Pests: Brown rot; bacterial canker. Peach leaf curl, which is best managed by growing resistant varieties: there is no point in growing susceptible varieties unless you are prepared to spray or grow them under a cover to keep them dry during the infection period early spring.

Varieties: Early varieties (e.g., Early Redhaven) have the best chance of ripening in coastal gardens. Several varieties have some level of tolerance or resistance to peach leaf curl (see Table 2.1): Frost is widely available; it has good resistance after it is three years old. Avalon Pride; Oregon Curl Free. Genetic dwarf peaches and nectarines can be grown in large tubs and moved under a roof overhang during the leaf curl infection period.

Pears

There are both European pears (well-known, sweet, pear-shaped fruit) and Asian pears (rounder, less sweet, with a crisper texture; also called "apple pears"). European pears are either summer pears, which ripen without a cold storage period, or winter pears, which ripen best after being chilled in a refrigerator for at least a month.

Culture: Pears enjoy good, well-drained soil, but tolerate less well-drained and heavy soils somewhat better than other fruit trees. Grow two varieties to ensure pollination or grow multi-graft trees. Dwarf pears can be slower than dwarf apples to come into bearing.

Pruning: Even dwarf pear trees tend to become rather large, but can be kept to 10 to 15 feet (3 to 4.5 m) with pruning. Left to their own devices, pears tend to grow tall, with upright branches and narrow crotches. Prune to keep trees shorter, and use spreaders to train the branches to grow at wider angles (young branches held in place for a growing season will keep that angle permanently).

Pollination: Asian and European pears are not good cross-pollinators for each other because they don't bloom at the same time (Asian pears bloom later). Some pears, such as Bartlett, can set a few fruit without pollination in warm weather, but it rarely happens in the cool coastal spring weather. All varieties produce much larger crops and bigger fruit when cross-pollinated. Note: Seckel pollen can't pollinate Bartlett.

Harvest and storage: Although summer pears can ripen on the tree, don't let them. They are much better quality, without brown mushy centers, when ripened off the tree (and early picking foils raccoons and other critters). Pears are ready to pick when the stem of the fruit snaps cleanly from the twig when you lift up the fruit. Hold summer pears in a cool dark place to finish ripening, or refrigerate for up to two months before taking them out to ripen. Winter pears are ready to pick September to early October. Refrigerate the pears for one month before bringing to room temperature to ripen. Winter pears can be kept for three to five months if held in cold storage at 35° to 41°F (2° to 5°C).

Pests: Pear trellis rust; European canker; pear scab (see Table 2.1 for resistant varieties). Pear leaf blister mites on leaves cause red bumps and blisters that later turn black; usually not damaging, but if necessary, control them with lime sulphur sprays when 90% of leaves have fallen in the fall and again just as leaf buds swell in the spring (no later as sprays burn leaves). Pear sawfly is occasionally a problem: they look like tiny black slugs, chewing holes in leaves between the veins. Wash them off with a stiff stream of water; they don't climb back up the tree.

Varieties: Summer European pears: Bartlett, Red Bartlett, Clapp's Favorite, Conference, Rescue, Ubileen, Orca. Winter European pears: Bosc, Seckel (small dessert pears, also called sugar pears). Anjou and Comice are notoriously poor croppers; Anjou blooms earlier than other pears, and Comice pollen is extremely short-lived. Many Asian pear varieties are available.

11.10 The arrow shows where the stem of this Red Bartlett pear will snap from the branch when it is ready to pick; it will take another couple of weeks to ripen to perfection indoors.

Plums

With sweet, juicy, and colorful fruit, plum trees are productive and usually reliable croppers. There are two main groups: European plums, which are oval with very sweet flesh and sweet skins, and Japanese plums, which are larger and rounder with tart skins.

Culture: Many, but not all, plum varieties are self-fertile and can provide a good crop with one tree; multi-graft trees are also available. Mature trees may set quite a lot of fruit in years with warm, dry weather during pollination. After the June drop, thin remaining fruit to 2–3 inches (5–8 cm) apart.

Pruning: Dwarf plums can be kept to 8 to 9 feet (2 to 3 m) high. Once tree shape is established, European plums don't need much pruning beyond removing crowded branches. Japanese plums put on a lot of shoot growth each season, so keep the vertical shoots pruned out in the summer.

Pollination: European plums generally bloom later than Japanese plums, which gives them a better chance of being pollinated in cool coastal spring weather. Some plum varieties require cross-pollination from a different variety; others are self-fertile, but cross-pollination improves fruit set in all. European varieties mostly bloom close enough in time to pollinate each other, but not early enough to pollinate Japanese plums.

Harvest and storage: Enjoy tree-ripened fruit immediately; plums picked before they are completely ripe keep in the refrigerator for over a month. For longer storage, they can be frozen, canned, or dried.

Pests: Aphids; brown rot; black knot is a fungus disease that causes rough, black, elongated tumours on branches.

Varieties: Examples of European plums (all self-fertile): Opal, Victoria, Stanley (very susceptible to black knot), Italian Prune (Fellenberg), Damson. Japanese plums (all self-fertile): Santa Rosa, Golden Nectar, Shiro. There are also complicated hybrids between plums, apricots, peaches, and related fruit (e.g., pluots, plumcots, apriplums); apparently these may not be as hardy as plums and may be somewhat more prone to diseases in the PNW climate.

Raspberries

Once raspberries become established, you may wonder why you planted such an invasive plant that sends up shoots everywhere—until you taste that first handful of ripe raspberries, of course.

Culture: Set plants 2 to 3 feet (60 to 90 cm) apart in rows. They must have well-drained soil, but prefer it to be cool and moist; therefore keep plants deeply mulched. They should have some kind of support to corral the canes because they get quite long. They can be tied in to parallel wires a foot or two (up to 60 cm) apart running along a fence or between posts or grown between supporting wires. Bush raspberries do not require supports.

Pruning: Simplest method for pruning raspberries: When plants are dormant, cut down all canes that bore fruit last year. The bark on these will be darker gray and rougher compared to the smooth bark of canes that grew in the last growing season. You can prune all varieties this way, but everbearing varieties can also be pruned in two stages. These raspberries produce a fall crop on the top third of new canes and a crop the following summer on the lower part of those same canes. When plants are dormant, prune off just the top part that has fruited and allow the bottom of the canes to produce fruit next year. Then prune out that entire spent cane the following winter. Try to keep only five to ten new canes per plant. Pull, cut, or dig out weaker shoots and those that come up away from the main plant. Raspberries tend to spread widely if left to their own devices.

Harvest and storage: Enjoy raspberries immediately or freeze or preserve them.

Note: When picking, hold the bucket away from the branch to avoid the risk of a stink bug falling into the bucket. They are common in bramble fruit and drop when disturbed. If they drop in the bucket, they will fire off a stink that taints all the berries.

Pests: Spotted wing Drosophila has become the number one pest for later summer and fall raspberries (June to early July fruit, so far, generally escapes infestation). Phytophthora root rot often appears in older plantings, especially in poorly drained soil. Affected plants have yellow or reddish leaves, canes wilt, and plants may die suddenly or decline slowly over the year. Replant elsewhere with resistant varieties (see Table 2.1). Raspberry crown borer is sometimes a problem: The larvae overwinter in cocoons at the base of canes; in March, they start feeding on buds of new shoots, then burrow into the lower part of canes, which die back. In early spring, pull back the soil and look for larvae to destroy before they move into the canes; prune out attacked canes at the base. Keep plants growing vigorously to provide many replacement canes.

Varieties: Summer bearing: Tulameen; Malahat. Everbearing (fall bearing): Autumn Bliss; Heritage. By planting several varieties, you can extend fresh harvest from June to early November. There are also golden, pale yellow, and black-fruited raspberries: flavors are generally a little less sweet than red varieties. Bush raspberries (e.g., Raspberry Shortcake) have been developed for containers, but are happier planted out; the short, compact thornless plants are productive (fruit flavor is good, not quite as sweet as some) and easy to cover with insect netting against fruit flies.

Rhubarb

I know rhubarb isn't really a fruit, but everyone thinks of it as one, so here it is. Tuck a plant into the back of a flower bed or in a corner where it won't be disturbed, and enjoy this earliest fresh "fruit" of the year.

Culture: It would be the rare household that needs more than one of these large productive hardy perennials. Plant offsets or crown divisions in late fall or early spring, and keep plants well-watered and mulched. Every spring, apply a thick layer of compost to plants.

Pruning: Snap off flower stalks as they form.

Harvest and storage: Start harvesting for a week or two when plants are two to three years old; by the time plants are five years old or more, you can harvest up to eight weeks. Remove stalks by pulling them, instead of cutting them, which leaves a stub that can rot back into the crown. Holding the base of the stalk, tug it sideways or twist it slightly, and the stalk will pop off without damaging the crown.

Pests: None. Well, almost none: Deer are not supposed to eat it, but they often do. And occasionally, older plants fail from root disease (replant with new plants in a different location). Leafminers make brown blotches in leaves but have no effect on the crop.

Varieties: Most gardeners get a plant from another gardener and don't know the variety. Some people prize plants with the reddest stalks: Crimson Cherry, MacDonald, Strawberry. Others like Victoria, a vigorous old variety with greenish stalks.

Strawberries

Strawberries thrive in coastal gardens. There are two main types: June-bearing varieties and everbearing/day-neutral varieties that fruit from late June to

October. Although not exactly the same thing, everbearing and day-neutral strawberries behave similarly in coastal gardens to produce berries all season.

Culture: Start a new bed with certified virus-free plants. For everbearing varieties, space plants 1 foot (30 cm) apart; space June bearers 18 inches (45 cm) apart. The wider spacing accommodates the greater number of runners that develop on June-bearing varieties. Set plants with the crowns slightly above the soil line. Well-spaced plants in fertile soil can produce well for three years or more. However, beds usually become crowded and overgrown after several years in one place, which reduces pollination and increases Botrytis infections on the fruit. I plant half of my total area of strawberries new each year, to have one new bed and one two-year-old bed. Top-dress beds with compost in the spring. Mulch plants with leaves or straw in the fall to protect the crowns from frost heave.

Pruning: Remove excess runners, which are string-like shoots that produce new plants on the end. Everbearing varieties generally produce fewer runners and require less pruning than June bearers. You can allow a couple of runners from each plant to take root and fill in between older plants. Or, peg down the developing plantlets in small pots of soil (still attached to the runner); in early fall, when plants are well-rooted, cut the runner and plant them.

Harvest and storage: Strawberries have a short shelf life, but freeze well and make classic jam. To avoid damage from slugs, millipedes, and Botrytis/gray mold, pick when berries are barely ripe (i.e., one side is still a lighter red than the ripest side), and allow them to finish ripening indoors.

Pests: Spotted wing Drosophila: June berries usually finish fruiting by the time populations become high; cover everbearing varieties with insect netting from midsummer onward. Botrytis/gray mold

11.11. Tristar is a winner—as this September harvest shows.

on overripe berries. Birds; slugs. Leaf diseases occasionally appear and are best managed by replanting beds with new disease-free plants.

Varieties: June-bearing: Shuksan, Rainier, Hood, Puget Reliance. Everbearing/day-neutral: Tristar (excellent flavor, resists red stele root rot, leaf spot, powdery mildew); Albion (large, sweet); Hecker (smaller berries, disease-resistant); Quinault (soft berries, excellent flavor, susceptible to Botrytis/gray mold); Seascape (large, showy berries). White berries/pineberries: Aloha (very susceptible to powdery mildew).

Resources

Soil Testing Laboratories
British Columbia
MB Labs Ltd.
2062 Henry Avenue West, Sidney, BC, V8L 5Y1
Phone: 250-656-1334; mblabs.com.
Soil pH: Up to 4 soil samples for $20; nutrient testing $37 to $70 (2017 prices).

Pacific Soil Analysis
#50150 – 11720 Voyageur Way, Richmond, BC, V6X 3G9
Phone: 604-273-8226; email: cedora19@telus.net
Soil pH $20, nutrient testing $70 (2017 prices).

AGAT Laboratories
#120 – 8600 Glenlyon Parkway, Burnaby, BC, V5J 0B6
Phone: 778-452-4000 or 1-800-661-7174
Samples can be dropped off at the Burnaby office (or any of their locations) or sent directly to the analytical lab: 2910 12th Street NE, Calgary, AB, T2E 7P7
Soil pH $17; nutrient testing $100 to $200 (2017 prices).

Washington & Oregon
OSU Extension Services provides a regularly updated list of PNW testing labs, *Analytical Laboratories Serving Oregon*, 2017. catalog.extension.oregonstate.edu /sites/catalog/files/project/pdf/em8677_0.pdf

Or search for the most recent edition in the OSU Extension Catalog: catalog.extension.oregonstate.edu

Soil sampling instructions [Some soil testing labs also provide instruction on their websites.]

A Guide to Collecting Soil Samples for Farms and Gardens free download from: catalog.extension.oregonstate.edu

WSU Extension added a submission form and information on how to understand the soil report to this, see: extension.wsu.edu/clark/wp-content/uploads/sites/36/2017/08/Soil-Sampling-Complete-Procedures-8-8-17.pdf

Compost Information & Products
Compost Fundamentals

whatcom.wsu.edu/ag/compost/fundamentals/index.htm
A thorough, scientific, and practical review of everything there is to know about composting from Washington State University, Whatcom Co. Extension.

Fish and Wood Waste Compost Products

Check supplier websites for store locators.

Sea Soil™ Foenix Forest Technology Inc.,

2175 Mine Road, Port McNeill, BC, V9T 6S3
Phone: 1-866-732-7645; seasoil.com
Products widely available in British Columbia and other provinces.
OMRI certified.

Earthbank™ Fish Compost

1424 Hodges Road, Parksville, BC, V9P 2B5
Phone: 250-954-0118; fishcompost.com/compost_info.htm
Available at garden suppliers on Vancouver Island. OMRI certified.

Oly Mountain Fish Compost®

northmasonfiber.com
Widely available in Washington at garden centers from wholesaler North Mason Fiber Company. Certified for organic growing by Washington State Dept. of Agriculture.

Pest Management

West Coast Gardening: Natural Insect, Weed and Disease Control, 2nd edition.
Linda Gilkeson, 2013.
lindagilkeson.ca/books.html
Detailed entries for common pests of vegetables and fruit, lawns, and ornamentals in the Pacific Northwest. How to identify insects and diseases, prevent pest problems, and use safe, effective controls, including beneficial insects.

Garden Insects of North America: The Ultimate Guide to Backyard Bugs,
Whitney Cranshaw, 2004, Princeton University Press, Princeton, NJ.
THE definitive photographic reference for identifying insects and looking up life
cycles (does not provide control information).

Plant Health Diagnostic Labs: British Columbia
Plant Health Laboratory
BC Ministry of Agriculture, Abbotsford Agriculture Centre,
1767 Angus Campbell Rd., Abbotsford, BC, V3G 2M3
Phone: 1-800-661-9903
Provides identification services for most plant pathogens and cultural and
physiological conditions that may cause plant health problems. Fees $16 to $32
per sample, depending on how quickly diagnosis is required. See website for
submission form and sampling instructions.

Plant Health Diagnostic Labs: Washington State
Washington State University operates two Plant Pest Diagnostic Clinics.
Both labs provide plant disease and disorder diagnosis, pest identification,
and management strategies to homeowners and commercial growers.
Submission forms and sampling instructions online.

WSU Plant Pest Diagnostic Clinic, Department of Plant Pathology,
345 Johnson Hall, 100 Dairy Rd., Pullman, WA, 99164-6430
Phone: 509-335-3292; plantpath.wsu.edu/diagnostics
Usually handles samples from eastern Washington.

WSU Puyallup Research & Extension Center,
2606 West Pioneer, Puyallup, WA, 98371-4998.
Phone: 253-445-4582; puyallup.wsu.edu/plantclinic
Usually handles samples from western Washington.

Pest Management Tools
Insect Netting
ProtekNet: wholesale distributor (Canada),
Dubois Agrinovation, Montreal
www.duboisag.com
Individuals can purchase a 328-foot (100 m) roll (cut it up and share with
friends). Sold retail in some local garden nurseries (Vancouver Island)
and by mail order William Dam Seeds, damseeds.ca

Agralan Enviromesh: Available from amazon.com and amazon.ca.

Kootenay Covers

kootenaycovers.com
Large bags of durable, knitted polyester fiber to cover whole fruit trees. The supplier also sells fabric separately in 100-foot (30.5 m) lengths.

Fruit Bags
ULINE

uline.com
Online wholesaler to both US and Canada. Organza gift bags sold in bundles of 100 in a wide range of sizes, also small glassine, kraft, white, and brown paper bags.

Matthew's Store Fixtures & Shelving

810 Shamrock St., Victoria, BC, V8X 2V1
Phone: 250-388-4123 or 1-800-964-1281; matthewsdisplay.com
Organza gift bags, small kraft, white, and brown paper bags

Eddie's Hang-Up Display Ltd.,

60 West 3rd Avenue, Vancouver, BC, V5Y 1E4
eddies.com
Organza bags and small kraft paper bags

Japanese Fruit Bags: Small quantities for US gardeners sold by amazon.com or Wilson Orchard and Vineyard Supply: wilsonirr.com/ecommerce/
Neither source ships to Canada.

Wireworm Trap

Noronha Elaterid Light Trap (NELT™) is a pitfall trap that uses a solar powered light to attract male and female click beetles.
Growing Forward Solutions, Inc.
Phone: 902-439-6316; growingforward.ca

Motion-Activated Animal Repellents

Sensors in these products automatically detect animals moving in the area and trigger a short but startling burst of water to frighten them away.

Contech ScareCrow® Animal Deterrent

Connects to a hose, sensor is battery powered. Widely available in garden centers and online. $60 to $70

Spray Away® Elite Hoseless Motion Activated Sprinkler Repellent
Available from Woodstream Brands, woodstreambrands.ca
Contains a water reservoir, solar powered sensor. $140 to $200

Tools & Equipment
Lee Valley Tools
leevalley.com
Mail-order supplier of tools to US and Canada, with retail stores in some cities.
Their extensive line of garden tools includes ten-year garden journals, electronic
and manual min-max thermometers, rain gauges, dehumidifiers for seed storage,
irrigation systems, cultivating tools, including the U-Bar Digger (broadfork).

Gardening Advice and Pest Identification
Master Gardeners Association of British Columbia
Phone: 604-257-8662; mgabc.org;
email: plantinfo@bcmastergardeners.org
Includes list of local chapters. Plant information line for Vancouver gardeners.
mgabc.org/content/vancouver

University of British Columbia Botanical Garden
ubcbotanicalgarden.org
Hortline: 604-822-5858; Open year-round, seven days a week, and answered
every Wednesday between 12:00 p.m. and 3:00 p.m. Questions are received by
telephone, email, mail, and in-person at the Campbell Building at UBC Botanical
Garden.
Mail: UBC Botanical Garden, Attn Hortline, 6804 SW Marine Drive,
Vancouver, BC, V6T 1Z4
Email: garden.hortline@ubc.ca
Online forums: ubcbotanicalgarden.org/forums

Gardening in Washington State, Washington State University
gardening.wsu.edu
Links to information on all aspects of home gardening.

Washington State Master Gardener Program
mastergardener.wsu.edu
Provides links to Master Gardener contacts for each county.

Oregon State University Master Gardener Program
extension.oregonstate.edu/mg
"Ask an Expert" service: extension.oregonstate.edu/extension-ask-an-expert

Horticultural Myths
Linda Chalker-Scott, a professor at Washington State University, has a website with information on the science (or not!) behind gardening methods; her research focuses on landscape vegetation, but much of the information is also useful for food gardeners.
puyallup.wsu.edu/lcs

Seed Saving
Books
How to Save Your Own Seeds: A Handbook for Small-Scale Seed Production
Excellent how-to manual from Seeds of Diversity Canada, with detailed instructions for saving seeds from all kinds of vegetables; 68 pages, well-illustrated with photos, $15 (includes postage).
Seeds of Diversity Canada, PO Box 36, Stn Q, Toronto, ON, M4T 2L7
Phone: 866-509-7333; seeds.ca/publications

Saving Seeds As If Our Lives Depended On It,
Dan Jason, Salt Spring Seeds, 2006, 54 pp.
Both a personal overview of how seed affairs have gotten to be what they are today and a practical beginner's guide to saving seeds and the joys thereof.
Available by mail order, $14: saltspringseeds.com

Seed Preservation Organizations
Seeds of Diversity Canada
PO Box 36, Stn Q, Toronto, ON, M4T 2L7
Phone: 866-509-7333; seeds.ca
Canada's largest seed exchange also maintains other information and educational resources, including the Canadian Seed Library (over 2,300 varieties available to members), master list of Seedy Saturday events, directory of community seed libraries, and Canadian Seed Catalogue Index of vegetable varieties and companies that carry them.

Organic Seed Alliance

PO Box 772, Port Townsend, WA, 98368

Phone: 360-385-7192; seedalliance.org

Non-profit supporting the ethical development and stewardship of seeds; carries a complete listing of organic seed suppliers in the region, extensive publications, reports on variety trials and breeding programs, resources and webinars on seed growing and plant breeding.

Seed Savers Exchange

3094 North Winn Rd., Decorah, IA, 52101

Phone: 563-382-5990; seedsavers.org

A non-profit organization dedicated to saving and sharing seeds of culturally diverse but endangered garden and food crop heritage, they maintain a collection of over 20,000 heirloom and open-pollinated vegetable, herb, and other plants. Many interesting varieties available for sale; will ship seeds to Canada.

Regional Seed Companies

There are many more seed companies than listed here. I have cited these because they are particularly good sources of varieties for West Coast gardeners and carry a crops for winter harvests. Local Canadian seed growers are often represented at Seedy Saturday events (for dates see seeds.ca/events).

Canada

West Coast Seeds

5300 34B Ave., Delta, BC, V4L 2P1

Phone: 604-952-8820 or 1-888-804-8820; westcoastseeds.com

Full range of summer crops plus a large selection of winter-hardy vegetables for the PNW, including winter broccoli and cauliflower. Seeds also available at the retail store, 4930 Elliott St., Delta, BC, V4K 2Y1, and regional garden centers. Will ship seeds to the US.

Salt Spring Seeds

Box 444, Ganges PO, Salt Spring Island, BC, V8K 2W1

Phone: 250-537-5269; saltspringseeds.com

Locally grown, unique, and heirloom vegetables and herbs; specializing in tomatoes, garlic, dry beans, and other pulses. Source for Purple Cape cauliflower and other vanishing winter varieties. Does not ship to US.

Full Circle Seeds

PO Box 807, Sooke, BC, V9Z 1H8

Phone: 250-642-3671; fullcircleseeds.com

Organic OP heritage seeds with a specialty in tomatoes and lettuce, some hardy greens. Source for unique leeks. Will ship to the US.

William Dam Seeds Ltd.

279 Hwy 8, Dundas, ON, L9H 5E1

Phone: 1-905-628-6641; damseeds.ca

Supplier of untreated and some organic seeds; many European varieties, including red torpedo onions, Namenia, corn salad, Dutch varieties of winter cabbage, chicory, endive, kale, and root vegetables not found elsewhere. Does not ship to US.

USA

Territorial Seed Company

PO Box 158, Cottage Grove, OR, 97424-0061

Phone: 1-800-626-0866; territorialseed.com

An extensive spring catalog carries a large selection of summer crops; a later catalog carries a wide selection of winter greens, lettuces, kales, winter cauliflower, purple sprouting broccoli, and roots crops. Seeds also available at local garden centers. Will ship seeds to Canada.

Osborne Seed Company

2428 Old Hwy 99 South Rd., Mount Vernon, WA, 98273

Phone: 360-424-7333 or 1-800-845-9113; osborneseed.com

Wholesale supplier of a wide selection of local adapted summer and winter crops, including winter broccoli and cauliflowers, lettuce, kales. Quantities larger than a home gardener would use. Will ship seeds to Canada.

Victory Seed Company

PO Box 192, Molalla, OR, 97038

Phone: 503-829-3126; victoryseeds.com

Pretty good selection of heirloom varieties adapted to the local climate; a couple of winter broccoli and cauliflower, also winter hardy lettuce. Will ship seeds to Canada.

International
Chiltern Seeds
114 Preston Crowmarsh, Wallingford, OX10 6SL, England

chilternseeds.co.uk

One of the only European seed houses that still sells retail internationally. Source of many excellent winter vegetables suited to the Pacific Northwest, including celtuce, purple sprouting broccoli, broad beans, parsnips, and other hardy vegetables beloved of British gardeners.

Unusual Plants
Fruit Trees and More
724 Wain Rd., North Saanich, BC, V8L 5N8

(on Vancouver Island near Sidney/Victoria)

Phone: 250-656-4269; fruittreesandmore.com

Specializing in temperate zone fruit trees and berries, citrus and Mediterranean fruit for coastal gardens, including figs, olives, persimmons. Most orders are picked up at the nursery, but arrangements for shipping can be made.

Figs for Life
76508 Marcus Rd., Denman Island, BC, V0R 1T0

figsforlife.ca

Hardy fig trees (100 varieties) and other permaculture plants for coastal gardens. Canadian orders only.

Raintree Nursery
391 Butts Road, Morton, WA, 98356

Phone: 1-800-391-8892; raintreenursery.com

A full range of fruit trees and nursery stock, including figs, citrus, nuts, and unusual fruit for home gardeners. US orders only.

Mapple Farms
129 Beech Hill Rd., Weldon, NB, E4H 4N5

mapplefarm.com

Specializing in sweet potatoes for northern gardens (including orange-, purple-, and white-fleshed varieties. Also interesting collection of seeds of other plants. Canadian orders only.

Territorial Seed Company
20E Palmer Ave., Cottage Grove, OR, 97424
territorialseed.com
See above; also carries sweet potato plants, including Georgia Jet and a mixed color collection (2017). US orders only.

Index

Bold page numbers indicate main discussion of topic.
Italic page numbers indicate figures and tables.

About the Author

Linda Gilkeson is a keen organic gardener with a passion for insects and 30 years of gardening experience on the West Coast. After earning a Ph.D. in entomology, she worked as the research director of a biological control company and then for the British Columbia government coordinating programs to reduce pesticide use. She is the author of *Year-Around Harvest: Winter Gardening on the Coast* and *West Coast Gardening: Natural Insect, Weed and Disease Control*. Linda is also a regular instructor in Master Gardener programs and is kept busy giving talks and workshops on organic gardening and pest management for community education programs, garden clubs and other groups. She currently lives on Salt Spring Island where she enjoys harvesting food from her garden all year round.

Visit her web site at www.lindagilkeson.ca

ABOUT NEW SOCIETY PUBLISHERS

New Society Publishers is an activist, solutions-oriented publisher focused on publishing books for a world of change. Our books offer tips, tools, and insights from leading experts in sustainable building, homesteading, climate change, environment, conscientious commerce, renewable energy, and more—positive solutions for troubled times.

We're proud to hold to the highest environmental and social standards of any publisher in North America. This is why some of our books might cost a little more. We think it's worth it!

- We print all our books in North America, never overseas

- All our books are printed on **100% post-consumer recycled paper**, processed chlorine-free, with low-VOC vegetable-based inks (since 2002)

- Our corporate structure is an innovative employee shareholder agreement, so we're one-third employee-owned (since 2015)

- We're carbon-neutral (since 2006)

- We're certified as a B Corporation (since 2016)

At New Society Publishers, we care deeply about *what* we publish—but also about *how* we do business.

New Society Publishers
ENVIRONMENTAL BENEFITS STATEMENT

For every 5,000 books printed, New Society saves the following resources:[1]

49	Trees
4,446	Pounds of Solid Waste
4,892	Gallons of Water
6,380	Kilowatt Hours of Electricity
8,082	Pounds of Greenhouse Gases
35	Pounds of HAPs, VOCs, and AOX Combined
12	Cubic Yards of Landfill Space

[1] Environmental benefits are calculated based on research done by the Environmental Defense Fund and other members of the Paper Task Force who study the environmental impacts of the paper industry.

MIX
Paper from responsible sources
FSC® C016245